D1707704

Polling, Policy, and Public Opinion

Polling, Policy, and Public Opinion

The Case Against Heeding the "Voice of the People"

Robert Weissberg

POLLING, POLICY, AND PUBLIC OPINION

First published 2002 by
PALGRAVE MACMILLAN™
175 Fifth Avenue, New York, N.Y. 10010 and
Houndmills, Basingstoke, Hampshire RG21 6XS
Companies and representatives throughout the world

PALGRAVE MACMILLAN is the global academic imprint of the Palgrave Macmillan division of St. Martin's Press, LLC and of Palgrave Macmillan Ltd. Macmillan® is a registered trademark in the United States, United Kingdom and other countries. Palgrave is a registered trademark in the European Union and other countries.

ISBN 0–0–312–29495–6 hardback

Library of Congress Cataloging-in-Publication Data

Weissberg, Robert, 1941–
    Polling, policy, and public opinion : the case against heeding the "voice of the people" / by Robert Weissberg.
        p. cm.
    Includes bibliographical references and index.
    ISBN 0–312–29495–6
    1. Public welfare—United States—Public opinion. 2. Public opinion—United States. I. Title.

HV91 .W4659 2002
361.6′0973—dc21   2002068427

A catalogue record for this book is available from the British Library.

Design by Newgen Imaging Systems (P) Ltd., Chennai, India.

First edition: August, 2002
10 9 8 7 6 5 4 3 2 1

Printed in the United States of America.

Contents

Preface   vii

Chapter 1   Public Opinion, Polling, and Politics   1

Chapter 2   From Wishes to Hard Choices   17

Chapter 3   Civic Competence   49

Chapter 4   Public Opinion I: Policies and Questions   71

Chapter 5   Public Opinion II: Fervent Desires   95

Chapter 6   Bestowing the Democratic Mantle   139

Chapter 7   Conclusions   175

Appendix   The Daycare Questionnaire   195

Notes   203

Bibliography   217

Index   229

Preface

*P*olling, Policy, and Public Opinion argues that the hundreds of garden-variety polls ostensibly revealing public appetite for expanding social welfare are seriously misleading. Moreover, heeding these demands is not "true democracy." It is not that these thirstings are insincere or totally valueless. Democratic elections may be entirely about best appeasing these cravings, and clever candidates may heed them carefully. The key is separating unthinking, poll-induced wishes from sound, hardheaded counsel. Majorities, as the polls relentlessly proclaim, *really* do yearn for government subsidized medical care, old-age assistance, lavishly funded education, and all else that Washington labors to supply. Unfortunately, that millions genuinely lust after something hardly makes this longing authoritative, let along sensible. Everyone covets an illness-free life and government rightly spends billions to eradicate disease, yet it would be preposterous to hold public officials accountable for eternal life. Ceaselessly pursuing the hopeless is a sign of mental illness. Legitimizing the parade of "government should provide more help to …" poll responses is equally dangerous. No matter how heartfelt, they are not policy directives, and to label them authentic "democratic mandates" is duplicitous.

Thus stated, *Polling, Policy, and Public Opinion* appears polemical, another battle cry over the welfare state, regardless of scholarly window-dressing. Reasonable truth resides in this accusation insofar as its data will undoubtedly provide ammunition to antistatist plotters. We also reaffirm Madison's antique warning regarding the havoc unleashed by catering to the public's passions. Conceivably, a handful of Republicans might repeat our conclusions to justify "mean-spirited" resistance to the erstwhile "compassion." Conservatives long suspecting that today's social scientists covertly impose liberal ideology to skew "scientific" research will likewise appreciate our messages. And, for good measure, the liberal faithful intent on denouncing this "reactionary screed" will easily prevail given today's peculiar academic evidentiary rules. Their misguided inspection will quickly bare "depraved" funding sources, "politically incorrect citations," and untold other smoking-gun clues exposing yet one more Vast-Right-Wing-Conspiracy exemplar.

Reality is a bit more complex, and an irony exists here begging to be told. Some personal history. This enterprise germinated during the late 1970s, and its overall thrust—deep skepticism regarding the *vox populi's* pseudodemocratic social welfare cravings—was present at inception. Launching an ideologically tinged crusade never crossed my mind, however. The goal was a technically oriented research project, nothing else. Ideologically, I was still a "big government" disciple, although my optimism was slowly eroding. If this disinterest is not to be trusted, let me confess: I voted for McGovern in 1972 and Carter in 1976! "Moderate liberal" would aptly describe my views back then. Ideological apostasy occurred years after launching this project.

As I understood it, only conventional political behavior research was being pursued. My sole aim then—as it is now—was to demonstrate that altering questionnaire construction was a political act. Such endeavors typically went absolutely unnoticed by the guardians of disinterested disciplinary science. Surely, for example, substituting "Russia" for "the Soviet Union" in a questionnaire experiment hardly invited charges of covert revisionism regardless of outcomes or who utilized the results.

Still, two recent changes might give credence to the ideology mongering accusation. First, let me concede that I have steadily gravitated toward free-market oriented solutions to social welfare dilemmas. The shift has been entirely pragmatic. Observing a parade of failed bureaucratic intervention has weakened my faith in big government as the mighty engine of genuine compassion. Although this personal conversion might explain some of the book's language, even occasional passion, I seriously doubt whether it has altered its conclusion one iota. Had this study been executed twenty years ago, the outcome would be nearly identical.

This project's alleged polemical coloration flows far more from transformations within the craft of professional political science than research bias. The intellectual context in which this research now exists has metamorphosed from its commencement. With scant exception, the liberal views once coloring public opinion research are now front and center. For example, a new scholarly public opinion book, issued by Columbia University Press, prominently announced the book's intended contribution to left-wing politics (Lewis 2001, xiv). This ideological openness would probably been unthinkable thirty years back.

This ideological penetration is hardly some nefarious, conscious bias. Rather, the culprit is an encompassing *Zeitgeist* directing intellectual traffic in some directions but not others. Many younger scholars barely notice its force—its norms are unspoken. And, this infusion has been welcomed, even judged legitimate, as "progress" although not too loudly, lest outsiders, particularly scientific inquiry benefactors, become alarmed. This politicization may even be a more general phenomenon—just read the inaugural speeches now annually offered by American Political Science Association presidents or the proliferation of ideologically driven convention panels.

When I first entered disciplinary life in the mid-1960s, disdaining "normative" analysis (addressing values beyond scientific proof) was *de rigueur* among those seeking political *science* prestige. Future progress, it was heartily declared in all best places, required abandoning advocacy and letting the empirical chips fall where they may. Partisans of "values" would be consigned to discipline's dustbin; virtuous analysts labored merely to prove or disprove factual statements. Today, by contrast, advancing one's career, even without publishing, demands a fresh sensitivity to the political winds blowing from the spectrum's left side. Heretical views are to be kept quiet. Anonymous reviewers attuned to "social justice" or some similar bandwagon cannot be challenged as one might contest false criminal accusations. The unnoticed exodus of unemployable nonbelievers or those morally uncomfortable with acquiescence compounds this penetration. Even disbeliever survivors within the profession must be wary of "harmful" unflattering implication or favorably citing *The Bell Curve*-like books.

In this newly political sensitized setting, the once appreciated "just the facts ma'am" style easily becomes an ideological assault if the facts are "wrong." Worse, conventional let-the-chips-fall-where-they-may 1960s behavioralism is now *inherently* "political." This transformation flows from today's academically fashionable view that everything, absolutely everything including hard science, is at heart political. In that context, escape from ideological labeling is futile; it comes with today's disciplinary territory. In the case at hand, then, demonstrating public social welfare thirsting shallowness can *only* be interpreted as right-wing counterrevolution vindictiveness against the truly compassionate modern state. In short, what originated as dispassionate social science, albeit with "real world" implications, is now judged mean-spirited polemical thanks to a shifting backdrop.

If my "objectivity" is still not believed, the doubting reader should read the concluding sections of chapters five and six. Here I briefly explain that if there were an "alternative universe" in which Libertarians dominated Washington, these warnings regarding poll influence would be equally fervent. Make no mistake, I personally dislike "made-in-Washington" grand social engineering remediation schemes. Even worse, however, is the transformation of the

Republic into governance by hidden-hand plebiscite. In the final analysis, the bumbling welfare state can be survived, wastefulness and all. I am less optimistic about surrendering power to a nonelected clerisy aided and abetted by a mass media intoxicated with superficial outrage. The dangers here far exceed extravagance.

Let me also address this enterprise's heft considering its modest aim. Even ideological sympathizers, let alone believers in cold-hearted social science, might wonder why two hundred plus pages of labored academic prose are necessary to announce points obvious to the economically literate. A few terse sentences regarding the silliness of heeding poll advice on labyrinthine public policy should be sufficient. Why not just execute a few differently worded polls and let the results speak unadorned—if confronted with costs, externalities, nonoptimal choices and similar inescapable real-world complexities, "public opinion" differs substantially from what conventional simple-minded surveys show. Do we honestly need verbiage galore to certify that citizens are generally befuddled by most public policy debates? Are we not beating a dead horse far beyond strict federal guidelines regulating battering expired equines?

Our response is that a few "counterpolls" cannot dislodge the giant edifice called "The Standing Consensus Regarding Public Support for Social Welfare Expansion, As Told to the Ever Attentive Pollster." This beast is impervious to a single well-aimed bullet to the brain. This is hardly speculation—the National Taxpayers Union (NTU) has regularly commissioned well-crafted polls showing opposition to increased federal spending or higher taxes. Despite the NTU's eager publicity efforts, these data are virtually unknown outside of conservative circles ever anxious for a glimmer of hope. An entire lifetime could be spent analyzing surveys without encountering the NTU's dissenting findings, especially if one toils in the academy. In an environment overflowing with public pulse-taking, merely adding a handful of divergent findings accomplishes zero. Ditto for all the qualms regarding *vox populi* wisdom to set public policy. The existing entitlement consensus is smothering. At best, survey data collectors might mention "but a tiny number of other polls utilizing different formats challenge public veracity and report somewhat different results." Securing a footnote is not our aim.

Bulkiness flows from the deceptively intricate nature of this meretricious survey created consensus. Undergirding the "we want more government aid for [fill in the blank]" question parade is an immense web of critical methodological and theoretical connective tissue. "Theology" replete with vast catechism is a more apt depiction. Elements range from slippery "democracy" and "civic competency" definitions to catalogues of anfractuous opaque statistical techniques useful for uncovering furtive, though desired, outcomes. Also scattered about are alleged axiomatic truths surviving only by repeated citation and untold misrepresentations on "sensitive" topics. Outsiders cannot possibly appreciate the extent to which these subterranean mental habits thrive as scholarly research conventions. If statist survey outcroppings should mysteriously vanish tomorrow, identical fresh poll results would instantly reappear. An army of well-schooled analysts would have the data factories up and running within days. If a convincing counterargument is going to be advanced, this thesis must address what lurks below, the genetic DNA blueprint, so-to-speak, not the individual progeny. In military campaign terminology, our analysis might be likened to tedious infantry ground assaults reclaiming territory foot by foot, not launching a few cruise missiles at enemy headquarters.

Equally important is a goal wholly disciplinary in character. The dictates of modesty aside, my hope is to redirect public opinion research away from today's infatuation with statistically extracting "deep meaning" from inconsequentiality. You can't get blood from a turnip even with a high-tech turnip press. To further compound this immodesty sin, this endeavor hopes to render the present crude questionnaire item obsolete. Current public thinking probes are hardly more sophisticated than when George Gallop launched the first primitive inquires some seventy years ago. The exigencies of telephone polling have compounded this shallowness. Only our statistical extraction techniques have grown more refined, not measurement itself. Perhaps this effort can redirect scholarship toward greater measurement precision.

Centuries ago, Tacitus wrote that history's highest purpose was "to let no worthy action be uncommemorated, and to hold out the reprobation of posterity as a terror to evil words and deeds." Scholarly convention regarding acknowledgments entails a lengthy compilation of helpers plus the "and all the others too numerous to mention by name." I certainly will honor this venerable custom of acknowledging the commendable, although, truth to be told, I wish that this list were longer. More about this unsettling point below. The Sarah Scaife Foundation, whose most generous financial support made this project possible, is deeply thanked. John Baden, erstwhile Montana farmer, Beau Brummell free-market intellectual, and all-purpose *mensch,* also deserves eternal gratitude. Fred Wall, Martha Roberts, and all the other Angus Reid Group experts did a superb job of data collection, analysis, and insight into a world beyond my ken. I could not have asked for a more stellar performance. Dixie Trinkle skillfully transcribed interviews and corrected untold typographical errors. Charles C. DeWitt, as usual, provided his invaluable stealthy assistance. The Social Philosophy and Policy Center at Bowling Green University generously afforded me the time and support to complete this manuscript. Toby Wahl at Palgrave deserves endless praise for his careful editing, but I'll skip the details since he would undoubtedly remove them in the interest of brevity. And, speaking of the "usual suspects," once again Erika Gilbert was always there with her superb free advice, a nice cup of coffee (not too much sugar!), and, most critically, the emotional support absolutely vital to a project of this magnitude.

Now, alas, to depart radically from custom. An unpleasantness has infused this project, and these "evil words and deeds," too, deserve proper mention. After all, we are obligated to future historians curious about academy-based intellectual life. We'll start gently. On innumerable occasions, I sought reactions from fellow academics, only to be greeted with stone silence. Even a handful with an "obvious" interest in this project—including a few known to me personally—unexpectedly became mute. Venturing beyond familiar intellectual turf is always arduous, and friendly encouragement, together with wise (if discomforting advice) is essential if all the obstacles are to be conquered. Writing books is always lonely, but this project was more solitary than necessary. Maybe everything got lost in the mail or intercepted by space aliens.

More serious are those unnamed souls whose conduct might charitably be depicted as poisoning the intellectual soil. These deeds, as Tacitus admonishes, cannot go unrecognized, however fleeting the notice. Each culprit, in his or her own distinctive fashion, made a difficult task even more vexatious. Although these painful events deserve itemized public commemoration, the repeated sage advice of wiser heads will be heeded. The careful telling of these horrid tales must wait another venue.

Why even acknowledge sordid episodes in a place universally reserved for cordiality? This is not a petty settling of scores; the issue is more serious. Today's academy is troubled; anti-intellectualism grows stronger, often welcomed by anxious-to-please amateur administrators. What makes—or should make—academic life supremely enjoyable is, to invoke that venerable cliché, the life of the mind. Uncovering truth is the *raison d'être* of our profession. We are scholars, not factory workers plying our trade with tools, training, and methods to increase piecework productivity. When intellectual life is reduced to industrial production tempered by petty squabbling and chronic mendacity, what is left?

CHAPTER 1

Public Opinion, Polling, and Politics

Public opinion is a permeating influence, and it exacts obedience to itself; it requires us to think other men's thoughts, and to speak other men's words, to follow other men's habits.
— Walter Bagehot, *National Review,* July 1856

Today's polls have achieved a prominence inconceivable fifty years ago; even disbelievers pay homage if convenient. They far surpass all rivals in proclaiming our collective self-definition. Are we a liberal society? Is America racist? Only the pollster can stare into our minds and answer authoritatively. Scarcely any cause can prosper without recourse survey-driven arguments while the court of public opinion renders its verdict via polls. Matters once determined solely by judging outward behavior, for example, an office holder's honesty, is now, thanks to polls, translated into "peoples' attitudes about his or her honesty." Wars are now "won" if a majority of interviewees believe this to be true.

This power is most apparent in presidential conduct, although this transformation is hardly unique. Since Franklin Roosevelt's day, presidents—save Truman—have heeded their pollster confidantes as French monarchs once confessed to private clerics (Bradburn and Sudman 1988, 38–49). The Reagan White House yearly spent about a million dollars on polls, all paid by the Republican National Committee (Brace and Hinckley 1992, 3).[1] The Clinton presidency nearly conflated leadership and marketing with its incessant fingering of the public pulse, and his soaring ratings confirmed the tactic's wisdom. According to John Harris's peek into Clinton's inner sanctum, last-minute poll results decisively shifted the president's legislative agenda on allocating the budget surplus to funding Social Security, promoting medical privacy, and abandoning a needle exchange to combat AIDS (Harris 2000). Even programs popular among other advisors, for example, parental responsibility for their children's crimes, were squashed by the poll data. Indeed, Clinton impeachment opponents often insisted that his upbeat ratings, not legal or constitutional dictates, constitute the supreme judgmental standard.

The poll's burgeoning authority rests on the steady embrace of science. Early collective portraits, the classics, offered scant professionally certified data and were oblivious to intricate statistical analyses; personal insight coupled with informed speculation were the accepted scholarly currency. Like primitive calendars guiding agriculture, calculation was crude, idiosyncratic, and surely mysterious. Skepticism was therefore predictable, indeed commendable. Today, by contrast, public opinion analysis moves closer to scientific exactitude, and greater insight appears imminent. One recent overview proudly compared today's poll with microscopes, telescopes, particle accelerators, and seismic sensors. Nowhere in this celebration was accuracy discussed (Brady 2000). This admirable reputation is powerfully reinforced by its stunning commercial success. "Mopping up" within a mature paradigm might be one way of depicting future evolution.

Not surprisingly, this triumph of polls is widely and enthusiastically welcomed. Social scientists know that the premodern, nonquantitative era was not a golden age meriting resurrection. Philosophical reservations about polling have been banished to the dustbin of disciplinary history. Survey neophytes cannot recall once-renowned skeptics such as Herbert Blumer, Lindsay Rogers, or even Walter Lippmann. The latter's detailed rejection of government by public opinion has not been refuted; it has, instead, suffered the indignity of being forgotten. No contemporary career-savvy academic would even hint, as Lippmann did, that "where mass opinion dominates the government, there is a morbid derangement of the true functions of power" (1956, 19). Insisting that this hunting and gathering of mass sentiment may be a pointless political gesture catering to popular foolishness hints a reactionary detachment from disciplinary progress.

Far more consequential is the ebullient welcome from those regarding polling as the harbinger of energetic direct democracy (or, in journalistic language, government by public relations). For these devotees, polling refines civic life—creating a Shining Oracle on a Hill, so to speak. Humphrey Taylor (2000), chairman of the Harris Poll, insists that polls play a vital democratic role in supplying leaders with information and preventing electoral fraud. Taylor likens "the right to poll freely" as fundamental to democracy. Another distinguished pollster insists that today's daunting problems are addressable only if power is removed from expert hands and returned to public opinion's enlightened forum (Yankelovich 1991, xii). It is often alleged that polls happily serve as the coequal of elections as public guidance (for example, see Crespi 1989, ch. 5). George Gallup proclaimed, "Polls can report what all the people think about a given issue, not just those who take the trouble to vote." They also, allegedly, more accurately assess public thinking (Gallup 1980, 174).

Political scientists heartedly echo this enthusiasm, or at least doubters remain unpublished. Sidney Verba, in his 1996 disciplinary presidential address, expressed an undoubtedly "obvious" fact to fellow practitioners: democracy implies elites heeding mass preferences, and surely the opinion poll is the premier facilitating tool. In his words, "Surveys produce just what democracy is supposed to produce—equal representation of all citizens" (3). Moreover, given the inequality virtually inherent in other means of communicating preferences, the survey is the superior instrument (Verba 1996).[2] James Fishkin, a political theorist whose polling innovations attract ample media attention, interprets this newfound attentiveness as an enduring and distinctly American democratic reinvention (Fishkin 1995, 17). Henry Brady's gushing commemoration of poll accomplishment states, "They provided the gold standard for measuring citizen opinions that are at the heart of democratic deliberation and they provided a powerful technique for ensuring the openness and transparency of the democratic process..." (2000, 47).[3] In their paean to public opinion as a worthy guide to elite decision making Jacobs and Shapiro treated the poll–democracy nexus as so axiomatic that justification seemed unnecessary (2000, preface).

Over fifty years ago, George Gallup optimistically foresaw that polls would raise democratic governance to unimaginable lofty heights (Gallup and Rae 1940; Gallup 1944). Like power station technicians, elected officials, unhindered by self-serving lobbyists, could dispassionately consult the gauges monitoring true public sentiment. The nefarious interest groups deceptively speaking on the public's behalf would be banished forever. No doubt, Gallup's contemporaries (save lingering Progressives) rarely shared his plebiscitory enthusiasm. Sounding an alarm about this fantasy was unnecessary. Such musings were Utopian, given obvious technical imperfections and prodigious cost.

Now, however, Gallup's "all-power-to the-people-via-polling" vision grows quite credible. In a historical millisecond, poll results have imperceptibly gone from infrequent curiosities to seemingly endless messages requiring earnest attentiveness. And, thanks to instant telephone badgering, these pollsters can pronounce nearly any time, on any issue, with unlimited vigor. One might also presume that rapid technological changes, especially the Internet and spreading wireless communications, will bring incessant opinion monitoring ever closer.

Interestingly, the public itself (like Narcissus) grows enamored of its own poll-expressed wisdom. In one 1999 survey, majorities repeatedly expressed confidence in their own superior judgment vis-à-vis that of elected official (Kull 1999). Some 80 percent believed that the nation would progress if leaders abided by public views. Sixty-seven percent agree that members of Congress should monitor polls when voting, while an almost identical number concluded that opinion polls generally serve the public interest. Nearly 85 percent endorsed greater public influence over elected officials. No doubt, these data reflect offhand responses to enticing verities, not reasoned assessments. Fortunately for these self-professed "experts," the interviewer did not inquire, "If you're so smart, how should we fix Social Security?"

A profound political transformation has transpired here: public passion, so feared by Madison and other founders is to be harnessed for civic betterment by those able to extract poll counsel. This change is deceptively fundamental, even radical, not mere mechanical perfection. Those commanding polls into existence are now political virtuoso "players" to the extent that they can freely define public discourse. The national sample stealthily surmounts the firewalls of decentralized federalism. Constitutional designs impeding public outbursts (e.g., calendar fixed elections, supermajorities) are now rendered obsolete by the majoritarian "morning after" survey. Metaphoric expressions such as "guilty in the court of public opinion" edge closer to concrete realities. The once feared, excited *vox populi* now provides wise counsel, or at least so it is argued.

This is an important shift. As Benjamin Ginsberg's *The Captive Public* (1986) makes plain, for centuries prior to scientific polling, control was widely diffused. Modern polling does not create "public opinion;" it only facilitates—even centralizes—its collection. In the premodern era, fabricating "public opinion" was volitional, an act open to every willing participant, not just those lucky enough to be solicited. Few gatekeepers controlled pamphlet writing, soapbox oratory, or joining an unruly mob or similar expressive acts. Nobody silently waited until the Royal Sampler arrived with the Imperial Questionnaire. Only having something to declare mattered. Interpretation was similarly decentralized. Only overt behavior counted; unexpressed "inner-thoughts" had no standing other than idle chatter. "Public opinion" on weighty matters erupted via behavior. Evicting the tax collector or cheerfully paying could voice conviction regarding taxes. A monarch erroneously advised that the peasants happily accepted their tax burdens might have these "data" disconfirmed by rioting. All the Royal Statistical Manipulators and all the King's Spin Doctors could hardly alter this disquieting plain-to-see fact.

The scientific poll has yet to replace this jumbled, fluid mosaic. Those dependent on public sentiment's shifting winds still must harvest bits and pieces of data well outside the poll. Newspaper stories, stirs in mass culture, letters to the editor, and untold behavioral manifestations remain integral to any full, well-rounded picture. Yet, just as "superstore" chains supplanted "Mom and Pop" commerce, this decentralized information gradually succumbs to the professionally run survey. Compared to its primitive rivals, the modern survey is faster, easier to execute, more sharply focused, and, most critically, it drapes itself in the mantel of science. A poll regarding tax burden fairness can be done almost instantly, and who will disbelieve all the Ph.D.s certifying the results? By contrast, personal observations on tax avoidance and widespread cheating tales constitute "vague anecdotal impressions." In a contest for authenticity, the poll data will outrank "impressions" even among those skeptical of interviewee honesty. Flippant thoughts anonymously expressed via the telephone are the "hardest of the hard data," provided the right inquisitors collect these musings.

This analysis rejects this polling-based truth celebration. To our mind, this plebiscitory vision is deeply flawed, both politically and technically. Gallup's enticing mission remains as hopeless and undesirable today as before, technical advancement notwithstanding. Not only is this plebiscitory vision unreachable, but its pronouncements are often rigged. When polls "advise" government on what "the people want," they egregiously distort, and this distortion, ninety-nine out of one hundred times, is systematic in a liberal ideological direction. Today's polls, in a concatenation of seemingly technically neutral steps, inevitably entice people to express unmeetable wishes that, ironically, may well be rejected if these cravings materialized. These unveiled, distorted appetites are then artfully raised up to legitimate democratic instructions. The political polling industry is not analogous to some faceless federal agency mechanically issuing statistics on, say, quarterly housing starts. What is being promoted as a superior, although colorless, way of extracting public pronouncements is part of the political struggle.

This problem lies not in minor wording defect or faulty sampling; it resides at the center of our analytical habits. By ceaseless repetition, these distortions have evolved into an unchallenged methodological orthodoxy. A more forthright depiction of the polling enterprise is that it coaxes statist urges from a cooperative public. Of course, industry experts would claim that our characterization is misguided: Americans *really* do covet these policies and polls faithfully announce the results. This rejoinder is nominally correct, but it misses the larger point, for not every personal wish is a collective command. Heeding popular aspirations for eternal life is pure foolishness although this sentiment is, technically, 100 percent "authentic." To be sure, poll defenders would agree that imperfections exist, for example, ambiguous terminology, but would argue that a little tinkering, not wholesale refurbishment, is the cure. We remain unconvinced; the disorders run far deeper than minor hindrances. Professional avowals aside, today's polls are not akin to a yardstick that indifferently records immutable data. The very ascertainment of public sentiment, *as presently executed and interpreted,* almost always constitutes a political act; "measurement" and "meaning" are often seamlessly blended. Rather than being a yardstick, the poll more closely resembles a rigid container into which liquids can be poured. No matter what the liquid's initial form, when poured it follows the container's shape. All the methodological controversies only obscure this Procrustean bed. The messenger is as much the message as what is inscribed on the delivered document.

This study zeros in on a single, though substantial, facet of polling, namely surveys eliciting public policy preferences regarding social welfare, broadly understood. The archetype is the, "What should the government do about [some problem]," question with the blank item covering virtually every modern governmental function, present and future. Actual question form (i.e., forced-choice vs. open-ended) is unimportant for our purposes. Nor are we especially concerned about the usual details that fascinate pollsters—fluctuating response distributions or demographic divisions. Although the livelihood of data millers, those finer points are secondary here. It is the assembling of a massive, though selective, poll data corpus as our political self-portrait that invites our attention. As in impressionistic paintings, the thousands of individual brushstrokes are subordinated to the overall representation.

Since our argument will undoubtedly appear hostile, even polemical to those laboring amid surveys, two qualifications—one philosophical and the other personal—should be registered at the onset. First, our argument fully accepts that public opinion does, in fact, exist. "Deconstructing" mass sentiment or otherwise advancing a thesis that "public opinion" is inexorably subjective, perhaps subordinated to the power imperatives of race, class, and gender, is not our intent. Nor do we reopen the more methodologically tinged debate regarding "nonattitudes" and similar challenges to the survey's authority. Our dispute is not an assault on the social science edifice or polling itself. That something properly labeled "public opinion" concretely exists is accepted axiomatically. Inquiry concerns how we grapple with the phenomenon, not its epistemological authenticity.

The second point pertains to practitioner research motives. To state that contemporary polls suit liberal statist ideology hardly indicts researchers for *personal* political bias. Inquiry stresses measuring strategies, not psychoanalyzing practitioners. Quite likely, those mining poll data typically welcome modern liberalism's entitlement promises, so earning a livelihood and advocacy are affably mixed. This happy, fortuitous marriage of politics and vocation is not, however, what we intend to expose. It is the deeper crafting of our *Weltanschauung* or worldview that demands watchfulness, not crudely cooking results. This ideological gravitational pull holds regardless of who commands the survey enterprise.[4]

To appreciate the shallowness of poll advice, consider the generic defense-spending question, a popular poll staple that has passed technical inspection by all reputable practitioners. It is almost always asked with a three-part fixed alternative menu—increase, keep the same, or reduce. Substantively, these polls regularly find an aversion to "more" defense spending (Page and Shapiro 1992, 265; Mayer 1992, 248–251). What might these findings tell us about public opinion on military polity? Not much—the entire exercise is beside the point politically.

First and most plainly, its very usage assumes that the public can play a useful role in deciding Pentagon budgets. This is highly debatable. Note well, it is the pollster, not government officials or the public itself, that has extended this invitation. Just why the public should pronounce on this subject is hardly self-evident. Conceivably, the public cares little about this matter and offers an opinion more out of politeness than a desire to shape policy. Moreover, budgets are certainly not decided in national referenda, nor does Congress anxiously await public advice. Even if public sentiment informed the decisional equation, this sporadic datum is rarely synchronized with the legislative calendar; it also fails to provide the nuanced message politicians need, for example, a division of sentiment according to upcoming district voting intention. It is almost unthinkable that any specific poll outcome would be construed as a mandate (see Cantril 1980, Part III; Robinson and Meadow 1982, ch. 3, among others, for how officials treat polls). This is not to say that officials are wholly insulated from public attitudes regarding military appropriation. Wildly erratic decisional shifts, for example, instantly doubling or halving outlays, is wisely understood to invite public outcry. Rather, the pollster-supplied details seldom dictate marching orders on matters on the legislative agenda.

The foolishness of following this counsel here becomes even clear when we consider public knowledge. It is quite unlikely that those answering this question fully grasp the nature of "defense spending." The phrase denotes a vast enterprise, and polls do not prudently exclude the ignorant or, better yet, offer learned tutorials to the ill-informed. Bona fide national security budgetary experts often confess sporadic bafflement with Pentagon disbursement. Try, for example, dividing purely warlike expenses from military social welfare—health care, pensions, childcare, psychological counseling, and sensitivity training. The authentic expert also would add that gross spending levels are secondary to overarching foreign policy debates, and divorcing spending from mission is inane. Perhaps isolationism versus global interventionism is paramount, not some gargantuan abstract dollar figures. There are also innumerable complexities involved in drastically altering defense budgets, for example, the disruption of local economies or wastefulness of rapid expansion–contraction cycles. Judged by the question itself, one might surmise that questionnaire crafters—like their respondents—are clueless regarding defense policy.

The enterprise's shakiness grows more apparent when we scrutinize the questionnaire's fixed choice menu. Judgments about "increasing" or "decreasing" assume respondent acquaintance with existing military outlay figures. In other words, a typical (and reasonably well-informed) respondent privately thinks, "the Pentagon's budget is now [at least in the late 1990s] about $260 billion, and I want expenditures boosted, so I'll say 'increase.'" Another equally conversant respondent answers "reduce." Survey experts assume this condition—everybody shares identical, factually correct starting point referents. This knowledge assumption is patently problematic. Data abound, at times elicited in the same survey, indicating widespread glaring ignorance of spending levels. In the late 1960s, for example, when the guns and butter dilemma was in the forefront, one national survey found 22 percent of respondents could not even offer a guess regarding the defense percentage of the federal budget. Among those venturing an opinion, only about half were even remotely accurate (Weissberg 1976, 40–41). And, it is within this exceptionally generous "accurate" range that actual legislative debate transpires over defense outlays. A mere 1.5 percent of those offering some answer knew the precise correct figure (about what one would expect by chance). Once this knowledge accuracy assumption is relaxed, the "meaning" of this question becomes wholly unascertainable.

Judicious statistical toying illustrates this message vagueness. Suppose that one subsample widely exaggerates defense spending—believing it to be nearly a trillion annually—and prefers something less grandiose, conceivably about $350 billion. Here "reduce" means, in fact, a call for *greater* generosity since current levels fall below $300 billion. Meanwhile, others mistakenly believe the "true" budget number is $100 billion and elect a $50 billion hike. They honestly answer "increase," although a spending reduction (to $150 billion) is what is truthfully desired. If one reasonably assumes ample knowledge variance, and since correct figures are withheld from respondents, the expressed desires cannot possibly be certified as informed policy guidance. *Any* outward response conceivably corresponds to *any* other reply in meaning. More plausible is that "defense budget" is an amorphous, murky symbol drawing uncertain popular reactions.

Even if defense budget figures were known, the "more" or "less" questionnaire alternatives are almost meaningless. Do cost-cutters wish reductions of $5 billion? $10 billion? $100 billion? Who knows, and conceivably everyone possesses an idiosyncratic choice. If a specific figure were agreed on (highly unlikely), what outlays require trimming or expansion? Or, if fiscal levels are untouched, are prevailing intrabudget allocations to remain intact? It is entirely possible that two respondents, both correctly knowing initial budgetary figures, requesting identical increases, diverge substantially in preferences. Smith, for example, craves a high-tech Star Wars missile defense system; Jones favors enhanced salaries and personnel benefits.

Inserting the inescapable factor of payment further compounds the message's imprecision. Citizens here (and elsewhere, as well) are permitted cost-free indulgences. Obviously, those favoring "increase" are implicitly requesting either tax hikes or corresponding reductions elsewhere. Or at least this is what they *should* be thinking, although such awareness cannot prudently be presupposed. Perhaps their desires are more akin to fantasy—they covet the infamous free lunch. If respondents do think realistically, how might this revenue juggling be effectuated? Should the Treasury borrow? Might entitlements be cut? If so, by what precise amounts? Might inflation solve the problem? The funding possibilities are infinite, and choices are politically critical yet are invisible in the survey question.

Finally, once these certified public desires are announced, researchers commonly conclude with a vague genuflection toward "democracy." Some may stop short of claiming a revealed mandate, yet always implied is that this enticed message surely must color public discourse. At a minimum, the poll is the public's contribution to our national colloquy. The supposed missive in our illustration is that the public generally rejects Pentagon budget expansion. Even when such a clamor momentarily exceeds 50 percent, do not be misled, for this "bump" can be explained as reasoned reactions to episodic international events (see, for example, Mayer 1992, ch. 4). In more normal times, stinginess is the default option. *Quod erat demonstrandum* (QED): raising defense budgets generally contravenes the democratic public will. Precious tax money is better spent elsewhere.

Lest we be accused of throwing out the baby with the bath water, this illustrative excursion is not a reactionary assault on survey research. The matter is one of prudent limits, not a social science apostasy. Within appropriate theoretical contexts, these defense spending data *are* the legitimate materials of scientific inquiry. It is certainly proper to align these outpourings with events or demographic shifts to grasp more fully what drives public opinion. Bartels (1994), for example, adroitly uses this defense-spending question to assess how momentous world events often fail to shape domestic public opinion. It is equally worthy to correlate such sentiments with endless individual level traits to paint a rich portrait of public thinking. Recall Gertrude Stein's deathbed rejoinder to Alice B. Toklas's query, "What is the answer?" To which Stein replied, "What is the question?" These defense spending data and all their close relatives clarify innumerable inquests; "What should government do?" is not, alas, one of them.

The key issue here is the usurpation of authority, not flawed survey technique. Our political tradition, formally or informally, scarcely authorized pollsters as *éminence grise* custodians of obscure Oracles. They certainly are not elected, nor popularly authorized. Selection is entirely volitional and, as in sausage making, who knows what transpires behind closed doors? Those drafting questionnaire items, many of which pertain to immensely complex debates, may be ill informed. One attentive review of fifty-one separate survey questions regarding the 1977 Panama Canal Treaty found that ten of these questions contained factual errors, for example, misstating treaty terms or recounting faulty history to interviewees. Numerous other queries were ambiguous or clearly biased (Smith and Hogan 1987). Becoming a pollster, frankly, is commensurate with announcing one's standing as a "certified psychic advisor" and is light-years away from the rigors surmounted by economists or lawyers.

If these insufficient portrayals merely constituted shoddiness in some obscure academic corner or political hucksterism, little else need be said. Chalk up another exposé regarding maladroit, overambitious social science. Unfortunately, the repercussions are greater, even if leaders honestly assert their indifference to this concocted *vox populi*. These indistinct snapshots, endlessly repeated by authoritative scientific Oracles, incorporated into civics textbooks, and portrayed daily in the mass media, help certify the "givens" defining our ever-shifting political culture. It is a smothering "atmosphere," not a precise mandate, that is being fashioned. These data provide a backdrop engulfing day-to-day policy deliberations. Leaders may nominally ignore surveys or contemptuously dismiss them, yet these seemingly endless missives silently infiltrate civic consciousness.[5] Individual poll finding may be forgotten, but each one joins an already immense "what everybody knows" body of public knowledge. Brick by brick, poll by poll, a new self-definition emerges. To dissent from this fabricated consensus perchance hints of dangerous quixotic disengagement from "reality." This catechetical fashioning of "what everybody knows to be true" is consequential for it automatically, with scarcely a moment's reflection, consigns certain goals to worthiness, while making others "unthinkable." Here the "reasonable" political agenda draws its concrete meaning.[6]

A *vox populi* reinforcement of bountiful state welfare intervention, to invoke a beloved Soviet expression, is no accident; it is widely welcomed. Above all, there is a happily arranged marriage between the pollster and the modern welfare state. Benjamin Ginsberg has shown that the modern bureaucratic state absolutely depends on mass support (Ginsberg 1986). The Leviathan's energetic activities, from financial extraction via taxation to achieving compliance to its innumerable regulations, could never survive amid a hostile citizenry. This is hardly slavish state attentiveness to popular cravings; rather, via such techniques as education and election campaigns, government ensures a "comfort zone." The trick is to insure that proposals seem "conventional" and "reasonable." The operative concept is state-secured popular acquiescence. The marshaling of this legitimizing consensus only superficially resembles the contractual mechanics of plebiscitory democracy, rhetoric aside.

The polling industry, regardless of its primary scholarly or commercial motivation, expedites this legitimizing apparatus and is therefore a welcome political player. At a minimum, conspicuously pushing survey results into the public debate outwardly confirms the public's "importance" as the ultimate policy arbitrator. As the Preamble announces that the people "ordain and establish" this Constitution, polls similarly drape state aggrandizement with the cloak of popular sovereignty. Poll results provide fortuitous standing orders for modern government to shoulder responsibilities previously left to citizens themselves. Tales of legislators suspicious of "big government," yet still opportunistically willing to expand government largess, are unexceptional. The arrangement is "win–win," since pollsters agreeably market their product commercially while the *apparatchiki* are happily "implored" to expand their domains.

To condense a lengthy account, the public is routinely probed regarding "helpful" social welfare programs providing fresh "compassion" opportunities.

Wording is one-sided, so respondents must select between government-instigated betterment versus, ostensibly, no ameliorative action. For example, the generic educational policy choice is between "government assistance" and "no assistance." Left unsaid, of course, is that "no assistance" *ceteris paribus* means lower taxes. The real option might more accurately be expressed as a mandatory $200 tax increase for education versus a $200 tax cut available for any purpose, including education. Not unexpectedly given the lopsided menu, robust majorities generally endorse state bounteousness, and this has prevailed for decades, transcending multiple diverse issues. With some reflection, this thirsting is virtually preordained—who can reject the enticing civic betterments? To be sure, as minor experimental details may momentarily derail scientific laws, similar exceptions can afflict polling, for example, substituting "welfare mother" for "impoverished mother needing assistance" seemingly reduces liberal generosity. Nevertheless, the authoritative interpretation of the overwhelming data merely announces the self-evident: to resist this public predilection entails a wearisome battle.

The revelation's tangible impacts are readily seen. Potential office seekers skeptical of New Deal style entitlements are effortlessly consigned to the political fringe. Few newspapers cover Libertarian campaigns. Bennett and Bennett's aptly titled survey, data-rich *Living with Leviathan: Americans Coming to Terms with Big Government* conclude "… that there will be no constituency for smaller government in the foreseeable future (1990, 134). Cook and Barnett's careful analysis of welfare state backing shows that Ronald Reagan's high-profile animosity came to naught—public support, although hardly strident, was sufficient to protect these besieged programs (1992, 4–6, 70; also see Coughlin 1980, 18–19). Recall the unenthusiastic, if not disapproving, public reaction to the 1994 Newt Gingrich led "Contract with America." Smaller government devotees were not merely refuted; their case was *ipso facto* bizarre in the court of public opinion. The unexpected GOP capture of the House clearly did not translate into a roll back of the public social welfare consensus.[7]

The argument is not that dismantling social welfare is an inherently superior choice but that pollsters (backed by a liberal-dominated media) obstruct this as an option. Nor are we hinting that leaders "really" oppose this liberalism but cravenly acquiesce to guarantee reelection. Neither assertion seems plausible: the welfare state *is* popular, deeply entrenched in and outside of government, and picking apart questionnaires cannot reverse this acceptance. Polls unfailing reflect public sentiment and may well reinforce it, but to suggest that surveys *create* citizen entitlement appetites exaggerates. Our point is less ambitious—poll generated consensus virtually smothers opposition by consigning to the statistical margins and, for good measure, mislabeling it. For opponents of this poll assembled *Weltanschauung,* the battle entails establishing a credible ideological beachhead, not merely a technical demonstration.

The perceptive reader undoubtedly detects an odd conundrum, even paradox, infusing our argument. On the one hand, we assert that surveys allegedly ascertaining public preferences are deeply flawed, so imperfect that the results verge on unintelligibility. People seek enticements that they may, if made fully aware of their predilections, reject, while accompanying "expert" interpretations confuse more for less and vice versa. Furthermore, the chorus pleading for the liberal social welfare state (among other benefits) may be delirious, given questionnaire inattention to costs, alternatives, and misinformation. Yet, on the other hand, we frankly acknowledge that this passion for state supplied benefits is real: people *authentically* want the requested health care, improved housing, lavish educational facilities, and so on. Is it possible that from this garble articulated messages worth heeding emerge? Are surveys simultaneously accurate and inaccurate, at once pertinent and irrelevant?

Further confounding our analyses is that these prosocial welfare opinion poll messages, regardless of their intelligibility, are *de facto* heeded democratic mandates. Majorities hunger for increased government benevolent intervention, and, since the 1930s, officialdom has graciously complied. The public speaks and, evidently, the government listens. Even President Reagan essentially acquiesced to these appetites, despite periodic grumblings. That perhaps leaders should have ignored these meretricious big government cravings cannot repudiate this "democratic" connection. The bottom line is that government accommodated public desire, no matter how ineptly expressed or ill-advised.

Our response to these apparent contradictions is unashamed agreement with everything: the polls typically express garbled messages, yet this thoughtlessness reflects a tangible underlying reality. But, admitting this odd truth only disguises a fundamentally false, deceptive picture. As subsequent chapters will show, polls typically elucidate the *wrong* data, not inaccurate data; the culprit is misleading results. It would be as if one sought a lost car key and eventually did locate some keys. Finding car keys *per se* is not the issue. More crucial is whether the key in hand precisely fits one's own car. Only a careful application can answer that question. In analyzing the opinion–policy nexus, the *politically* pertinent data are citizen responses to situations closely corresponding to actual political choices, not fantasy menus. If the poll wishes to assemble mandates, citizens must emulate relevant officials. Apples to apples, so to speak. Citizen wants are irrelevant, even in a democratic Utopia: *only what they can have under difficult, realistic circumstances is germane.* Avoiding this perplexity escapes into a world of political reverie that no amount of statistical manipulation can hide.

Plan of Analysis

We contend that the ubiquitous everyday snapshots presented by today's polls displaying the social welfare state's popularity are either incorrect, grossly exaggerated, or—at best—undemonstrated. Disputing this conventional wisdom will be daunting and, to exacerbate the task, we assert unfamiliar analytical distinctions applied to well-known subject matter. An entire industry, unchallenged since the early days of the social science behavioral revolution will assuredly feel threatened. If these assaults were insufficient to guarantee enduring unpopularity, we further seek to roll back the infatuation with the plebiscitory style that daily creeps closer to legitimacy. George Gallup notwithstanding, democracy and polling are not symbiotic, and announcing this fact will surely draw the ire of professional pollsters.

In the following chapter, we offer our most controversial theory. We investigate the very meaning of "opinion" in "public opinion." It is here, in some conceptual sleight of hand, that the rush to generate easily manipulated, unambiguous results engenders a disregard for intimidating, yet vital, political issues. "An opinion about government policy" entails far more than those facile utterances routinely expressed within the generic poll. We begin by distinguishing types of public sentiment often obscured by pollsters. We shall see, for example, that coveting the unobtainable, no matter how candidly articulated, differs enormously from intelligently selecting among harsh reality-imposed options. Hidden complexities bedevil these choices— imposing priorities across issue domains, willingness to bear policy burdens or tolerating nonoptimal preferences, among others. Contrary to devotees of plebiscite style guidance, correctly assessing public preferences may be hopelessly indeterminate.

Chapter Three takes up the theory underlying the public's capacity to render informed policy judgments under realistic circumstances. Public competency is an inescapable element in creating today's poll-defined consensus, yet our knowledge (and theory) here is deceptively inadequate. Citizen proficiency will be explored both generally and specifically: competence required of all citizens, simply by them being citizens, versus the highly specific capacities needed to navigate policy dilemmas. We show that today's scholarly "civic competence" measures are essentially irrelevant to ascertaining citizen decision-making skill. We then formulate a more appropriate assessment instrument. The accurate calibration of citizen capability is essential for we cannot expect an incompetent public to guide government. Moreover, falsely attributing collective wisdom is mischievous—recall our defense expenditure example of the public's ill-informed "pronouncements." Reaching a judgment on this capability matter is exacting and, as in properly calibrating "opinion," this task may exceed today's polling reach.

Chapter Four sets the stage for more realistic probes into the American public's putative social welfare state infatuation. We consider two policy initiatives—Washington subsidies to hire more grade-school teachers and greater daycare accessibility. Both are "classic" seductive entitlement lures. Analysis sharply breaks with survey research tradition and explores these two proposals in great detail. We show, for example, that lurking behind these popular measures are serious difficulties and uncertainties, all conveniently ignored in conventional polls. Our questionnaire on one of these topics also will be given close scrutiny, given its divergence from the usual "quick and dirty" probe.

Chapter Five examines data drawn from two national polls expressly conducted for this project. We shall see that "public opinion" is far more complicated than is extracted from the familiar "Do you favor..." type poll. Not surprisingly, support for a worthy aim can wilt when citizens are confronted with drawbacks and risks. We also show that citizen competence to address these seemingly "easy" issues is problematic. "Buying" improved education or federal daycare subsidies is hardly on a par with purchasing humdrum consumer goods. Our aim is not to reveal that people misspeak or that stealthy liberal pollsters manipulate surveys. Rather, the enterprise itself, no matter how proficiently executed, elicits public responses that are better characterized as lofty aspirations, not choices corresponding to realistic policy options.

Chapter Six, "Bestowing the Democratic Mantle," scrutinizes the easy conflation of poll results (and other direct democracy devices) with an alleged "democratic mandate." This flattering connection grows ever more ubiquitous, especially among academics and self-appointed direct democracy tinkers. Nevertheless, infatuation aside, this imputed nexus demonstrates both a profound twisting of "democracy" and disdain for already established sturdy citizen influence channels. Relentless survey-inspired initiatives are not the preordained next step in the march toward democratic perfection; worse, an estimable status quo is radically subverted. The plebiscite poll and comparable contrivances authorize a potentially dangerous shift in power away from accountable, elected officials to obscure technocrats marching to a wholly different political beat. This conscripting of ordinary citizens as "unofficial political advisors" facilitates the most craven political manipulation and empowers untold unelected players at the expense of duly constituted authority.

Finally, having navigated the survey's many uncertainties, we explore the poll's legitimate democratic role. The distinction between generating "interesting curiosities" and "useful advice" is fundamental. The former is perfectly legitimate in its proper sphere, mainly as public self-inspection, for example, polls regarding morality or similar topics where "an opinion" is inherently subjective. There is nothing inappropriate about inquiring into the neighborhood's *Zeitgeist*. Such extracted musing may even inspire policy. When the aim is soliciting firm popular counsel, admission standards must, necessarily, be much stricter. Governments are not department store Santa Clauses. Such public testimony must be carefully evaluated and, conceivably, the populace will be wisely excluded from public deliberations. The proper focus is one of appropriateness, and debates over "elitism" only distract from this arduous task. Disbanding the polling enterprise is uncalled-for; rather, as in utilizing any instrument, suitability is the true test, not abstract worthiness. Analysis ends with a ringing defense of elections, not polls, as the superior democratic method.

CHAPTER 2

From Wishes to Hard Choices

What we call public opinion is generally public sentiment.
—Benjamin Disraeli, Speech, August 3, 1880

If public opinion is to guide our politics meaningfully, messages must be accurate and applicable. As the blind must lead the blind, the disconcerted must not direct the confused into the wilderness. Critical is the distinction between accurately measuring respondent views and extracting messages providing sage counsel. Although the former has been the object of immense scholarly attention, the latter has barely been noticed. The two concepts routinely diverge under ordinary circumstances. For example, a poll may solicit opinion on what the government should do next on education. Every respondent may answer absolutely accurately in a way satisfying the technical perfectionist. Yet, this avalanche of passionate outpourings will undoubtedly be useless to officials seeking public guidance. This erstwhile "mandate" will surely be an amalgam of idiosyncratic views, fantasies, misunderstandings, and garble mixed in with a bit of realism. Paradoxically, individual accuracy is superb; civic usefulness is near zero.

This neglect of "politically useful messages versus accurate personal views" involves far more than scholarly carelessness. Nor is more adroit statistical processing of commonplace survey data the cure; deficiencies are far more conceptual than technical. Here we begin explicating polling's shortcomings. We argue that the prevailing survey methodology, regardless of how superbly it might assess an individual's thinking, falls short when judged against the worthy counsel standard. That conventional survey data might conveniently be deciphered as advice hardly certifies this substitution as appropriate.

What is needed, then, is a reconceptualization of public opinion itself, a shift away from probing inner-thoughts toward how best to elicit political realism. Although today's survey research vocabulary is woefully inadequate to our task, progress has been made to extract worthy advice, although it may not have been labeled as such. Though each alternative enterprise might be judged evolutionary "dead ends," they are profitably resuscitated if realism is our authentic aim. More important, their resurrection sheds light on the prospect for the poll-driven direct democracy so favored by today's practitioners.

Delineating the Cosmology

What do we label poll results regarding government aid to education? Sentiments are typically assigned various descriptors: preferences, attitudes, views, choices, and similar synonyms connoting wants and desires. Terminology substitution undoubtedly reflects a commendable effort to enliven readability, not substantive or theoretical distinctions. Few readers might even notice shifting phraseology, and certainly favoring one term over another implies nothing special theoretically. Nevertheless, at the risk of inviting accusations of scholasticism, consider certain distinctions in this haphazard vocabulary.

Let us call an expressed public desire for an amorphous proposal far distant from the public agenda a "*wish.*" Wishes, by nature, properly bear on anything conceivable, no matter how unobtainable, impracticable, political, or nonpolitical. They are cravings, thirstings, even fantasies. A longing for world peace and economic equality exemplify "wishes." Moreover, despite this potential for detachment, public articulation is unquestionably democratically legitimate and authentic. Idealism, after all, is a worthy civic culture ingredient. Public thirstings for glittering vagaries may be the singularly most dominant feature of public opinion—they define those collective "givens" of public discourse. A discerning candidate might well craft his or her electoral messages to satisfy these urges, for example, pander to a "law and order" clamor. They are "real" thoughts, regardless of their dreamlike coloration. Still, as counsel directing government, they resemble children's Santa Claus "wish lists." Opinion polls in such circumstances only serve to announce the obvious—people covet prosperity, peace, tranquility, and so on. To reiterate, wishes are not "wrong" or ephemeral; they just do not comprise serviceable political guidance. Surely, no sane person opposes majority appetites as a "decent idea," but this flattery does not certify these messages as marching orders.

The term *"preference"* advances one step closer to political reality although the journey still remains incomplete. Preferences are, at least nominally, politically realistic and more focused. Support for greater government efforts to promote education illustrates "a preference." Separating wishes from preferences is hardly self-evident, but this disconnecting is a prerequisite to transforming wishes into realistic messages. Several factors provide useful separation criteria. Most evidently, a preference must, at least in the foreseeable future, conform to guiding constitutional and legal principles or else it reverts to "wishfulness." In the illustration of government education assistance, a "preference" acknowledges traditional legal constraints, the decentralized federal character of school policy plus untold other gridlock inducing controls. Desiring augmented local school expenditures is a preference; demanding that Washington outlaw Catholic schools is wishful thinking. That wishes may ultimately become preferences (and vice versa) cannot abolish this distinction. Everything depends on reasonable feasibility within some immediate future. A few may desire public education to be eradicated altogether, yet, within the context of "reasonable politics," this desire should properly be classified as a wish, not a preference. Politics customarily involves transforming the outlandish into the conceivable.

Additionally, a preference must, at least in principle, be achievable over and above its legality. This may entail adequate financial resources, technical acumen, ample motivation, or countless ingredients typically entering the accomplishment equation. Requesting the local school board to abolish football is an achievable (although undoubtedly long-shot) preference; insisting on uniform mathematical proficiency is hopeful thinking. Again, the boundaries are not forever permanent and some disagreement is inevitable. Mathematical excellence is conceivably reachable if only colossal resources were committed or some new miracle teaching method arrived. Many a political wish—women's suffrage, African American voting rights—have evolved from "pie-in-the-sky" daydreams into hardheaded preferences. Yet, it is foolishness to contend that anything imaginable is doable, so all desires are equally serious. The political landscape is cluttered with endless failed quixotic schemes. Potential agenda items might require biological engineering or harsh draconian measures, and these can surely be legitimately monitored via polling. Perhaps "long-term future-oriented preference" should artfully describe wishes possessing some tiny, although not infinitesimal, likelihood of success.

The final step in our march toward political relevance we shall label *"hard choice."* The defining element is an option array realistically corresponding to decision makers' choices. Hard choices are firmly rooted in political reality.

Conceive of "a poll" in which fifteen hundred ordinary citizens joined Congress (or the relevant executive branch agency) when it came time to enact policy. Moreover, these newly anointed "lawmakers" would be responsible for their choices: they might, for example, be asked to explain or justify themselves by colleagues or pressured by outsiders. "Bad decisions" would have discernable negative consequences, for example, removal from "office." Choice would occur within the context of all other competing obligations, for instance, voting for increased spending might contravene past promises to cut taxes. "Hard choices" differ absolutely fundamentally from diverse populist projects mimicking leadership decision making by inserting discussions into the polling progress (see, for example, Fishkin 1991; Fishkin 1995). Having citizens collectively discuss their choices is a far cry from insisting that they wrestle with obstinate dilemmas or pay for ineptitude.

Nothing here stipulates wise choices, informed choices, or the rational pursuit of self-interest. The shift from wishes to hard choices refers only to the character of the decision-making process. Hard choices are realistic in the sense that a multitude of inescapable, tangible variables *must* now inform decisions. We are merely putting ordinary folk, to the extent feasible in a poll, into the shoes of those who must ultimately decide. Citizens, like our esteemed leaders, have every right to stupidity. Insisting on hard choices is not to concoct clever schemes to extract blood from turnips. Foolishness always remains possible, even likely. Comparability with the political process, not uncovering abstract excellence, is the aim.

Proceeding from wishes to preferences and then to hard choices makes the public's message more politically relevant, perhaps more legitimate, to actual decisions. A normative argument also informs this transformation: to be heeded, public messages *should* pass this equivalency test. Make no mistake, leaders in any political system, democratic or not, are always free to pander to any ruinous public passion. Polls will always be free to solicit wishes and, no doubt, examples of "give-them-what-they-want" imprudence are eternal. No constitutional or statutory obligation commands "obey only sensible public opinion."

Nevertheless, leaders cannot reasonably be held accountable to obeying nonsensical, unconstrained Utopian mandates. Office holders are not wizards who can square budgetary circles or magically flatten economic inequalities, if only they "truly" desired. Officials may publicly compliment such utterances, prudently incorporate them into electoral strategy, or adjust their daily rhetoric accordingly. It is preposterous, however, to insist that every survey-solicited, instantly concocted whim be awarded legitimate political standing. Governance cannot be guided by backroom question-formulators free to propose attractive absurdities to the gullible. Majorities might well express enthusiasm for bizarre recommendations, yet this "advice" is dismissable on its face.

Soliciting responsible recommendations regarding at-hand perplexities is the implicit model. As the advice-giver becomes more acquainted with a situation's intricacies, and the wages of shoddy guidance become more consequential, proffered advice is taken more seriously. A professional accountant intimately acquainted with a client's options professionally vouching for one's tax return receives a more receptive audience than a stranger's flippant harebrained scheme. The latter's counsel may indeed be attractive, but it is not in the same league as legitimate expert opinion, obviously. In short, unlike wishes, sentiments comprising hard choices are the stuff of serious policy deliberation.

From Free Choice to Constraint

To appreciate current political polling's deceptively problematic nature, hypothesize commercial market research imitating the quintessential political survey. That is, the interviewer presented respondents with "What do you want from car manufacturers?" or "Which features do you prefer in an automobile?" style inquires. Answers were then aggregated and presented to the sponsor. The manufacturer would indubitably reject the resultant portrait as fantasy, no matter how technically adroit the statistical analysis. Surely, the client would explain, *nobody* could build a vehicle that performed like a Corvette, was as crashworthy as a Volvo, as luxurious as a Rolls Royce, as reliable as a Lexus, while being Yugo priced. Yet, this is *exactly* (hypothetically) what the best and brightest practitioners have expertly revealed. The survey's patron would assuredly challenge this methodology without impugning public candor. He or she surely asks if these respondents could afford a car, needed a vehicle, or even intended to enter the automobile marketplace. None of this would have been extracted in this wishlist poll. The survey is accurate, the customer is always right, but inapplicable information has been recovered.

Now imagine that our poll respondent actually sought to purchase an auto. Initially, this mythical Corvette-Vulvo-Rolls-Lexus-Yugo (Cvrly) might be sought, but preliminary marketplace tours would quickly disclose the quest's hopelessness. One-by-one, each of these desired ideals would be abandoned or drastically downgraded and, in the end, the final pick will be totally unlike survey-expressed ideal model. The consumer's purchase will doubtlessly cost more than a Yugo, be less opulent than a Rolls, handle less brilliantly than a Corvette, and so on. Perfect fantasy seldom—if ever—survives harsh reality. Moreover, the car might be a lemon, not the "demanded" phantasm.

Now suppose a second marketing firm joined this project. Here, however, uncovering public desires stressed consumer behavior, not wishful verbal fantasies. It was axiomatic that when it came to actually writing a check, resources were scarce, priorities arrayed, tradeoffs made, and all else that goes into making "real choices." The research would reveal, for example, that Honda Accords far outsold Lincoln, Jaguar, or Mercedes although, if tastes could be painlessly indulged, many Honda owners might prefer untold grander, even technically superior autos. If these data were then combined with survey information it might be disclosed, for example, that Honda owners commonly made their pick because Honda did everything commendably, though nothing extraordinarily well. It was, in fact, not "the best" car or even among the top ten; it was merely the better car across multiple criteria. Moreover, deeper probing revealed that Accord owners "really" coveted BMW 740s but, even those few who could afford this $75,000 engineering masterpiece, believed that the marginal improvement exceeded the added $55,000. Repeatedly, respondents volunteered, "with an extra fifty-five grand, I could buy three Hondas or pay off the mortgage." If Honda management did commission a "wishlist" market-research survey, it would probably delve into details, for example, favorite colors, versus transforming plain-Jane Accords into high-performance luxury vehicles.

Which of these alternative methodologies correctly applies to public opinion assessment? Judged by fashionableness, the first—the "anything goes" survey—wins hands down. This approach is obviously simpler methodologically and therefore more alluring. By contrast, the second stratagem's application is exceptionally vexing. Save periodic elections plus an occasional voter initiative, citizens cannot "purchase" policies as they do with groceries. Convenient, collective hard currency "policy supermarkets" are nonexistent outside governing institutions. Citizens may buy individual health care or home security, but they cannot decide *public* policy in these areas. Thanks to unconstrained surveys, however, citizens are "allowed" to demand the political equivalent of Cvrlys for *everyone*. Compounding this mismatch, when Cvrlys are unavailable, grumblings are heard that "the system" is unresponsive and, horror of horrors, democracy itself is under siege. One can only conjecture if GM stockholders "demanded" that this wondrous Cvrly be built. Management would unfailingly dismiss this clamor as nonsensical, and even GM's harshest critics would concur. Manufacturing—like politics—is the art of the possible.

Have we unearthed a deep incompatibility dooming public guidance? Not exactly; it is only a matter of rendering unto Caesar what is Caesar's. Today's generic polls cannot disentangle unfettered thirstings from hard choices; they can only reveal wishes and, at best, preferences. But, the matter is not forever closed, and it may be possible for the polling format to proceed beyond wishes. The emphasis is on "possibly" moving from wishes to hard choices. This task will be addressed in two parts. First, what theoretical components comprise hard choices (rather than wishes and preferences); second, can practical survey techniques mimic market decision making? Put concretely, since citizens do not periodically purchase military defense as they might acquire automobiles, how can a survey make defense buying resemble consumer choice?

Fabricating Hard Choices

If we take the legislature process as our model, certain elements should inform a realistic tapping of public pulses. Consequentially is essential—those venturing opinions must "live with" their choices. After all, those lawmakers proposing chancy schemes afterward answer to voters and/or fellow public servants, interest group leaders, campaign contributors, and innumerable others. This requirement need not imply a particular direction. For example, both financial frugality and abundant wastefulness may be enticed by "face-the-music" requirements depending on conditions. One might also append susceptibility to challenge—proposals will undoubtedly be denounced and thus must be defensible. Outrageousness may be indulged, but it will have repercussions.

Equally germane is the proliferation of options confronting decision makers. Legislative menu alternatives, even on narrow issues, may run into the dozens, not the two or three options proffered to survey respondents. Choices, moreover, are inescapably linked, not independent; generosity in one realm may oblige parsimony elsewhere. One cannot at roughly the same time have both A and not-A, however great the temptation. Finally, the dictates of collective choice ineluctably propel expressed preferences toward consensus. Why express ideas lacking any chance of adoption where majorities rule? The aim is securing the best possible "sellable" deal, not achieving perfection. Again, the introduction of a correspondence formula is not a stricture for wisdom: the endeavor only insists on public opinion–policymaking comparability.

Although this equivalence problem remains to be more fully explored, let us consider three inescapable elements: (1) accepting non-optimal preferences;

(2) paying for preferences; and (3) fashioning tradeoffs across competing wants. No doubt, other ingredients comprise this virtual reality recipe, although these three are prominent starting points. Each component seemingly infuses real-world decision making lacking in the conventional approach. Our thrifty perspective Honda owner, for example, only wants to spend roughly $20,000, desires a satisfactory—though not necessarily brilliant—performance on multiple criteria, and ranks trustworthy resale investment over exotic luxury. The bottom line, then, is a willingness to pay something reasonable for a decent car, and this buyer will gladly settle for a fifth or sixth choice vis-à-vis a BMW or Mercedes. Olympian perfection is off the agenda. Further excluded from this calculation is informational accuracy or astuteness. Incorporating consumer sagacity is, at least temporarily, beyond this hard choice virtual reality—the Honda may turn out to be a lemon.

Measuring Hard Choices

Accepting Nonoptimal Choices

The typical poll question offers respondents a menu from which one, and only one, item is selectable. Individuals insisting on electing two or more options would, no doubt, be asked to pick only "the best." Selection variability over successive trials is interpreted as either instrument unreliability or preference instability, both defects to be expunged in future questionnaires. It is assumed that this single choice best approximates the "most preferred" choice of the array, and that what is rejected is wholly unacceptable. Designs inevitably impose this singularity assumption definitionally, for example, "yes-no" or "more-same-less" choices are exhaustive and exclusive. Geometrically, a survey response is conceptualized as a single point on a one-dimensional line defining all possible, mutually exclusive policy choices. The poll objective is locating this unique point as accurately as possible.

In pedestrian "give-and-take politics," this assumption of a sole acceptable alternative to the exclusion of all else is plainly preposterous. The poll inquiry indubitably masks ample willingness to accept multiple nonoptimal outcomes, at least under common situations. This acceptability may range from "excellent" to "barely acceptable under the worst possible conditions." For example, respondents endorsing government health care spending increases might prefer a $50 billion jump but, plausibly, could acquiesce to $60 or $40 billion, as well. Indeed, a few preferring $50 billion hikes might embrace a $1 billion increase provided this figure was the single viable option and the initial extraordinarily high number was a strategic ploy. Faced with imminent health assistance cutbacks, our "spend $60 billion more" advocate might well settle for zero expansion as the most advantageous deal under horrible circumstances.

The political ramification of formulating public opinion as an acceptable options range is immense. In the world of "wishes" impractical policy options such as doubling the health care budget may well elicit majority endorsement. In vaudeville language, a wishful populace constitutes a "tough crowd." In a "hard-choice" setting, however, such detachment from realism is impermissible. Here the menu is dictated by harsh actuality, not a fantasizing clientele: one eats at McDonald's, not dines on customized gourmet meals prepared by a famous private chef.

In the hard-choice environment, *any* or nearly every current agenda item might fall into the zones of "acceptability," although each one may lie quite distant from perfection. Or, nothing might be appetizing, and one selects only by dint of interviewer pressure. It all depends on momentary tangible political constraints and the structure of proffered options. Typically, to the extent that policy is routinely adjusted at the margin, *every* publicly presented agenda alternative might be sufficient, although hardly the most preferable to popular majorities craving momentous improvements. Options that patently lack notable support or are unfeasible have long been winnowed by the time the issue ripens for resolution. Political necessity may engender watered-down compromises only minimally satisfying a bare majority. In the case of health care proposals, contrary to what menu a pollster might offer, the choices are *not* between government increases versus zero intervention. Rather, for the most part, the debate centers on relative details on top of an ample status quo: coverage extensions, altered copayments, enhanced private entity participation, and the like. Conceivably, many program expansion fans might well be minimally content with sustaining the status quo.

Banishing suboptimal choices from the proffered options menu loads the dice toward poll-constructed policy-preference disjunction. What might be an easy-to-please customer is now converted into a picky one by virtue of available questionnaire options. Proceeding one step further, picture a highly incremental policy process whereby government action gravitated toward the majority's optimal choice. If only the majority's singular optimal demand was visible via the survey, each separate preceding opinion measurement reveals plebiscitory unfaithfulness. Yet, judged against the standard of adequacy, the opposite holds: government has continually acted to satisfy. As in Zeno's Paradox, progress is continuous but, alas, the destination is never reached.

Can this fuller picture be obtained without making untenable assumptions regarding popular calculating skills to sort among optimal and nonoptimal preferences? This is surprisingly achievable, but, as we shall see, only up to a point. One small research island counsels optimism, although the "bulkiness" of this technique explains its current obscurity. This is the "social judgmental" approach, a technique invented primarily to theorize about individual-level attitude change. Nevertheless, it serves our purposes admirably well. Central to social judgmentalism is an expansive conception of "attitude." As outlined by Sherif, Sherif, and Nebergall (1965), an "attitude" is a person's evaluative stand toward an object, other people, groups, issues, or institution. Most relevant for our purposes, this "stand" is defined as a *range* of graduated evaluative reactions, not a single optimal point. This definitional acceptance of multiple preferences, all part of the same attitude, is fundamental.

This expanse of points can be conveniently divided into latitudes of "acceptance," "rejection," and "noncommitment." These vary across individuals and within individuals by issue domains. For example, a religious fanatic might judge religious objects with a highly truncated, binary standard—the single "true" faith and everything else, all of which is uniformly negative. A secularist conceivably exhibits a quite different stand: a murky "good" faith cluster, indifference to sundry other creeds, and a brief list of "bad" sects. The fervent believer cleaves the theological world into cherished Roman Catholic and all else. The political phenomenon of avid partisans imposing microscopic distinctions among those nearby while grossly characterizing opponents is also frequent. Evidence also hints at cultural differences, for example, one study found that compared to Americans, Japanese were inclined to bunch up their evaluation in the middle or more neutral category of evaluative scales (cited in Sherif, Sherif, and Nebergall 1965, 100).

Attitude assessment mechanics here are technically esoteric compared to today's conventional questionnaire despite straightforward underlying assumptions. Assessment commences with collecting issue positions via content analysis drawn from social life and generally known to respondents. These snippets encompass the full range of publicly exhibited (not hypothetical) debate. The difference between this design and the more prosaic questionnaire construction is subtle, yet sharp. Drawing issue points from ongoing disputes interjects valuable fluid up-to-date realism—for example, today's health care debate may be quite unlike the 1960s controversies, when deliberations first entered public consciousness and "founding" questionnaire items initially surfaced. After all, why solicit public counsel on matters long since settled? Reliance on political arena expressed views similarly interjects authenticity, no small gain since questionnaire drafters may be policy novices. Choices are no longer between *a priori* content-free options on forever-fixed questions, for example, "Should we increase/decrease spending on X?" Their replacements are generally closer to what we have deemed "hard choices." And, by insisting on some minimal respondent acquaintance with the issue domain, we withdraw invitations to those incapable of entering public discourse.

It is assumed that positions culled from ongoing disputes can be respondent-arrayed according to personal favorableness. Naturally, those oblivious to the policy universe will be challenged. One can only imagine, for example, rural Bolivians grappling with divergent U.S. health care policy alternatives. It must be assumed that the assignment entails familiar material. Nevertheless, this assumption aside, this ranking exercise is straightforward. No fixed set of researcher-supplied set of categories is mandated. Some participants might impose a bipolar classification scheme; others may infer minute distinctions. As Eskimos have multiple words for "snow," a few respondents may finely delineate "accept" and "reject." This seeming technical detail interjects valuable political realism. To wit, innumerable public disputes involve conflicts between "hardliners" unwilling to accept anything less than perfection confronting "softies" promiscuously embracing nearly everything. Views that are respondent-defined as nonsensical, ambivalent, or otherwise meaningless are simply excluded from the sorting process. Nor are intervals between categories assumed to be equal. This is unimportant politically thought, pertinent for statistical computation. To reiterate, the aim is to discover roughly structured collections of preferences for current political agenda options, not exposing the most preferred choice among researcher-devised options.

To illustrate this approach, consider various experiments assessing racial integration views conducted among University of Oklahoma undergraduates during the 1950s (Sherif, Sherif, and Nebergall 1965, 109–126). That era's conventional poll questions were of the "Do you favor or oppose racial integration of schools?" type. Respondents there could only oppose or favor crude alternatives, and, in retrospect, one can see how ineptly this coarse polar opposite formulation foretold future racial divisiveness. This stark "either-or" menu may have reflected questionnaire formulator viewpoints plus the need to obtain quick clear-cut data. In our example, by contrast, analysis began with 114 statements covering the full range of race-related issues. Care was taken to include subjects known to possess strong views, for example, black student civil rights activists and white members of anti-integration fraternities. Respondents sorted these 114 statements into piles reflecting similarity of content. The number of categories was respondent prescribed. This assignment completed, instructions were given to sort the most objectionable to the least objectionable within each grouping. Neither category number nor evaluative phraseology was researcher determined.

The results generally confirmed expectations regarding interindividual differences. Those outwardly expressing vehement stands applied fewer evaluative categories while gravitating toward extreme positions. Blacks in particular found few positions even nominally acceptable. Interestingly, when respondents were subsequently told to utilize an eleven-point scale, they generally continued to stick with their "own" (briefer) classification format. This is deceptively important for it demonstrated that at least some respondents refused to make distinctions among views that, we can assume, were arguably distinct abstractly. This is no small matter when polls supposedly demonstrate one stand generally preferred over another. Conceivably, every position in a grouping might be judged as roughly interchangeable.

Similar experiments also revealed that statement mixes given to respondents shape the sorting process. For example, among those personally favoring extreme views, the inclusion of immoderate alternatives "pushed" more middle-of-the-road views away from acceptability. In other words, a once acceptable temperate stance may well become unsuitable, depending on what lies at the outer edges. The political relevance here is obvious—the poll's range of proffered choices frames what might accept independently of what one "really" prefers. Why settle for a perfectly serviceable Honda, if a coveted BMW is remotely feasible? The perfect is the enemy of the good, as the old adage goes.

The work reflecting this approach is assuredly fragmentary, even obscure, especially in comparison with the thousands of conventional poll inquires. The social judgmental technique flourished briefly in one small corner of psychology and has, seemingly, vanished from today's research landscape. Sadly, this demise assuredly reflects more on the technique's arduous implementation than the quality of extracted data. Just compare the simple battery of "yes–no" probings on general at-hand topics with tediously assembling dozens of positional statements and statistically analyzing data where response categories (and total items selected) fluctuate individually. Rendering social judgmental data "meaningful" via a standard computational procedure overwhelms, while the simplest informational display taxes the eye. For those desiring quick reads of public sentiment, this technique imposes prodigious burdens.

Our mini-review nevertheless offers some potentially helpful lessons. Policy choice "meanings" evidently vary across people and domains.

A sharply delineated choice menu to one may be indistinguishable sameness to another. Imagine an isolationist answering a poll about U.S. overseas intervention in which all options entail degrees of foreign involvement? While activists might rush to the barricades over seemingly trifling differences, the average person might gladly accept *every* option in an array of choices. Equally apparent, capacity to distinguish among preference may be constrained and, significantly, issue-domain dependent. Recall how multiple, supposedly distinct statements were compacted into a few categories, even when respondents were invited to employ more differentiated measuring sticks. Forcing picks from among items in a broad category may unintentionally impose nonexistent differences. A particularly intriguing possibility is that wide conceptual gulfs may exist across subpopulations. We cannot assume that the poll question writer's world corresponds to a universal reality. Finally, beware of the "too-good-to-be-true" option inserted willynilly into the poll's array of picks. Such Utopianism may render the once acceptable unacceptable.

Still, this technique takes us only half way (perhaps less) if our goal is ascertaining nonoptimal choices from survey data. This pessimism holds even if this technique could be made amenable to today's analytical conventions. Assembling all these citizen nonoptimal preferences, regardless of how nuanced, says nothing about arriving at a final *collective* choice. Remember, in the above experiments respondents could elect from among dozens, sometimes one hundred plus choices. Respondents who might be allies will in all likelihood differ in just how they sort their choices, even permitting crude grouping of dissimilar picks.

This method cannot elicit majorities, a key ingredient in formulating poll-derived counsel. Perhaps only when a majority evinces the identical first choice is this dilemma solved; otherwise a governing majority must be created from innumerable less than perfectly satisfactory preferences. This majority extraction is a nightmare when a supposedly collective, *public* opinion is to be extracted from individual responses voiced by people who will never negotiate among themselves.

Hypothesize a legislative body considering health care. Each legislator will begin with his or her assortment of ranges: "most preferred," "acceptable," and so on. Desires may exceed dozens and, to add an extra dollop of realism, identical issue stands may range from indifference to fanatical advocacy. As this topic meanders along the legislative process, initial ranges will evolve as circumstances shift and new information emerges. A few lawmakers will surely grasp that even their initial fourth or fifth desired choices are unobtainable and that the best available option now lies in their once "barely acceptable" category. Meanwhile, others pleasantly discover that they have more like-minded colleagues than formerly believed and that their first choices are feasible politically. The upshot for the latter group is that positions once assigned to the "indifferent" class now may well become unacceptable. Over time, harsh realities force opinion adjustments just as the expression of other people's views alters the reality governing what is possible. With vote trading, opportunistic alliances, and all the other negotiation features necessary for legislatures to reach majority consensus, initial viewpoint configurations *must* be transformed by the exigencies of majority decision making. Put differently, initial first-choice only positions can *never* be the final word in achieving a majority save the simplest cut-and-dried situation (e.g., there are only two genuine options).

The poll, by its intrinsic atomistic nature, precludes those interactions necessary to transform atomized multipreference positions into a consensual majority. Collecting a thousand interviews does not create an assembly of citizens, and this fact is critical. Even if our sample were assembled, the quest remains formidable. Social choice theorists such as William Riker (1988, especially ch. 10) have long argued that amalgamating individual choices into singular, indisputable collective outcomes is nearly impossible. Note well, these social choice exercises do not preclude obtaining *a* majority. The problem is that any number of democratically (and morally) justifiable aggregation rules can yield notably different outcomes with the identical data. Put concretely, with all the abundant data generated by the social judgmental approach, a "majority" flows from researcher-imposed counting rules, not some obvious, indisputable trait of the opinion data.[1]

There is a notable irony here. Practitioners always fear "outsider" influence on responses, for example, the impact of social desirability or unintentional interviewer cueing. Such "social pressure" distorts the individual's true opinion, forcing him or her to, alas, voice only situationally determined, hedged stands. Researchers would be horrified if respondents consulted others so as to please friends before answering questions. Yet, this conferring with others, giving and taking, in which acceptable views are adjusted to attain a situational consensus is *exactly* what *must* transpire in decision-making bodies, be they legislatures or samples. Without this horse-trading, abandoning one's initial ideal, and all else that smacks of pragmatic *realpolitik* to get the best deal possible, a majority outcome is often unachievable in equivocal situations. Tales of legislatures enacting laws not quite favored by anyone, far removed from initial proposals as the best deal possible, are endemic. Congress would fail miserably if lawmakers, like steadfast poll respondents, said: "This is my first choice, and I will not be swayed by such extraneous factors such as trying to please others." Enticing a majority from amorphous arrays of individual views cannot be solved by mere discussions among sampled citizens, either. Final decisions must be negotiated with a singular outcome imposed if equivalence between the poll and the legislative act is to be maintained.

Willingness to Pay

A disposition to finance one's expressed choices absolutely inheres in any realistic public opinion portrait. Demanding a plethora of lavish goodies while refusing to reimburse costs renders this craving nonsensical and therefore dismissable. For the poll to cultivate public rapaciousness only summons national ruin, not enlightened guidance. Elected public officials certainly grasp this fact—few readily embrace tax increases, no matter how fervent their ostensible civic generosity. Surprisingly, in stark contrast to commercial inquires regarding consumer purchases, polls seldom extract financial eagerness on public goods. The acknowledged state-of-the-art University of Michigan's Survey Research Center's surveys have for decades touched on virtually every topic imaginable. Probes regarding payments are, alas, conspicuously absent.

This neglect is typical, even in sophisticated academic-administered instruments and largely goes unnoticed. In economic terms, the typical survey is an extravagant free lunch buffet. For both respondent and interviewer, anything is possible. Respondents thus regularly indulge themselves with zero cost health care, benefits for the elderly, and a clean environment. Nobody, apparently, worries about future bills (Page and Shapiro 1992, ch. 4, well documents this feasting). Green (1992) has suggested that pollster inattention to cost explains the unanticipated null relationship between opinion and economic self-interest revealed by questionnaire data. Nevertheless, even if an explicit cost/benefit balance were sought, its achievement is deceptively troublesome while adding multiple technical obstacles to smooth data collection.

For one, the true costs associated with expressed wants are oftentimes unknown and, in some situations, unknowable. Who can attest that the unadorned figures accompanying "Would you be willing to pay X dollars more a year in taxes to accomplish policy Y?" are, indeed, accurate? Calculating future tax invoices fazes even experts, let alone dilettante questionnaire fabricators. Tales of alluring "affordable" entitlement, for example, Medicare and Medicaid, financially exploding beyond the wildest preliminary estimations abound. Future outlays are often devilishly uncontrollable or unpredictable—demographic shifts, technology changes, foreign interventions, and similar factors can engender skyrocketing costs. Acrimonious conflicts frequently center on contending cost estimations, not policy itself. It is far easier to skip this quagmire than hazard guesses regarding bills due.

A corollary of the accurate estimation quandary is likely citizen confusion between increased outlays and heightened benefit. Money and impact can effortlessly be conflated. It is axiomatic that expanded financial commitment may bring declining marginal benefits. Doubling the police budget will unlikely half the crime rate. Overall, given that government already spends prodigious amounts on virtually every problem eliciting public concern, the marginal betterment may be slight, despite expensive "wars" on crime, poverty, inadequate health care, and all the rest. To compound this troublesome matter, experts will inevitably disagree in calculating these ever-shifting investment returns. To expect citizens to comprehend these cost-benefit perplexities, let alone align future outlays with anticipated gains, may be unrealistic, even assuming that a questionnaire can convey these dilemmas.

The sheer magnitude of foreseen burdens might make cost estimation moot. Conceivably, $10 billion plus numbers (or trillions, over a person's lifetime) are concretely meaningless to those believing $100,000 a colossal sum. Must we also take seriously the mathematically untrained "buying" of a $75 billion antimissile defense system? Judged by such exercises as calculating lottery odds, figures exceeding $10,000 may be intuitively meaningless. Perhaps costs should be personalized as in "each taxpayer (in your tax bracket) would pay an additional X dollars." Presentation details are not, alas, politically inconsequential, and may bias outcomes. Green (1992) reports that respondents grow thriftier as they are peppered with "Would you spend ... ?" questions. Conversely, "small" enticements to unsophisticated consumers—those "E–Z" low weekly payment ruses—often mask outrageous total prices. For example, in one seemingly innocuous 1999 poll, respondents were asked about increasing taxes to improve education. Various dollar amounts were suggested, and 55 percent said that they were willing to raise taxes by $500 ("Public Agenda Online," n.d.). If we assume that this jump will come entirely from state and local taxes, this generosity would be approximately a 50 percent per capita increase for education spending![2] Imagine running for office on this hypergenerous platform? Obviously, these "generous" citizens are unaware of just how philanthropic they are (no doubt, many erroneously conflate net tax with marginal tax). A dollar or two in tax money can, unexpectedly, yield *billion* dollar outlays—in 1997, every dollar added to a federal tax return meant a $120 million increase.

Assessing possible nonmonetary costs is even more vexing. Free lunches abet overeating and this, in turn, might bring uncomfortable indigestion. All enticements possess potential dark sides. Unfortunately, polls routinely disregard these unavoidable, nonfinancial addenda. Seldom do we find cautions asking, "Would you approve this policy if the probability of some (specified) potential debacle were, say, .2? .5?" The seriousness of this oversight is immense, as revealed in those rare polls that do insert nonmonetary costs. For example, a spring 1999 ABC/NEWS poll asked respondents about sending in troops to Kosovo if the air campaign failed. When "the send in troops" alternative was posed by itself, 57 percent supported this venture. However, when the possibility of casualties was broached, enthusiasm plummeted. When "some casualties" was mentioned, 44 percent still endorsed the ground troop option. A possible one thousand casualties reduced support to a mere 26 percent! In other words, a majority wanted a ground war sans U.S. soldiers being killed (Langer and Fitzpatrick 1999).

This ABC/NEWS poll offers only hypothetical costs, and this raises the bothersome problem of calculating costs or assigning risk probabilities. This assignment can baffle even experienced public officials. Untold hugely expensive projects often began life as cheap undertakings. Especially critical for polling, the decision to accept one set of costs over another may be decisive in eliciting public support. Imagine if pollsters adopted a cautious stance and appended near worst-case scenarios. Appetites for novel enterprises might vanish if grim cigarette package-style warning labels were attached to questionnaire items. Some of these costs can only be imagined, not put into precise dollar figures. Can most citizens, unassisted, anticipate the possibility that an alluring, innovative education scheme may well aggrandize entrenched bureaucracies while depressing test scores? Might creating bucolic urban sanctuaries boost housing costs to unaffordable levels? Risk must be upfront if costs are to be assessed but, alas, this seldom transpires.

Sincerity is notably troublesome—saying, "yes" to costly invitations knowing full well that bills are hypothetical is all too inviting. Economists divide on whether "talk is cheap" or whether pledges will be honored (Green 1992 offers a brief overview). Respondents may opportunistically conclude that "somebody" else will pay—a cigarette tax on smokers, if they are non-smokers, or a "tax on the rich," if they are poor. Firm answers may be impossible in the typical polling situation. Can we genuinely label as "sincere" respondents who agree to pay the piper after they committed themselves to government largess?[3] The pollster is not the IRS or the local tax assessor and, as is well known, attitudes need not predict behavior on subjects far distant from daily experience. Public generosity in the survey stands in sharp contrast to niggardliness on tax referenda or votes for big-spender office seekers. One can only imagine if profuse public spending rested on voluntary levies.

Finally, is "buying" personal merchandise comparable to endorsing the acquisition of public goods? Purchasing national defense may be entirely unlike purchasing a car, and commendable habits developed in the latter may be inapplicable to the former. A car buyer may gladly pay an extra $500 for a lifesaving safety package, yet the same individual might be far less agreeable to funding an extra $500 worth of highway construction, although each, technically, may actuarially yield identical safety benefits. Discrepancies doubtless increase as the public good becomes less personal, for example, willingness to subsidize distant redwood forests or foreign aid to nations with unpronounceable names.

Can this tremendous obstacle be conquered? Various solutions have periodically been proposed, and we can only highlight a sampling. In general, the results will probably fail to convince skeptics of words and deeds connection, though the outcome data are always deemed authoritative. A plain-Jane tactic is the two-step approach; for example, ask respondents if they support a specific program and then inquire if they are satisfied with paying required taxes (Cook and Barrett 1992, 66–70, and Citrin 1979 offer a sampling of this method and its variations). Even more straightforward is asking, "Would you be willing to pay X dollars to secure some specified public benefit? (Green 1992, Appendix B, compiles many of these questions). Although these simple strategies are disciplinary conventions to the extent that any cost is broached, the problem is hardly solved.

The singularity of these "willingness to pay" inquiries is especially troublesome. Judging by interview dates and sponsorship, these are "stand-alone" questions. An October 1989 Gallup Poll is typical. It inquired as to whether respondents would pay $200 a year more in taxes to reduce pollution (cited in Ladd 1990, 13). At about the same time, a national *Los Angeles Times* poll asked about willingness to spend tax money to save endangered wild life (cited in Green 1992). A handful of other questions on different polls likewise asked similar, "do good things with tax money" questions during this brief time span. Respondents were not, however, asked these divergent questions *simultaneously*. Apparently, only *one* tax increase item per poll was utilized (if there were indeed additional items per poll, the outcomes were not pooled). It is virtually certain that if interviewees were given, say, twenty "Would you spend more on…?" items, including competing personally salient topics (e.g., police protection, education), environmental beneficence would diminish (as it were, only a minority supported the environment and wildlife items when costs were inserted).

Compounding the deficiency, these probes share an odd predilection toward cost figures. Most critically, it is impossible to disentangle demands for marginal fiscal increases from pleas for total benefit packages. Respondents are *not* informed of *existing* expenditure levels. What people believe regarding the status quo is wholly unknown, and guesses would undoubtedly be inaccurate. Questionnaire wording conceivably may inadvertently encourage people to believe that zero is currently allocated toward saving wildlife or environmental protection. And, to facilitate the seduction to "do good," the proffered sums are hardly burdensome—typically $100 or $200 per policy.

This differs substantially from the incrementalism transpiring within even a legislative body of modest astuteness. A lawmaker would certainly be informed of both current outlays prior to deciding changes and the how revenue changes would be managed by expense shifts. Most likely, it is this *marginal* shift in policy, not the ongoing total expenditure level, drawing lawmaker attentiveness. Alas, pollsters do not grant these elementary courtesies to citizens asked to play-act as legislators. For the unsophisticated to confuse absolute financial commitment with marginal increase is almost inevitable, given the question's highly incomplete information. "Some" thus easily becomes "more" via researcher interpretation. Imagine if respondents knew that the typical U.S. taxpayer (in 1992) averages $5,500 on federal obligations, and that the Environmental Protection Agency (EPA) had a 1992 budget of $5.95 billion, and "spend the extra $200 per taxpayer for this alluring project" means a 3.6 percent tax hike?

The tempting, oversimplified figures in these "expert" questions also are worth scrutinizing, yet one more time. Consider the 1992 Gallup question soliciting a $200 tax boost to help Washington combat air pollution. In 1992, nearly 114 million individual tax returns were filed, and if we added $200 to each return, some $22.8 billion would be generated (*The American Almanac, 1996–1997*, 339). This constitutes a nearly *fourfold* expansion in the EPA's budget, and if one strictly honored the public's mandate, every additional nickel would be dedicated to fighting air pollution (which, of course, constitutes only a fraction of the EPA's mission). Visualize EPA administrators testifying before Congress pleading for a $22.8 billion allocation for air pollution work, when their entire existing budget was less than $6 billion! This testimony would be dismissed as absolute idiocy. No sane bureaucrat would dare act so outlandishly, regardless of the public's clamor. Nor, for that matter, could any realistic candidate run for office proposing a 3.6 percent income tax boost to improve air quality.

Similar examples of generating messages, divorced from political reality, abound when these "Would you be willing to spend X for Y?" questions are utilized. This Gallup item is not atypical. One must ponder if these figures—whether $5 or $200—are plucked from the air, for they are, apparently, unrelated to tangible budgets or even wished-for agenda items. More important than inappropriateness is their incompleteness. These queries comprise only the first step in a lengthy willingness to pay assessment. A suitable instrument would surely include: (1) the full range of to-be-altered budgetary items (surely exceeding a dozen); (2) existing expenditure levels for each policy; and (3) the total tax increase or decrease from *all* budgetary changes, adjusted to respondent marginal tax rate. A further stipulation is subordinating individual generosity or cheapness to consensus building. Under these circumstances, what might initially begin as widespread easy generosity might grow miserly as the outlays accumulated. In our $500 education benevolence example noted above, bountifulness may engender bitter gridlock-producing skirmishes. And, a single dollar extra—a seeming mere pittance—might be withdrawn, if the extracted sums violated legal taxation ceilings. Or, the very opposite is possible: the possibility of paying a few pennies a day for a currently fiscally starved program might excite immense generosity. Who can really say, given all these uncertainties plus the ways of posing the questions.

One cannot help but compare this polling exercise with how deliberate political bodies, whether lowly town councils or the mighty Congress, address this problem. Here there are required mechanisms for reconciling expenditures and projected revenue across all policy domains. This is a tough job, and few experienced legislators can track these interconnections without elaborate accounting mechanisms and specialized staff personnel. And, as critics of Congress are quick to acknowledge, constraining mechanisms can fail or succumb to sabotage. At a minimum, poll respondents should have running tallies of outlays and incurred tax obligations as they move across the policy menu.

One attempt to address these deficiencies is the Contingent Valuation Method (CVM). Initially developed from the 1960s onward, typically favored by economists and almost entirely absent from conventional polling. It aims to put dollar figures on public desires for collective nonmarket benefits, for example, how much a person might spend for clean water. This methodology's impetus partially lies in government's legally mandated attentiveness to costs/benefits in undertaking expensive, low use projects—creating wilderness areas visited by a relatively small handful of campers.

Distinctive about "public goods" is their nondivisibility, that is, everybody (at least in principle) shares in these commodities. As such, public goods differ from values that could be consumed personally—for example, one might pay X dollars for a New York to Chicago airline ticket, but everyone "buys" national defense, regardless of feelings toward militarism. A particularly intriguing feature is that a clever person might volunteer zero contribution recognizing that he or she will nevertheless receive identical benefits as those who pay (the so-called free-rider problem). After all, you cannot deprive nontaxpayers of breathing clean air resulting from multibillion dollar antipollution campaigns.

This comprises a far more tricky, demanding probe than the commonplace one-shot "Would you be willing to pay X dollars for some government benefit?" instrument. Not unexpectedly, given the newness of the method, the technique has aroused sizable technical disputes, for example, whether verbally expressed largesse is as trustworthy as substantive consumer choices. Analysts typically hedge regarding the exercise's hypothetical character and the possibility that savvy respondents manipulate answers to secure selfish benefits (these issues are examined in Cummings, Brookshire, and Schulze 1986, chs. 1–3). Perhaps this doubtfulness, coupled with its time-consuming bulkiness, explains its rarity in mainstream polling. Nevertheless, applications have occurred in both traditional-type surveys and small-group experimental settings.

Although particular studies have their unique variations, the CVM contains certain essential features (Mitchell and Carson 1989, ch. 1). First, respondents receive itemized descriptions of situations requiring taxpayer resource allocations. This problem to-be-addressed is accompanied with baseline expenditure levels, fund allocation stratagems, available substitutes, and varying expenditure methods, among other details. Willingness to pay (WTP) is then solicited under various scenarios. The "bidding game" technique is one common elicitation technique. Here, a respondent might be asked if they would pay $1 for a benefit. If the answer is "yes," the amount increases to $2 and so on, until a maximum WTP ceiling is reached. Care is usually taken not to bias the outcome toward easy generosity, for example, portraying impending world cataclysms escapable by a miniscule tax hike. A variation is "Willingness to Accept" (WTA)—how much the respondent would demand to forego a public good, for instance, the required compensation for drinking dirtier water. Finally, background information is collected, from demographic data to, more importantly, information about valued goods utilization. These are considered particularly relevant for validating WTP. These elaborate, multiple responses, it is hoped, can answer questions as, "How much is the space program worth to the American public?"

To illustrate this novel approach, consider one archetypal CVM study (Mitchell and Carson 1989, ch. 1). The Clean Water Act of 1972 mandating the purification of every national freshwater body to permit boating, fishing, and swimming instigated the research. A forty-five-minute interview painstakingly explored how this legislative goal was to be pursued. The amount of policy-relevant information conveyed and solicited was formidable, vastly beyond what infuses the quintessential Gallup poll (Mitchell and Carson 1989, Appendix B). For example, respondents rated the nearest body of fresh water in quality. The perceived valuation of water purity was similarly ascertained. Notably, respondents were informed of their current tax burdens, together with their individualized dollar outlays, for competing public good programs, for example, funds already committed to education, police protection, highways, and other budgetary categories. The respondent is led through a concatenation of choices (complete with paper and pencil work sheets) permitting small increments in tax money allocated to specific goals, for example, making 99 percent of all national freshwater bodies useful for boating. Options are expressly offered for "no tax increase" and preferences are alterable as the informational context evolves.

CVM variants have ingeniously sought realism. One study (Jones-Lee, Hammerton, and Philips 1985, cited in Mitchell and Carson 1989) tackled the irksome problem of having respondents face exceptionally rare risks. Subjects were asked their willingness to pay extra in bus trip tickets to reduce the mortality risk from 8 in 100,000 to 4 in 100,000 and, finally, to 1 in 100,000. This task was presented as imagining 100,000 squares in a grid with 8 (or 4 or 1) blacked out. Whether these experimental subjects— or anybody, for that matter—can visualize one hundred thousand squares accurately is, apparently, undisclosed. To asses the aesthetic benefits of hiding a proposed lakeside power plant from public view, interviewees in another study received pictures portraying various degrees of visibility, for example, the power plant being barely discernable, just having the smoke but not the building seeable, and so on. A "bidding game" was employed with the opening "offer" to achieve maximum beauty being $1 per day per family (Mitchell and Carson 1989, ch. 1).

A particularly noteworthy way to increase realism is to use test populations with actual experience in judging costs for public goods. After all, a hardcore urbanite might be baffled about spending a dollar to beautify the unimaginable Grand Canyon. One study (Davis 1964, cited in Mitchell and Carson 1989, ch. 1) asked 121 Maine hunters and recreationists about their willingness to finance wilderness improvement. Respondent discussion during the "bidding game" mimicked savvy shoppers weighing costs and benefits. When respondent income, length of stay in the area, and similar pertinent factors were factored into consideration, WTP evinced considerable economic rationality. Several other recreation expenditures explorations (cited in Mitchell and Carson 1989, ch. 1) likewise focused on actual consumers, for example, hunters, hikers, or swimmers.

The CVM has spawned a vast industry among economists, particularly since public policy legislation often insists on measured public appetites for government projects. The EPA has been a major benefactor in this proliferation. CVM is, to say the least, an endeavor generating immense controversy. Even admirers confess that progress remains intermittent and that the robust CVM literature may rest more on expectancy than demonstrated accomplishment. Whether this technique will conquer these vexing issues surrounding the public's pricing of collective goods remains uncertain. Let us, however, consider briefly just four features of this methodology particularly central to formulating our "virtual reality" via the survey.

The first concerns applying a tedious, time-consuming technique to extracting preferences. What makes CVM so powerful also imposes practical limits, especially in a telephone poll. Application typically requires upward of thirty minutes (or more), and these tasks far exceed respondent's industriousness demanded by conventional "yes" or "no" inquiries. Sustaining interviewee interest is also daunting, given that no actual personal money will be expended and a long obscure parade of facts is explicitly hypothetical. Formulating CVM questions correctly is also labor intensive, for example, collecting details regarding interviewee tax rates and accurate project costs. It is arguable whether those writing questions possess the adequate expertise to formulate queries across multiple technical areas. These impediments may well be fatal where poll costs must be minimized. It is no wonder, then, that the CVM technique has seen only modest application and we might predict that left unsubsidized, it will never enter the poll industry's standard repertoire.

Second, the assumption that payment intention is expressed absolutely truthfully remains moot (see Cummings, Brookshire, and Schulze 1986, chs. 1, 2, for a brief overview of this vexing issue). Even accuracy champions make their case only circumstantially—for example, payee volunteers enjoy higher incomes while WTP declines if cheaper substitutes are available. Everything constitutes *intent*. As far as the published literature contends, no interviewee is subsequently solicited for contributions to endorsed causes. Aligning actual tax data with interview response is pointless given taxation's nonvoluntary character. One research corpus suggests that WTP is really little more than an attitude reflecting policy support, not a separable economic act (Kahneman and Ritov 1994; Kahneman, Ritov, Jacowitz, and Grant 1993). Perhaps future research will correlate user fees for facilities such as national parks with questionnaire responses.

Much suggests caution regarding WTP forthrightness (see especially Mead in Hausman 1993). Most notably, the CVM rests on hypothetical scenarios, and respondents, despite fulfilling their demanding assignments, may not fully grasp these inexplicable issues. The interjected realism only disguises respondent bewilderment. The proof is that solicitations may yield wildly divergent, even financially bizarre, WTPs. One study, for example, reports the public's *minimum* commitment to spend $8.3 billion a year to protect old growth forests and spotted owls (Hagen, Vincent, and Wells 1992, cited in Mead 1993). Surely, only the most fanatical environmentalist would endorse this bounteousness. Another investigation finds the public willing to allocate $32 billion to save the whooping crane (cited in Green, Kahneman, and Kunreuther 1994). Even extremist Greens would demur on this figure! This outrageous generosity is not unusual and, again, suggests that the questions tap diffuse attitudes, not hardheaded economic thinking. Seemingly trifling differences in how respondents "pay" for their choices often elicit immense WTP variations (see Cummings, Brookshire, and Schulze 1986, ch. 4, for a review). More generally, slight question wording details or including an outwardly minor item (e.g., being reminded of payment details) may have a disproportionate impact (Green, Kahneman, and Kunreuther 1994).

A similar puzzle also concerns large differences between how much respondents would pay for a benefit (WTP) and what sums they would accept for surrendering a benefit, the WTA (Cummings, Brookshire, and Schulze 1986, 35–36). An interviewee might willingly pay $10 to construct a new water treatment facility, but if questioned, "How much compensation would you demand for eliminating an existing facility?" the probable demanded figure would be far greater—double or even triple. Ample research reveals that proclivities are easily shaped by momentary high profile, uncertain events, informational deficiencies, and overtly minor aspects of question framing. A dramatic oil spill might artificially inflate lavishness to repair environmental damage. Being quizzed about a dollar or two to beautify a distant lakeshore is radically different from shopping for breakfast cereal where an unexpected $1 increase can inspire consumer rage. That CVM apparently works well with highly experienced populations, for example, deer hunters, hikers, is irrelevant, if 99.9 percent of taxpayers are outside that category.

Third, and more theoretically central, policy choices are inescapably imbedded in competing alternatives, and fixating on one item, independent of rivals, is wholly detached from decision-making actuality. A singular preference, if even ascertained absolutely perfectly, is not a public mandate.

The overall context—guns versus butter—is inescapable. Our hunters might gladly pay $1 for more sportsmen amenities, but—conceivably—*not* if this dollar is sliced off a more cherished budgetary category. Obviously, political meaningfulness requires interjecting multiple, competing values, and this likely overwhelms even the most patient, earnest interviewee. Expanding the typical forty-five-minute interview to several hours is hardly workable. That such a labor-intensive exercise may be theoretically conceivable hardly certifies its future implementation.

Finally, aggregating individual general preferences into a collective mandate regarding more sharply defined policies is not easy in this format. Outwardly, aggregating dollar figures derived from a bidding game into a majority choice seems simple enough. For example, while some may flatly refuse anything for a new wilderness park, others will gladly pay $5. Most will fall in-between. Statistical analysis may reveal a majority tolerating a $.75 tax increment for "some improvement." Unfortunately, in messy, real-world horse-trading politics, this revelation only begins resolution.

The "how" to spend may be highly contentious despite a dollar figure consensus. Hunters might prefer that their dollar go toward breeding more game; hikers may fear hunters and seek more trails, which, conceivably, could disrupt hunting. Lumber companies want more trees planted for future harvesting, an aim wildly unpopular with both hikers and hunters. Strict conservationists want the money spend to buy more land to be kept absolutely pristine. For hunters, the $.75 may be a priority, while for hikers, it may be subordinate to more attractive enticements. It is no exaggeration to say that the combinations are virtually infinite.

Clearly, a solution demands several successive polls plus bargaining among poll respondents. The final outcome *must* be negotiated, not extracted by the almighty researcher from one-shot poll data. Even the most sophisticated, powerful statistical resolutions of this situation are but hypotheses, not confirmed political mandates. Respondents, not researchers, must decide. If realism is the aim, these WTP data are essentially opening offers in a context where no one participant can impose his or her will. The final compromise might conceivably resemble *nothing* initially proposed. Logrolling and side payments are virtually certain. Issues ostensibly far removed from the survey exercise might be dragged in via consensus building. Hunters and hikers might agree to fund urban daycare centers to secure their enhanced recreational needs! Hence, the real tax increase necessary for the nature project might be huge although, technically, only a tiny portion of the total expenditure eventually goes to these nature lovers. The rest might be called necessary though personally nonrewarding "political costs."

Making Tradeoffs

Among all the elements comprising tangible individual consumer choice, making tradeoffs is undoubtedly the simplest. Resource paucity *imposes* constraint. One cannot possibly devour everything, whether this "everything" comprises tangibles, edibles, recreation, leisure time, or any other resource-consuming activity. Millionaires, too, cannot pursue unremitting gluttony. When public goods define the poll-defined choice menu, this constraint is dramatically less true. Behaviorally, gluttony imposes costs; in the world of public opinion assessment, having it all is possible. Respondents craving every imaginable enticement, including the reduction of taxes, are not expelled from public discourse, let alone chastised for extravagant foolishness. Nor are elected officials compelled to correct such impossibilities: flattering every aspiration and then violating these vows is a time-honored custom. Historical examples abound of officials wildly accumulating public debt to satiate constituent cravings.

What the material marketplace effortlessly decrees becomes deceptively vexing when mimicked via the poll. A shopper daily deftly navigates thousands of tradeoffs may be overwhelmed in the civic arena and collapse into inanity. The familiar pairwise "guns versus butter" scenario works satisfactorily, provided one subsists in a two variable world. Still, this two-variable problem affords innumerable combinations regarding just how many guns (and what sorts of guns) versus how much butter (salted, nonsalted, whipped?). Deriving a satisfactory, collective allocation solution is hardly straightforward, even if we assumed requisite citizen capacity and possessed accurate collection devices. Hard-pressed decision makers might well elect to follow a more practical path of juggling guns and butter within a broad range of "good enough" combinations, all of which facilitate reasonable domestic quiescence rather than an optimal solution.

Abandoning this two-variable scenario changes matters fundamentally. In principle, ordering a preference hierarchically typically entails huge (perhaps infinite) collections of items—besides guns and butter, one also has to consider bullets and bread, holsters and mayonnaise, and virtually everything else imaginable. The modern government provides thousands of values, all of which are configurable in endless combinations. There is also a nonlinearity of this tradeoff process across varied individuals. Marginal expansion of an already huge medical assistance program will undoubtedly yield a lesser return on investment than initial outlays. Yet, for some, for example, those with expensive-to-treat diseases, this marginal benefit increase may be identical—perhaps even greater—in utility to earlier, more productive expenditures. We cannot limit what citizens might legitimately covet, and the possibilities are mind-boggling. Respondents can assuredly demand both guns and butter, while insisting cuts be made elsewhere, and this "elsewhere" varies idiosyncratically across respondents. It is even arguable that this "elsewhere" need not be specifically defined and may be vacuous, for example, "cutting waste." Perhaps only an all-knowing supercomputer can "solve" these puzzles.

Nevertheless, daunting problems aside, researchers have periodically attempted to secure tradeoff data via polling-like devices. One method in particular drew ample attention during the 1970s—the budget pie. Each researcher added a few wrinkles, but the technique itself is relatively straightforward (see Clark 1974; Birch and Schmid 1980 for overviews). Essentially, respondents are given a circle (the pie), or other representational device, and asked to divide it into budgetary segments. If, for example, municipal expenditure preferences are being ascertained, the categories might be police, education, fire protection, and so on. The various service expenses might also be given, for instance, it will cost $10 to have a police car patrol for an hour. The pie might also pertain only to within-agency allocation, for example, how the police should allocate departmental efforts such as patrols versus more detective work (McIver and Ostrom 1976). At the other extreme, respondents might elect across the entire public sector (all levels of government!), even the whole Gross National Product (Beardsley, Kovenock, and Reynolds 1974).

Payment can be "made" with poker chips, pegs in holes, or just drawing lines in the circles. Potential pie sections vary across studies, typically three to five categories, although one exercise (Beardsley, Kovenock, and Reynolds 1974) utilizes fifteen. This information is then integrated with various attitude and demographic data, often to serve as validity checks. Key for our purposes is that respondents *must* confront the restraints imposed by finite resources and spending in one area definitionally precludes generosity elsewhere. The method's great appeal, therefore, is its close resemblance (though substantially simplified) to the tradeoff choices faced by office holders working within a framework of multiple demands.

Beardsley, Kovenock, and Reynolds (1974) offer a particularly intriguing budget pie-size approach. Other studies assume either a fixed spending level or, if a change is presented, this is researcher-decided, with no chance for interviewee dissension. The conventional budget pie design thus offers zero policy leeway to those wanting more guns *and* more butter (or less of *both*). In one experiment, however, Beardsley, Kovenock, and Reynolds (1974) permit expanding overall expenditures via a tax hike or reducing public spending via lowering taxes. Specifically, to their initial supply of one hundred poker chips respondents could add or subtract up to an additional fifty with a corresponding tax adjustment. Either socialists or libertarians can now happily play the game.

A notable modernization cleverly uses the Internet to solicit expenditure opinion. Here interviewees not only visualized their choices, no small advantage over verbal telephone responses, but spreadsheet technology automatically guaranteed balanced budgets. Now respondents can carefully wrestle with twelve expenditure categories on their monitors to reach a $1,000 federal budged. The message pronounced by the Center on Policy Attitudes is that citizens and lawmakers differ profoundly in fiscal priorities (full study available at http://www.policyattitudes.org). On average, respondents would slash defense spending by 24 percent while dramatically upping funding for education (45 percent), job training (128 percent), and medical research (147 percent). Support for the U.N. and U.N. Peacekeeping received a whopping 218 percent increase over existing funding levels. In anticipation of a theme reiterated by the Gore campaign in 2000, the budget surplus would be largely allocated to shoring up Social Security, funding Medicare and paying down the national debt.

Unfortunately, budget pies have nearly disappeared despite initial high expectations. It is also doubtful that Internet-based variants will survive beyond an occasional novelty. Although lamentable, this is hardly unexpected. Poll practicality again intrudes. Regardless of clever format, slicing and dicing a budget is time-consuming and labor-intensive, no small commercial consideration. Its most promising applications were in small group settings where precise instructions can be offered face-to-face and respondents enjoyed ample time to practice budgetary skills. When inquiry moves into "real-world" conditions, administration shortcoming multiplied. This is especially true among poorly educated respondents unfamiliar with government services and inexperienced with abstract tradeoff calculations. McIver and Ostrom (1976) report that only about half the residents of a low-income neighborhood could even navigate a three-section budget pie addressing police functions. Another telephone-based study (May 1981) in an affluent, well-educated San Francisco suburb asked about five everyday municipal services. Residents were told that cutbacks were necessary, and that this cutback amounted to $100 per household. This was then to be allocated across the five policy areas. Regrettably, about a quarter of those contacted, in one way or another, could not complete fully the policy ranking exercise.

A far deeper problem concerns the correspondence between carving up a hypothetical, highly simplified budget pie and making realistic allocations. Those studies using categories such as police protection versus education do not even attempt this extrapolation given intrinsic crudeness. More plausible efforts, for example, The Center on Policy Attitudes exercise, are not genuine upgrades despite contrary intimations. For one, twelve items, though an improvement over the three or four categories employed elsewhere, hardly comprises "the federal budget." Inclusion and exclusion choices are obviously critical politically, not methodological details (and no rationale is provided for why some, but not other, items are included). Moreover, whether or not the public is fully conscious of its actions is highly debatable. There is certainly no indication that respondents were well schooled in the topics at hand. Judged against ongoing political debates, suggestions such as slashing the defense budget by a quarter or boosting Washington's educational spending by 45 percent are truly preposterous. Surely, if these sentiments were heartfelt as suggested in this experiment, they would have attracted opportunistic attention in the subsequent 2000 election. Yet, as was obvious, not a single candidate even hinted as such drastic reallocation. To embrace this "cut defense spending by a quarter" message as a party platform would have been suicidal!

The dozen or so studies comprising the tradeoff survey literature, taken as a group, do not foretell progress. As with willingness to pay, respondent truthfulness is always arguable. It is not dishonesty that concerns us for there is no reason to suspect mendacity in matters such as fire department budgets or unease over military spending. Rather, the apprehension concerns whether ordinary citizens genuinely know their own behavior if asked to hand over real cash. Remember, these allocation exercises are obviously understood as games, and respondents can indulge themselves as a Walter Mitty impersonates John D. Rockefeller when playing Monopoly.

More telling, the budget pie method and its variants, like CVM, may be too cognitively demanding, especially under surveylike circumstances. Can inexperienced citizens absorb and apply all the information required in tradeoff allocations, for example, the relationship between expenditure shifts and marginal government performance? It is no easy task to track all the decisions and their ramifications across categories. Professional legislators need years to learn these skills. This is not to argue that citizens inherently lack these mental capacities—judged by the marketplace, shoppers everyday execute far more complicated tradeoffs. The argument concerns whether this information processing can be transferred to billion dollar abstractions such as "health care," where essential learning feedback is wholly absent. A brilliant shopper need not be an instant federal budget expert. If these budget pies and their relatives are to be applied successfully, they will undoubtedly find their place in small group experiments, in which confused respondents can be intensely coached. Even then, judged by past encounters, a sizable portion of the population may be far too challenged to offer thoughtful reactions.

Conclusions

Our review began with a seemingly straightforward task—unearth survey techniques capable of mimicking political decision making. In terms of the distinctions raised at the chapter's beginning, the poll must replace elucidating wishes and preferences with establishing hard choices. We contend that it is inappropriate to compare mass sentiment with government policy if the two phenomena are fundamentally dissimilar in character. Decision makers cannot be held accountable to wishful nonsense or vague preferences, no matter how artfully these public musings are extracted. Lest pollsters defending the accuracy of their probes distract us, fathoming a respondent's "inner truth" is not the issue here. That quest for "real" thirstings can only supply inappropriate data, no matter how successful.

This march through sundry techniques engenders pessimism. The shadows on the cave wall still remain obscure, despite formidable ingenuity. Only the occasional promising possibility can be discerned, such as the social judgmental approach for uncovering suboptimal preferences or the contingent evaluation method for introducing essential factual detail into the questionnaire. Even with these, however, prodigious theoretical and technical problems remain unsolved; that these imbedded dilemmas are often blissfully slighted exacerbates the quandary. Repeatedly, clever, industrious researchers are stumped on how to proceed beyond the oversimplified Gallup-style formulaic inquiry. Revealing hard choices seems always just beyond reach.

Of course, this inadequacy is not entirely the pollster's fault. The most skilled chef cannot concoct a meal from nothing. Paradoxically, the more realistic the citizen interrogation exercise, the less its appeal to the pollster, and this certainly reflects on public capacity. Probing beyond superficial reactions often uncovers confusion on pressing matters such as taxation that are the *sine qua non* of intelligent public discourse (see, for example, Citrin 1979). A discouraging sequence regularly appears: a fresh technique is proclaimed, a handful of investigators optimistically experiment with it, flaws arise, and, alas, it soon slips into obscurity. Eventually, research defaults to the plain-Jane, grossly inadequate "Do you want government to . . . ."

This relapse is partially explained by today's scholarship incentive structure. Unlike the physical sciences or medicine, the social sciences seldom honor those struggling to perfect measurement. The comparison between the attentiveness bestowed on polling versus voting is instructive. The latter is politically central while the former is but a curiosity, legally speaking. Enormous attention thus attends the impact of voting rules on aggregating public preferences. Volumes on suffrage, districting formulae, vote counting schemes, ballot forms, and all else transforming citizen preferences into standing governments proliferate daily. Everybody acknowledges that the "merely technical" particular is illusionary—the process is not neutral. Litigation abounds on virtually every electoral detail, while social scientists and law professors galore expose the minutest impact of the slightest rule shift. To suggest that concocting electoral arrangements should be an exclusive social science responsibility is bizarre.

By comparison, those toiling to perfect polling so as to guide political decision making affect the indifferent demeanor of laboratory technicians searching for extraterrestrial life. They would assuredly reject a comparison to partisan legislators carving up district boundaries or tinkering with ballot minutiae. At one level, they are absolutely correct. Nobody sues the pollster to enhance political clout; the usually intrusive Department of Justice is silent here. It is assumed among these survey technicians that the public's voice, perhaps like distant galaxy radio pulses, may appear wildly incomprehensible, but with the correct application of filters, noise suppressors, and mathematical algorithms, obscured missives can blaze froth. The proper statistical manipulation of pooled survey items can surely detect meaning where none seems apparent. Cool headed, skilled professionalism will triumph over garble.

We disagree. Such "details" as inserting costs, suboptimal alternatives, and tradeoffs ineluctably fashion the *vox populi*. Grinding simplistic data with powerful statistical tools cannot surmount the absence of these desiderata. Nor can the insertion of more substantive information or policy complexity solve the problem. In Price and Neijens's (1998) superb overview of various "data-rich" alternatives to the commonplace poll query, they conclude that such "improvement" is fraught with hidden problems. Helpfully inserting facts or structuring alternatives inevitably changes the substantive outcome, and these impacts are seldom acknowledged or even understood. There can be no such thing as a perfectly politically neutral extraction of real public sentiment. Polling, unlike physics, lacks strict experimental protocols so the researcher can easily favor one substantive outcome over another all the while appearing technically "reasonable." Decades (if not centuries) may pass before we are able to insert policy details into a questionnaire without unwittingly manipulating the outcome.

More important, pushing these naive cravings into the limelight helps build an unwarranted case for their legitimacy. When pollsters ventures forth with his or her "What do you think the government should do about…?" the implied supposition is that polling *can* reveal legitimate messages to guide government. Reaffirmation transpires, regardless of how contradictory or unstable the results. Now, armed with easily launched polls, step-by-step, plebiscitory democracy becomes more intrusive, more "natural," and, seemingly, more feasible.[4] Moreover, opining that these data "messages" usefully guide government is far easier than expressing the opposite "elitist" inclination. Few wish to be stigmatized as "antidemocrats" and this agreeable scrutiny of public thirsting can supply handsome livelihoods.

No argument is being advanced that "the people" are—or should be—politically irrelevant. Challenging poll authenticity is not a covert assault on democracy. Resurrecting the wearisome debate over "elitism" is a canard. If the polls vanished tomorrow, ordinary citizens still possess ample power. Elections continue to terrorize office holders. Democracy did not suddenly materialize when George Gallup shouted "Eureka!" Our point is that, save a dramatic breakthrough in polling proficiency (highly unlikely), *today's polling cannot supply the detailed information necessary to inform the vexing choices made by office holders.* The public's guidance is highly constrained and, in all but a few instances, cannot be obeyed by the most ardent populist flattery, contrary assertions notwithstanding.

Although we cannot prophesize, this incomparability may be incurable. Or, to refresh our marketplace metaphor, purchasing public policies is fundamentally unlike securing public goods and no one can make it otherwise. Comparability requires inserting ordinary folk into the shoes of the elected. Let these newly anointed souls wrestle with all the grim governance dilemmas—the hard choices. If this exercise yields substantially divergent outcomes, then we can, and only then, speak intelligently about public sentiment and public policy fissures. Judged by our canvass here, polls cannot provide this virtual reality necessary for either sending legitimate messages or imposing accountability.

This last point gives rise to a message woefully neglected by pollsters but of paramount democratic importance: institutions—not polls—transform public cravings into hard choices. Congress is not constituted to ratify survey outcomes, and attempting to do so is pure foolishness. At best, the poll's numbers comprise one of innumerable raw ingredients comprising public policy. To intimate that polls should supercede deliberative bodies denies the very *raison d'être* of those bodies. In fact, to anticipate a point more fully developed in Chapter Six, even assembling citizens to create information-rich face-to-face "advising bodies" is senseless (see, for example, Denver, Hands, and Jones 1995). Put differently, hard choices cannot be outsourced. All the king's statisticians and interviewers cannot make Humpty Dumpty, no matter how wise, into a legislature.

CHAPTER 3

Civic Competence

Vox populi, vox humbug
— General William Tecumseh Sherman, letter to his wife

U p to now, I have only shown that current survey methodology cannot extract intelligible hard choices when citizens confront policymaking situations. Whether this problem lies within polls themselves or is, instead, a personal shortcoming is currently unclear. Conceivably, improved survey instruments could discover ample personal capacity. Uncounted physical properties, for example, the speed of light, were once judged unmeasurable, and perhaps a parallel exists for ascertaining citizen hard choices. If one blames flawed instruments, then mere questionnaire tinkering is the assignment. Upgraded education or other corrective actions are unnecessary. Alternatively, no amount of technical enhancement can uncover the nonexistent; respondents will always be flustered when wrestling with policy complexities.

What drives our inquiry is skepticism toward treating poll responses as authoritative policy guides, particularly social welfare desires. Public adequacy is front and center here solely because its ascribed presence legitimizes polling advice. Without imputed wisdom, heeding poll counsel from hapless interviewees is pointless. Devotees of economic populism must, therefore uncover proficiency or, where harsh reality refuses to cooperate, try for easy-to-accomplish remediation. Frankly stated, alleged civic adequacy undergrids the larger battle to mobilize "public opinion" to promote bigger government.

"Citizen competency" is a thorny subject hardly immune to the twisting of terminology and data to fit covert ideological agendas. A fair amount of what advertisers call "bait and switch" also transpires—civic competence in one area is used to assert sufficiency in quite different domains. Formulations can also be frustratingly casual, often scarcely more than grab bags of clichés or selective quotations. The contrast with legally defined suffrage requirements—age, residence, citizenship, and so on—is immense. Yet, this nebulous subject must be addressed systematically since public capacity lies at the center of citizen opinion worthiness debates. Analysis begins by probing the often-neglected problems infecting "citizen competence." We show, for example, that today's admonitions for "good citizenship" are often vacuous or subtly impose murky radical baggage. Our central point here is that the term's plasticity opens the door to politically driven manipulations. We then explore more concretely how investigators resolutely distill "competence" from doubtful data, even when scarcely evident. Politics here is subtly joined with scholarship. Finally, hard choice measurement strategies to uncover "citizen competence" in making tough policy choices are developed.

Disentangling "Citizen Competence"

Democratic "citizen competence" fascinates countless scholars. W. C. Fields said that giving up drink is easy—I've done it a thousand times, he mumbled. So it is with formulating democratic competencies—the task is seductively simple and has generated an entire cottage industry. Who can oppose adding yet one more attractive item to an already growing compendium of civic duties?[1] Nancy L. Rosenblum's inventory calls for treating others with "easy spontaneity" plus speaking out against day-to-day injustice (1999, 68). Radicals favor skills to challenge the inequality of power (see, for example, Gaventa 1995). Karol Soltan (1996) endorses "moral competence," by which he means awarding everyone political access (7–8). Elkin (1999) blithely calls for attributes necessary for "a well-designed popular regime" that "... citizens must be able to distinguish from among prospective lawmakers those who are disposed towards deliberate ways of law-making" (388). Ingenious citizens, then, reject office seekers who are "hacks," beholden to interest groups, constituency panderers and those seeking the material rewards of office.

A narrower, more influential stance is "informed activism." This vision deeply colors today's survey-based civic health inquires. Here, political passivity coupled with ignorance works against democratic worthiness. For example, Dennis Thompson (1970) depicts "democratic citizenship" in terms of "... the past and present capacity for influencing politics" (2). This entails an across-the-board activism in such endeavors as voting and discussion (2). Robert Dahl similarly calls for being attentive to public affairs, being well-informed, engagement with other citizens over issues, plus attempting to influence government (voting, attending meetings, etc.), as qualities all directed to furthering the general welfare (Dahl 1992, 46). Nie, Junn, and Stehlik-Barry (1996) also place a capacity for "political engagement" front and center in democratic citizenship (11). By this, the authors mean the citizen's ability to understand politics, identify preferences, pursue interests skillfully, and comparable traits essential for self-rule. Another study begins by stating that political knowledge (which included self-interest awareness and a grasp of government operations) constitutes a vital qualification for democratic governance (Niemi and Junn 1998, 1).

This approach, regardless of content or even ideological flavor, is seldom challenged. Why object to a better-informed citizenry, shrewder voters or a more politically engaged citizenry? Opponents of any particular catalogue simply list their own desirable requisite traits rather than dispute rival compilations. Like Australian rabbits, desiderata multiply unchecked, so those seeking a convenient benchmark possess abundant choice. Here we take a more critical stance. Obviously, we cherish "good citizenship"; our point is that these general criteria are inappropriate standards to appraise polling advice worthiness. Why should we think that just because citizens follow politics or discuss events with neighbors that they can necessarily offer sound foreign policy or health care advice to leaders?

In technical language, the commonplace general citizen competency standards (e.g., citizens should be well versed on civic affairs) rarely permit predictive validity regarding advice usefulness. It is impossible to know if citizens labeled as "competent" give worthwhile guidance unless government heeds it, and this exercise is seldom practical (and judgments of usefulness are fraught with difficulties). This assessment is customary in professional relationships—a stockbroker's competence is measured by portfolio performance, not his or her training.

The lack of proved links between capacity and outcome make it easier for researchers to treat them as "true." Because any single attempt at measurement is no better than any other, any claim of worthiness rests solely on inference and plausibility. With plenty of options available, a specific standard grows ever more "authoritative" by repeated citation. It would be as if those ever-agreeable comic characters, Alphonse and Gaston, were made responsible for deciding on a single standard. The existence of readily available data may push this truth-by-consensus further along. Eventually, an "others-do-it-the-same-way" reference becomes the rule. The educational equivalent would be "predicting" future college success by the student's height. Those intent on "proving" the future college success of tall students might argue that a height advantage permits greater visibility in lectures, and, with no firm data available, who can refute this link? Since student height is easily determined, and if enough scholars cite this conjecture via citation, the height–proficiency association would surely be transformed into a "fact."

A further common problem is a drift toward conceptual haziness. Many of the supposed competency attributes are so loosely formulated that they allow almost anything to be judged "proficient." To appreciate the latitude available to creative researchers, consider as an example Gerber and Lupia's assessment of referenda voting competence (1999; Lupia 1994 makes the same "demonstration"). The authors acknowledge that multiple factors conspire against adequacy here—issue confusion, the dispute's novelty, the absence of traditional partisan guidance, and so on. All these circumstances seem to predict widespread incapacity. Yet, fans of skilled direct democracy need not fear. Voters are competent here "if they cast the same votes they would have cast had they possessed all available knowledge about the policy consequences of their decision" (149). Most surprisingly, "Voters can know almost nothing and be competent ..." (149). What permits this *deus ex machina* salvation is for ignorant voters to (unknowingly) mimic better informed, demographically similar compatriots sharing the same substantive interest. Adequacy is handily acquired by joining the right herd. That the pack's "leaders" may be clueless despite passing brief general information quizzes is beyond discussion. Civic grace is bestowed by choosing correctly independent of skilled decision making. This would be as if one certified American consumers to be savvy engineers if they heeded *Consumer Reports'* expert car purchasing advice without ever reading the magazine. As a tactic to swell the ranks of competent citizens, this device is unbeatable. We shall have more to say on about concocting easy-to-pass proficiency standards below.

Vague paper and pencil predictions may be further complicated if actual power is a prerequisite to competency, however defined. As attitudes often fail to predict behavior, anticipating civic performances is uncertain until real decisions are confronted. Arguably, as current supporters of participatory democracy argue, *only* actual policymaking experience—not schoolhouse instruction or the survey experience—will raise up an inept *vox populi* to the level of an Assembly of Great Legislators. Political dolts may turn into brilliant activists when city hall tried to expand a hated nearby homeless shelter. Power produces competence, not vice versa (this claim is made by Elkin 1999, 394, among many others). Assessing "competence" via the conventional survey is thus pointless until that day when citizens are indeed true rulers. (Of course, the opposite may occur—geniuses may degenerate into nitwits once achieving power.)

The implied tie between competence and numerous idealized political arrangements is also troublesome. Some definitions hide their true meanings. Competence imposes change, and what is artfully labeled as "citizen competence" might be correctly grasped as civic transformation apart from improving status quo. This is especially notable when "competency" is designed to upgrade today's woeful citizenry to enhance some nebulous "true democracy." As a result, radicalism is easily dressed up in the sheep's clothing of "mere improvement." Insisting, for example, that "capable citizens" must crave social justice fundamentally challenges, not merely improves, the status quo. To claim that enhancing citizen political virtues leaves substantive outcomes unaffected is either naive or disingenuous (see Weissberg 1982 for this oft-hidden connection). Surely to push apathetic citizens to the polls in the name of "competence" might alter election outcomes. Witness today's clamor over high school "what should the 'good' citizen know" history standards. Is a politically competent student to comprehend, for example, that the 1950s was a period of oppression against women and minorities, as some high school textbooks allege? It is obvious that teaching America's shortcomings versus accomplishments is not politically neutral, although each instruction plan "enhances competence." The lesson, then, is that not all proficiency formulations are to be treated as merely improving that status quo.

"Competence" implies accomplishment, not a talent divorced from application. A skilled chef, for example, can prepare a tasty meal; an able policymaker fashions effective policy. Consequentiality of actions, not lofty intent, certifies proficiency. A competent citizen, it would appear, offers profitable advice if solicited by the pollster if wise counsel is the standard. Yet, as is plainly obvious, in some civic matters *there may be no such thing as solutions within the constraints of democratic policy.* Supporters of enhanced citizen capacity assume some betterment if these voices were heeded. Believing that surefire solutions exist to illegal immigration, health care, declining educational attainment, family disorganization, deteriorating urban infrastructure, and innumerable other public agenda items is fanciful, if not dangerous. Answers will not blaze forth if citizens master their high school civics lessons or dutifully watch C-SPAN. Imagine an M.D.-like competency exam whereby would-be citizen policy advisors would be asked, "How can inner-city schools be revitalized?" Try scoring answers "right" or "wrong," when the correct response is unknown.

This inability to determine what serves as "good advice" intrudes everywhere. Even the simplest political "fact" can melt away, if scrutinized closely, while the "expert consensus" might mask wildly divergent guesses. The debates over the alleged health insurance crisis or poverty figures exemplify the difficulty of ascertaining correct figures on pressing public issues. A similar confusion surrounds determining risk—what, for example, is the true peril posed by an AIDS epidemic or global warming? Who knows for sure? And, to borrow a page from the postmodernist, political sufficiency—read power—may *create* the competence test key, not vice versa. That is, the politically dominant use their superior resources to shape the range of "sensible" agenda options, including what constitutes a "fact" or "likely consequence." Thus, a "competent citizen" would answer "Medicare and Medicaid" in today's environment if asked: "How does the federal government assist citizens with medical care?" Yet, a libertarian, consigned to the fringes of societal power, could plausibly insist that statist questionnaire writers socially construct this "truth." To this libertarian, the "real" answer is that the federal government *does not* assist its citizens in medical care, and scoring this response as demonstrating "competency" only confirms liberal propaganda's reach.

This brief overview of "citizen competence" might seem unnecessarily harsh, a dreary example of Ivory Tower quibbling and inconsequential hair splitting. In addition, one might reasonably argue that efforts to enhance citizen capacity—however imperfectly formulated—are certainly worthwhile, even acknowledging shortcomings of vagueness, imprecision, and all the other deficiencies. What conceivable harm is caused by overblown rhetoric? Our misgiving is not with the good-heartedness informing these pleas. The focus is whether this vague approach is useful or not and the possible mischief its continued acceptance might create. Scientific adequacy is certainly not served by these lofty exercises. If citizen counsel extracted from polls is to be taken seriously, it must be held against clear, precise standards.

Contemporary Survey-Based Competency

Up to now we have approached "citizen competence" rather abstractly. Here we zero in on those investigations tackling the matter empirically. Our earlier warning deserves to be repeated: "citizen competence" seldom entails a dispassionate concern for civic health. Opinion data (of uncertain germaneness) is often crunched to "uncover" ample civic mastery, which, in turn, implicitly validates polls calling for government social welfare generosity. Although these "find-the-competence" exercises are often ingenious, usually displaying impressive statistical dexterity, we remain unconvinced. We now peek behind the curtain to expose how this alleged competence is contrived.

When moving beyond lofty admonitions into empirical demonstrations, Philip Converse's seminal work, concretely defining ideology by "constraint," is the place to begin (Converse 1964). This study profoundly molded subsequent research by substituting an easy-to-apply statistical approach for qualitative judgments regarding good or bad advice. Unfortunately, political relevance was sacrificed to ease-of-execution. Here's the way it worked. Converse contended that individual cognitive "quality" (labeled "ideological thinking") is displayed in *statistical patterns* of answers to a hodgepodge of policy questions. To repeat, quality of poll answers (for example, whether advice was sensible) was equated to the *pattern* of answers. Now respondents—at least as far as the investigator was concerned—could demonstrate political deftness[2] by: (a) evidencing predictable policy-issue preference patterns and (b) sustaining these stands over time. That is, a consistent liberal position across multiple issues on multiple surveys showed more competence than a mixed pattern. Counsel worthiness lay outside this research design—only consistency on several questions mattered. Although future inquires would pursue innumerable variations, the principle that "capacity" could be derived from analyzing humdrum poll interrelationships was now firmly established.[3]

Initially, constancy across separate questions showed immense citizen inadequacy, that is, the public's views were conflicting, ever shifting. Early analyses applied deprecatory terms such as "random," "nonattitudes," or "incoherent" to mass sentiment. The heyday of this disdainful assessment was brief, however. A robust revisionist countertrend soon emerged but, and this is critical, consistency continued as the proper indicator of opinion sophistication. The debate only shifted to whether consistency existed, not what it meant for poll-supplied counsel.

While the first "anti-Converse" articles merely doubted this pessimism (e.g., Nie, Verba, and Petrocik 1977, ch. 7), subsequent statistical efforts were more optimistic. By the 1980s Converse's gloomy conclusions served almost entirely as foil useful for proclaiming the opposite truth. Technical diligence had recovered the public's honor. Tom Hoffman's artful overview of this salvation aptly characterizes this shift as defining rationality down (1998). This is not the place to resolve this dispute, nor are we saying that the public remained incompetent. That comes later. Here we only illustrate how earlier gloomy judgments can be "rescued" via artful statistical manipulation, even when the data barely touches on the subject.

William G. Jacoby's "Public Attitudes toward Government Spending" (1994) is noteworthy for its technical dexterity. Using 1984 University of Michigan's Center for Political Studies survey questions regarding increasing/decreasing/keep same spending levels for Social Security, Medicaid, food stamps, unemployment, and similar entitlement policies, Jacoby attempts to unscramble the underlying "meaning" of these public preferences. Are these desires disordered and therefore insignificant? Using sophisticated statistical procedures, meaningful patterns are, ostensibly, visible in at least five of these ten items. In other words, the public speaks sensibly on at least some of these issues. Inspection of the actual content (notably the symbolic versus concrete programmatic content), combined with analyzing other questionnaire items (e.g., respondent's general orientation to government spending), further extends this initial optimistic finding. Overall, Jacoby renders an upbeat, confident certification assessment and concludes, "… public opinion on government spending represents a relatively high degree of rationality and apparently reasonable judgment on the part of individual citizens" (354). To be sure, Jacoby fully admits that his analysis skips over how these judgments arise. Moreover, not all government spending attitudes display this rationality although, he suggests, this shortcoming may be inherent in the questions themselves, particularly their distance from other political dispositions, rather than citizen capacity.

John Mark Hansen (1998) offers a second notable "find-the-competence" study in this tradition. Once again, response patterns among very simple questions, not asking, "Do these responses constitute wise counsel?" certifies public wisdom. Within this framework, even imprudent advice (e.g., cut defense spending entirely) might be judged "competent" if internally consistent with other choices. In this particular exercise respondents in a 1995 survey were asked twelve questions on two separate occasions (fifteen to twenty minutes apart) regarding taxes, budget deficits, and spending on programs "… like Medicare, education and highways" (labeled "domestic spending" and *never* differentiated).[4] Questionnaire options were exclusively "favor," "oppose," and "don't know." A person's policy knowledge, for example, actual expenditure levels, is unreported, as is the magnitude of the desired fiscal changes. Essentially, respondents had to choose among options so that increases and decreases ultimately balanced. For example, a "reasonable" citizen could opt to cut the deficit by raising taxes, slashing spending for domestic ventures and/or defense spending. Far less reasonable would be desiring reduced deficits, reduced taxes and more across-the-board spending.

Strong status quo support was evidenced. Respondents generally opposed tax increases, objected to domestic program reduction, and opposed federal deficit increases. The only change favored was cutting national defense to increase domestic spending or reduce taxes/budget deficit. This sentiment recalls the public's aversion to defense spending highlighted in Chapter One. More pertinent for our purposes, however, was the supposed coherence (the implied measure of "competence") displayed by answer patterns. First the positive news: only a handful of respondents failed to execute these instructions, and only slightly more favored outright contradictory policy combination. Score one for alleged competence.

The picture is foggier as to whether these citizens can logically organize their spend-cut choices. Keep in mind that this difficult assessment is inferred *entirely* from patterns of "yes" and "no" responses to twelve relatively crude survey questions.[5] Reaching this conclusion also depends on several nonobvious technical assumptions and complicated statistical analysis, including actually adjusting respondent answers to "improve" the outcomes. Still, when all is said and done, and without various adjustment, a mere 3.9 percent offer a strict ordering of preferences, while another 36.4 percent gain entry into this select group of competent citizens if their occasional indifferences to policy pairs are accepted. The remaining respondents offer, in varying degrees, inconsistent, incomplete patterns. These findings aside, Hansen still optimistically asserts, "... mass preferences over public finance are remarkably well structured, all in all" (1998, 517). To drive this upbeat point home, the conclusion repeats this message verbatim, and we are further told, "Most people have no difficulty determining their views" (526).

This exercise reveals just how energetically a positive judgment regarding poll advice usefulness can be pushed. The effort to make do with flimsy data is prodigious and no statistical effort is spared in to flatter the public's ability. Troubling contrary findings regarding proficiency are always refurbished via intensive mathematical reanalysis; the opposite never transpires. The enterprise also rests on a debatable definition of proficiency—internal consistency among very simple responses, not the soundness of advice. Even then, despite all the effort, the actual results hardly justify the author's upbeat assessment.

Page and Shapiro's *The Rational Public: Fifty Years of Trends in Americans' Policy Preferences* (1992) takes a different methodological approach, but here, too, the intent is to convert uncertain poll results into wise counsel. Unlike other scholars who at least superficially adopt the disinterested scientist demeanor, however, the ideological goal is openly admitted. The Preface boldly announces the book's aim: "... to show that public opinion is 'rational' in a specific sense of that term" (xi). Their commitment to poll-driven democracy is unconditionally forthright: "The chief cure for the ills of American democracy is to be found not in less, but in more democracy; not in thwarting the public's desires, but in providing it with good information and heeding its wishes." The authors further contend that American public opinion is "real" (not random), coherent, stable, understandable, and predictable (xi). In Chapter One, Page and Shapiro confidently reaffirm the public's capacity to hold sensible opinions and process available information (3).

And how is this upbeat impressive assessment to be reached with garden-variety poll data? That polls seldom elicit much more than "yes" or "no" responses regarding nebulous policy choices makes this task very difficult. Nor are the rationales for peoples' answers easily known. The authors are undaunted. The secret for Page and Shapiro lies in overall response patterns, particularly stability, across dozens of issues. In a nutshell, individuals offer expert advice *because* the overall patterns show certain regularities. While this use of *aggregate* figures to reach conclusion about *individual* capabilities is stated matter-of-factly, this shift is truly momentous. It is quite dubious logically and, frankly, impossible to prove empirically given the absence of other information. The equivalent would be insisting that since certain products sell year after year, buyers must certainly be intelligent consumers, and then making no further inquiry.

How can astute guidance flow from thousands of data points on dozens of policies, some of which bounce around while others remain virtually unchanged? The secret is to rely on the insightful researcher to distill guidance from jumbled data. Chapter Four of *The Rational Public,* "Economic Welfare," seemingly illustrates this knack using poll data on the welfare state's main pillars—income maintenance, medical care, taxes, education, economic redistribution, and the like—over several decades. What sensible advice might be conveyed by these bountiful but frequently confusing data? The answer is straightforward, or at least to Page and Shapiro. When the numbers show stability (as in enduring support for Social Security), one must conclude that the public speaks competently. It is not that every person holds durable, stable views. Rather, claim Page and Shapiro, individual volatility is irrelevant, since "... at any given moment, the random deviations of individuals from their long-term opinions may well cancel out over a large sample, so that the poll or survey can accurately measure collective preferences as defined in terms of the true or long-term preferences of many individual citizens" (1992, 16). In other words, if we see similar poll figures year after year for a particular entitlement, the message is worth heeding.

But what if poll numbers significantly fluctuate? Does this signify incompetent jabber? Hardly. Everything depends on whether this response instability is event driven, and if the researcher can align these ebbs and flows with changing situations, then the public's message remains as "reasonable" as if no shifts had occurred. After all, changing circumstances and new information can push popular sentiment to and fro, all the while underlying dispositions remain rock solid. For example, when enthusiasm for assisting cities increased sharply in the late 1960s, this shift was attributed to possible reaction against Nixon's "benign neglect" and urban riots (Page and Shapiro, 134–135). When backing for government medical assistance dropped in the late 1970s, this was explained by inflation, soaring medical costs and conservative rhetoric (131). In the case of education during the Reagan administration, however, the president's rhetoric failed to budge proentitlement support, so this evenness reveals public astuteness in the face of conservative propaganda (133). In sum, overall stability definitionally equals competence and flux also shows proficiency provided changes are explainable, and such reason always seem handy.

At least superficially, this rescue of the public's wisdom is impressive. Charts and tables are studied rigorously to unlock their secrets. Worthwhile messages *always* can be uncovered from poll data. Even on the obscure and exceedingly complicated MX missile deployment issue of the early 1980s, the public offers helpful counsel. That polls showed widespread public ignorance and experts themselves were often baffled makes no difference. Researchers can still penetrate the confusion to obtain marching orders. Indeed, after subjecting the data to close scrutiny and even applying the Law of Large Numbers, the authors proudly announce, "Despite the complexity and relatively low visibility of the issue, and the frequent 'don't know' responses, the data suggest the collective public opinion concerning the MX was real, measurable, stable and (given the information that was made available) rather reasonable" (22). For Page and Shapiro the lesson is plain: if the populace authoritatively about the tangled MX dispute, they can wisely pronounce on *anything!*

The author's alleged evidence on the public's willingness to pay (that Page and Shapiro assert on page 118) deserves special mention. Surely cost calculations must inform any proficiency judgment—citizens are hardly "competent" or rational if they want something for nothing. How is this largesse revealed? Page and Shapiro review various polls on taxation and conclude, sensibly enough, that the public generally rejects tax increases. To be sure, majorities periodically endorse increased "sin taxes" or higher levies on the wealthy, but, taken together, these approvals did not alter existing tax policy (163–166). In other words, if an observer only saw tax preference data, the unmistakable conclusion regarding welfare state expansion is "keep the status quo." Yet, repeatedly, Page and Shapiro's data elsewhere reveal a clamor for *more* spending for education, health care, and so on. How is this apparent contradiction explained? It is not—the book's conclusion simply proclaims the public's willingness to finance state growth (169). Techniques designed to extract this willingness explored in the past chapter (e.g., budget pie exercises), uncertain as they are, receive zero attention.[6]

Analytical neglect, not misrepresentation, is the culprit here. No logical contradiction exists between unchanged taxes and increased social welfare desires. Americans may reasonably reject tax hikes, but they simultaneously hunger for untold program increases. This circle can, in principle, be squared via reductions elsewhere, such as slashing military spending or through more efficient administration. Logically, these contradictory preferences are not firm proof of citizen inadequacy. Still, to conclude from these assembled data that the public is "willing to pay" for these social welfare enhancements is unwarranted, even a *non sequitur.* This may technically be correct, but *this assessment is nowhere supported in these data.* This is a giant, unsubstantiated leap. It is far more plausible to argue the opposite—the evidence only further confirms the public's "want-something-for-nothing" mentality.[7] One can only surmise that competence is wistfully assumed to award populist authority.

A final example of the lengths to which competence can be "discovered" is Delli Carpini and Keeter's ambitious *What Americans Know About Politics and Why it Matters* (1996). Although technically quite different from *The Rational Public,* both books share the Progressive's fondness for direct democracy. Once again, regardless of disconcerting contrary evidence, analysis will demonstrate sufficient citizen competence to justify heeding popular opinion. The Preface of this book declares, "… we find consistent support for the idea that given appropriate information, citizens are capable of making rational political choices" (xii). Indeed, the enterprise will evidently undertake a paradoxical task—vigorously proposing a case for heeding popular guidance while simultaneously displaying in immense detail public political ignorance.

This quest begins (without corroborating data or even an explicit justification) by asserting that democracy excels when citizens are politically informed. Familiarity with politics is fundamental: "Civic knowledge provides the raw material that allows citizens to use their virtues, skills and passions in a way that is connected meaningfully to the empirical world" (5). This knowledge, moreover, not only facilitates the democratic process, but helps secure a critical substantive goal, furthering the public interest. James Madison's fear of foolish, impassioned majorities is absent. Similar silence surrounds the possibility of indirect government being superior to direct citizen intervention, even with a more enlightened citizenry. Leaving these complications aside, the authors are clear that if one desires both democracy and the public interest satisfied, citizen knowledge is the key.

Unfortunately, mountains of data demonstrate pervasive civic ignorance among Americans. A dispassionate observer might conclude that since citizens have failed this singular competency test, today's efforts to upgrade or even sustain democracy are doomed. Worse, a despairing observer might argue that since the opportunities for civic knowledge now abound, from educational opportunities to a politics soaked mass media, hopes for increases in political knowledge are fantasy. If mass literacy, state-mandated civics instruction and round-the-clock news cannot do the trick, what can the future hold? Why invite disappointment by insisting on the unobtainable?

Delli Carpini and Keeter have appeared to box themselves into a despairing situation. However, like Page and Shapiro (and in the tradition of Houdini), they are able to escape with a little fancy conceptual footwork and "demonstrate" that extensive public ignorance need not nullify poll guidance. Civic competence primarily depends on data interpretation; from the authors' perspective, political ignorance is scarcely an obstacle. The *vox populi* is again rescued! The secret to this escape is to treat dreary information levels not as an incurable personal deficiency, but instead as a situation beyond respondent control. The inept are not really inept; they merely reside at society's economic bottom. The failures of ability and motivation say little about individual capacity because these shortcomings are system determined, shades of that popular 1960s slogan, "Don't blame the victim." Being short-changed economically or dreadful living conditions only reinforces political incapacity. In their words, "Our conceptualization does not eliminate the normative implications of low levels of political knowledge. Nor does it excuse citizens for their political ignorance. It does, however, shift the emphasis from the competence of individuals or group to larger issues of access and opportunity" (8).

Stated simply, the argument's peculiarity is inescapable: (1) democratic civic competence rests on political knowledge; (2) Americans are woefully politically ignorant; (3) the inequitable socioeconomic system engenders and deepens this imperfection; therefore (4) the people would be competent if the defective system would permit it. Pushed to its logical end, the unstated conclusion is that the socioeconomic system, not the people themselves, is "incompetent." It is this last step that is nonsensical but essential to this labored procompetency argument. Thus understood, the book's subsequent massive excursion into public ignorance is immaterial, at least theoretically. Reviewing question response on response, slicing the data by demographic group, and otherwise delving into our disorder's roots can *never* bring an inadequacy verdict, so long as people themselves are absolved.[8] Their conclusion confirms this point when it boldly announces, after pages and pages of recounting dreary political knowledge data, that, "... it is nearly meaningless to talk about how much the 'public' knows about politics" (269).

As in *The Rational Public*, this civic competency documentation is difficult to disprove. Inconclusive data notwithstanding, easy escapes are always found to flatter public capacity.[9] This is the triumph of faith. If the indigent are politically confused this inadequacy merely reflects the lousy hand dealt them by an unequal society. And how is this critical fact known? Where is the confirming empirical evidence that the public can be improved? Have these "victims" been tested to see if bestowing fresh resources can remedy their ignorance? No such inquiry transpires—the "society-did-it" account is axiomatic, totally proven by the fact that the rich are rich and the poor are poor. To admit that some sizable portion of the population can *never* achieve necessary civic competence, just as most citizens cannot master advanced calculus, is unspeakable. To doubt this "democratic competence" perhaps makes one a heretic.

While these four civic competency analyses are hardly exhaustive, they resonate well with current populist leanings among public opinion scholars. Other examples would only demonstrate even more technical ingenuity and logical leaps to arrive at comparable conclusions. Their strong desire to advance the faith, despite untold obstacles, is remarkable.[10] The civic competence case is going to be made, and that's that. If the data-at-hand are hardly appropriate, no matter; they are still used. Plainly, individual cognitive information processing may not be discernible from aggregate patterns no matter how artful the statistical twisting. Such dexterity no doubt could transform black into white and vice versa without violating accepted rules of evidence. The same for manipulating stability or event-determined opinion shift as "proof" of collective capability. Who could have imagined ample data documenting public political ignorance buttressing the case for heeding poll expressed desires? These arguments are blatant reaches pursuing a political agenda.

That ideology has trumped the principle of dispassionate analysis is inescapable. These are not polemics in the usual sense of that term. Every undertaking has passed strict scholarly dissection, and strident advocacy was probably not the research's main purpose. *Zeitgeist* (spirit of the times) better captures what transpires. This is a happy, though subtle, *ménage à trois* of advancing an ideology (liberalism), professional attainment (publications), and the psychological self-congratulation that derives from upholding energetic democracy. This "rescue" is hardly an inconsequential academic tour de force for, as we never tire of repeating, it helps bestow a mantle of legitimacy on public opinion polling.

Competency as Policymaking

The patient reader may well guess that navigating "citizen competency" is hopeless. Still, making distinction between those baffled by policy choices and those capable of *some* accomplished judgment is essential. Absolutely central to this enterprise is a standard regarding competency level. If citizens are suddenly asked snap policy choice questions, a judgment of competence is necessary if responses are to gain "advisory" status. It is pointless to say that mass sentiment is "meaningful" since citizens *are capable* of rendering wise opinion if better informed, or if the mass media was more dutiful, and so on. Additionally, proffered policy choices should be about "real-world" quandaries. Concocting imaginary over-simplified options is, as we saw in Chapter Two, mischievous. Why allocate precious resources to solicit popular advice about nonexistent disputes?

The task, then, is to formulate narrow-gauge standards applicable to hard choice, survey-based policymaking. Although predictive validity is impossible, face validity is feasible. Imagine a job description for "citizen legislator." What might this include? If producing reasonable, informed counsel is the ultimate aim, poll responses vocalizing mere wants are not good enough. The questions "Are you satisfied with water quality?" and "Should we increase spending on water quality?" both may elicit a "yes" response but the latter requires far more from respondents, *if the answer is to be taken seriously.* Both are legitimate expressions of popular sentiment. The "satisfied" question, however, reflects idiosyncratic standards while the "spend more money" demands policy astuteness. Alas, this distinction is absent when pollsters inquire about health, defense, education, and all the rest. Our previous distinction between polls eliciting "wishes" versus "hard choices" should be kept in mind. Here we outline the criteria necessary for a hard choice exam much in the same way that the Scholastic Aptitude Test (SAT) uses reading comprehension, mathematical reasoning, and so on to calculate likely college success.

Before proceeding to screening test components, certain objections can be anticipated. Admittedly, any "civic adequacy test" that stresses strong cognitive talents apart from current events knowledge will nonrandomly exclude people. Since this instrument will undoubtedly correlate with general intelligence, the "high" and "low" scores will follow familiar—and, for some, disputable—patterns within different socioeconomic groups. Make no mistake, only individuals, not demographic entities, will be rejected, but this will surely raise "unfairness" outcries. This is inevitable in any exercise of this type, and if demographic proportionality is mandated, this sorting endeavor will always be unpromising.

Let us offer two rejoinders to this "discriminatory" accusation. First, poll advice solicitations, unlike the vote, possess no official political weight. An adequacy hurdle is not a literacy-like test for prospective voters. Analysts might even include inept advice as a separate category, and egalitarians can generously aggregate the totals to show the public's voice in its fullness. Furthermore, even without this explicit sorting device, polls *already* impose similar selectivity. Sampling, filters, and the availability of "no interest" question options already disproportionately screen those less cognitively capable. Recall Sidney Verba's complaint about polls neglecting those further down the socioeconomic hierarchy (1996). Also, nothing prevents all but the least able from acquiring the civic proficiency to pass our proposed competency standard. Although demanding, a modest level of policy acumen is not mathematical physics.

Our second response is normative: incompetent advice givers *should* be excluded from advisory polls. Note well—we are saying dismissed from *polls* enjoying no official political standing or imperative; nothing is said about banishment from civic life. More generally, democracy is not a participation invitation without boundaries. Admission criteria are inescapable; the debate only concerns precise application. Age, citizenship, criminal record, mental capacity, and residency still restrict the franchise. Locating the voting booth bars the hopelessly bewildered. Statutes guide financial campaign contributions (including *who* can donate), while laws regulate fitness for office (e.g., only natural-born citizens can become president). Consistent with the first point above, banishment from the survey, based on inadequacy, violates no legal right. These "deprived" individuals undoubtedly still possess ample superior political resources, everything from contributing money to rioting, to advance their aims. Their views, moreover, will certainly carry weight in nonadvisory poll questions. Finally, poll responses are puny weapons compared to voting—no poll has ever removed anyone from office or decided binding policy.

What, then, are the hard choice test components? Though predicting future capacity is inherently difficult, civic advice-giving competency would seem to require the following six capacities:

1. *Estimating policy financial costs.* Government largesse is never free, yet one might never know this from poll questions silent on costs. Putting anticipated price tags on benefits is routine in the marketplace. Consumers are roughly aware of what a gallon of milk costs—$10 for a gallon of 2 percent is hardly "a deal." Unless citizen policy advisors can make these approximations, disentangling reasonable desires from fantasy is impossible. At a minimum, citizens should think about "How much?" when programs are suggested. Given that knowledgeable government agencies and interest groups do make ballpark estimates for concrete legislative proposals (albeit they may conflict), these

can be matched up with citizen guesses to assess similarity. Of course, this guesswork would be unnecessary if polls included accurate cost figures, but since they do not, competent citizens must supply them.

2. *Conceiving of drawbacks.* As polls seldom note cost, they rarely acknowledge potential, inescapable negative consequences. To believe a policy to be risk-free is fantasy and thus signifies ineptitude. Interviewees should consider risk without being prompted, and these volunteered responses should have some relationship to the policy. We expect, for example, citizens to grasp that a cleaner environment might raise consumer prices, reduce selection, or cause shortages. These disincentives are integral to informed judgments. Precise externality lists are not being solicited; it is the capacity to imagine reasonable drawbacks that is central.

3. *Calculating tradeoffs across multiple domains.* Government's resources are limited, and expanding one domain means reductions elsewhere or high taxes. As noted in Chapter Two, this difficulty is easily escaped by stand-alone "have-it-all" poll questions. At a minimum, respondents must acknowledge tradeoffs and, ideally, be willing to make sacrifices to achieve priorities. Refusal to surrender a benefit, while eschewing higher taxes or cuts elsewhere, indicates detachment from political reality.

4. *Willingness to pay for one's choices.* Short of interviewers asking for money, willingness to pay (WTP) is notoriously troublesome to measure. Nevertheless, without some expressed generosity, the desire for greater spending, while refusing the bill, is *prima facia* evidence of opinion unworthiness. WTP has to be made as realistic as possible, for example, what policy adoption would mean for the respondent actual income or property tax bill or hikes in the sales tax. "Do you want government fixing the highways?" is hardly the same item as "Would you be willing to pay fifty cents more per gallon of gas to improve roads?"

5. *Preferring only feasible alternatives.* All bona fide policy menus are constrained, legally and practically. Since polls often permit utopianism, a competent respondent must impose these restraints unaided. That means both recognizing broad legal limitations (e.g., due process) and what is feasible given current knowledge, technology, or resources. Citizens might wish to end homelessness, but competent citizens know that existing law bans forcing the homeless into shelters. Hence, to say, "government should solve homelessness by forcing the homeless to live in government run shelters" expresses a wish, not a hard choice directive.

6. *Ranking choices in terms of acceptability.* Politics, it is said, is the art of the possible, and competent respondents must accept nonoptimal choice. The quality not only entails an ability to rank choices, but it further implies a capacity for differentiation. If presented with several well-defined options on improving education (for example, school vouchers versus federal grants), a competent respondent would perceive differences among the options and, then, be able to rank them.

Plainly, these are demanding requirements, and we'd guess that few citizens could successfully navigate them, even if generous graded. Might they be unfair? Are we loading the dice toward incompetence for the devious purpose of discrediting greater social welfare spending? Hardly. First, if unfairness exists, the conventional polls are the culprit. We merely supply missing context for the questions. Everything on our list could readily be provided within the questionnaire—cost figures, potential policy downsides, willingness to pay or other materials assisting respondent mastery. Such fullness is unlikely to transpire, however. Not only would this raise interview costs, but perhaps more significantly, it might also elicit a newfound coolness toward the expanding Leviathan. It might also encourage second thoughts about the alleged viability of direct democracy, to boot. It is "the other side" that loads the dice by assuming competency, despite ample evidence elsewhere of its nonexistence. Our efforts should be commended, not chastised for unfairness.

Second, suppose *nobody* passed this competence test. What might this signify? This only tells us that the usual "Do you want the government to supply [some benefit]?" question is just a wish, not a hard choice. This is scarcely catastrophic—ascertaining popular wishes on any policy imaginable is perfectly legitimate. The query "Do you want low-cost government supplied health care?" does convey useful information but *not* a serious recommendation. Our qualm is not with wishlist questions; it is the acceptance of these ill-formed wishes as credible voices on policy decisions that draws our criticism.

Conclusions

For "citizen competence" aficionados this has been a gloomy account. We initially described various high-sounding pronouncements for an improved citizenry. Unfortunately, these requirements were usually vague and, most relevant for our purposes, has scarcely anything to do with providing sound counsel via the public opinion poll. More troubling, the practice of continually adding requirement for competence exercise quietly sets the stage for ingeniously discovering "some" proficiency, which, after some acrobatics of logic, justifies *vox populi* authority where none is credible. Our foray into data-driven "citizen competence" analyses confirmed the danger of this lax approach. Repeatedly, a below-the-surface political agenda trumped reality. Data of dubious relevance were artfully transformed "to prove" a citizen facility which, in turn, confirmed (seemingly) the value of public opinion poll advice. Finally, we presented a highly specific framework for assessing citizen policymaking proficiency that surely will prove daunting. Whether citizen adequacy actually exists according to our stern criteria will be pursued in Chapter Five.

Before turning to that empirical side, a few additional comments regarding "citizen competence" are warranted. Some upbeat news: citizen proficiency is far superior to what might be gleaned from preceding analyses. Americans are undoubtedly quite competent, and reaching this conclusion scarcely requires conceptual leaps or twisting data. The foregoing analytical efforts that we have criticized rest on scholarly myopia. Today's academic competency experts' search is misdirected, and when quests come up largely empty, analysts refurbish what they encounter. To invoke an old adage, "the perfect is the enemy of the good." Being informed, monitoring public debates, thinking "ideologically," and all the other comparable requirements are not the be all and end all of qualified civic life. Exposing that apathetic, factually clueless citizens are absolutely bewildered when navigating social welfare issues hardly sounds the alarm to "save democracy" via competency remediation, real or analytically contrived. Untold civic virtues beyond today's scholarly investigations are worthy of celebration, and formulating useful policy advice may count for less than half the test taker's total "civic worthiness" grade.

The broader idea of "good citizenship," as opposed to "citizen competence" better captures our focus. Today's democratic champions mostly ignore "civic virtues" (or "good character" in a bygone vocabulary) well removed from lively civic engagement. These attributes undergird democratic government without necessarily being quintessentially "democratic." In today's intellectual climate they might be judged unfashionable, even stodgy. Indeed, as we shall see, these virtues can sometimes be executed passively, a serious offense to today's competency formulators. To appreciate these neglected attributes, try imagining a polity overflowing with wise, energetic participants indifferent to all other citizen traits save democratically infused informed activism. Civic life would soon degenerate into chaos.

Where does one begin in this accounting of neglected talents? The eminent political theorist, Michael Walzer, offers a useful beginning (1974). These stipulations are hardly idiosyncratic and, most critically, reflect a long tradition of "good citizenship" firmly rooted in hardheaded experience. Paramount is the constellation of political loyalty, obedience to duly constituted authority, and, if necessary, a willingness to defend the Republic. No democratic arrangement (or any political order) could survive without these closely complementary attributes. Critically, such qualities must exist apart from police state coercion or constant bribery. This is the very glue of civic life, and the founders fully grasped this necessity despite their infatuation with impersonal governmental mechanics (see, for example, Budziszewski 1994). As John Adams proclaimed in 1776, "There must be a Decency, and Respect, and Veneration for Persons in Authority, of every Rank, or We are undone" (quoted in Wood 1969, 67). That these merits may not be distinctively "democratic" does not make their execution any less fundamental.[11] The "job" of political loyalty is especially critical, as distressing events in the former Soviet Union, the former Yugoslavia, and untold other disintegrating nations now make painfully evident. Imagine civic life with an informed, activist but politically *un*attached citizenry?

Today, of course, citizen loyalty and legal acquiescence are so presupposed that researching this question seems pointless. Why launch expensive surveys confirming the obvious—Americans, with scant exception, are patriotic and accept government authority as legitimate. Powerful evidence comes from what does *not* transpire. Outside of tiny political fringes, civic life is free of irredentism or attacks on the legal system's very legitimacy. Desperate would-be refugees from the United States seeking new national identities do not besiege foreign embassies. The impulses of separatism and tribalism, so commonplace worldwide, are entirely opportunist rhetoric among a handful of isolated agitators. Ditto for the rule of law—it is largely safe among today's citizenry. Deeply felt alarms over soaring crime confirm our attachment, not its disregard. Vigilante justice, a sure sign of popular disrespect of constituted judicial authority, exists only as an historical curiosity. And while draft-dodging is not unknown in today's culture, even among those seeking high office, it draws intense approbation.

To those virtues of obedience and dutifulness, we add a modicum of political tolerance and civility. These are the unstated *sine qua non* of the public life envisioned by nearly every citizen competence devotee discussed earlier. Unfortunately for activist-oriented competency examination takers, credit from this portion of the quiz is excluded from their final score. Lively public discourse is assuredly impossible if unfashionable speakers are forcefully silenced. Try picturing inclusive political activism—even the simple act of voting—under mob rule.

Once again, the public generally passes this civic job requirement with excellent marks. Regardless of multiple deep-seated antagonisms, the United States escapes the communal bloodshed endemic to Northern Ireland, India, Indonesia, Rwanda, and many other places. Speeches invoking specters of internal class or race warfare receive polite indifference. Even race-related antagonisms, perhaps our most contentious dispute, are largely limited to narrow gauge policy debates, not armed clashes. Without exception, today's elections include numberless mayhem-free rallies and assemblies; disrupting unpopular speakers and other politically motivated violence is newsworthy only due to its rarity. In addition, aside from occasional personal slights and insults, there is a general tolerance for diversity. A recent compilation of beyond-the-mainstream inclination found a thriving zoo of political and sexual penchants, all unchallenged by either government or citizens (Weissberg 1998).

In a similar vein, a competent democratic citizen must evince some degree of uncoerced willingness to submerge selfish interests to the public good. "Public-regardedness" is perhaps the applicable term. Unswerving, crass selfishness hardly permits civil society, let alone a democratic polity. As Sinopoli's close reading of the constitutional debate shows, the founders knew full well that a Republic was unthinkable without a "virtuous citizenry," and this meant a serious attentiveness to the common good (Sinopoli 1987). This theme appears in several of the *Federalist Papers,* notably numbers 51 and 57. To quote Vetterli and Bryner (1996), "It was expected that the people would voluntarily temper their demands and pursuits enough so that liberty could flourish. The ideal of virtue was an important source of personal restraint and willingness to contribute to the common good" (3). This feature of "civic virtue" has been a long-standing component of classical republicanism (see, for example, Burtt 1993). This obligation should not be exaggerated: saintly altruism is not needed. That would be unrealistic. Rather, the virtuous citizen knowingly accepts that *some* policies must be endured despite their personally irrelevant or narrow detrimental impact. For example, a pensioner pays taxes for schools for miniscule personal gain, while the affluent acquiesce in supporting thousands of never-to-be-encountered indigents. Citizens accept military duty knowing full well that adding one more soldier is militarily unimportant, but the action's cost may be disastrous personally.

This record is admirable and hardly requires proof by statistically manipulating irrelevant data. Willingness to shoulder tax burdens is especially pertinent on this point. Tax cheating plainly occurs, but—unlike Italy, Russia, and innumerable other nations—this practice clearly lies beyond civic respectability. Nor does avoidance seem particularly widespread or grievous, as evidenced by the relatively small costs associated with the IRS. More critical, escaping this liability is largely driven by personal greed, not a principled aversion to shouldering unwanted or nonutilized government policy. Incidents such as when Vietnam War protestors withheld 40 percent of their tax bill to defund Pentagon misbehavior are exceedingly uncommon, and never evoke public admiration. Today's tax evading militias are judged reproachable, not heroic. Ample philanthropic data, coupled with an unmistakable readiness by the wealthy to bear taxes to assist the needy, similarly reveals a communally attentive citizenry. When urban riots unexpectedly erupted during the 1960s, the "obvious" remedy was beneficent economic uplift, not brutal military intervention, and this charitable inclination still dominates. If one counters that such civil behavior is "merely human," and therefore undeserving of commendation, just visit any number of developing world nations where such public spiritedness is exceedingly rare.

To put our arguments into sharper perspective, imagine a help wanted ad for a "competent democratic citizen." The "employer," ever mindful of litigation from angry rejected applicants, takes nothing for granted. Emulating Marine Corps recruiting, the advertisement starts, "We are looking for a few good democratic citizens." Then, beginning with the most important qualities, it announced: "Must be loyal to the Republic, law-abiding, and willing to bare all responsibilities of citizenship, including (but not limited to) paying taxes, obeying the law, and supporting the military in time of need." A civil disposition and reasonable tolerance for a heterogeneous society would also be listed as "musts." Those disinclined to settling disputes peacefully or disdaining orderly elections need not apply. The announcement continues with, "Successful candidates must display ample public spiritedness though Sainthood unnecessary." Then, in a section labeled "helpful but not essential" flowed the parade of optional traits now exclusively informing the activist-infused competency literature: political attentiveness, current-events familiarity, ideological thinking, a talent for prudent policymaking, a taste for political engagement, and all else that today's scholars can append. In sum, nearly all of today's citizens would pass the obligatory requirements; far fewer would survive the "optional" job description section (while many overseas applicants might reverse this ordering). The "rescue" of ordinary citizen competence to bestow legitimacy to poll results is wholly unnecessary.

CHAPTER 4

Public Opinion I:
Policies and Questions

In every political meeting I have ever been to, if there was a pollster there his work carried the most weight because he is the only one with hard data, with actual numbers on paper. Everyone else has an opinion, the pollster has a fact.

—Peggy Noonan, *What I Saw At the Revolution,* p. 249

P olls assessing public appetites for social welfare typically center on generalities, for example, "health care" or "assisting the poor," not precise policy options. The usual list of response choices is likewise vague, often little more than "favor" or "oppose" government facilitation, while spending levels are usually reduced to the simplistic three-part "more," "same" or "less." To reiterate our *idée fixe,* these inquiries minimize potential negatives, especially costs, and thus painlessly promote strong support for unrealistic options. They tell policymakers almost nothing save, perhaps, the public's abstract compassion. Moreover, nearly any legislative proposal might be construed as advancing any diffuse aim (for example, excluding government completely from health might, conceivably, enhance overall healthiness). While such data are "real" in the sense of truthfully expressing public desires, and, indeed, may usefully portray "moods," this methodological orthodoxy offers but conjectural or even misguided counsel. As mentioned in Chapter Two, unrestrained "wishes" are confused with hard choices.

Here we view the conventional public clamor for heightened government benevolence from a radically different perspective. This strategy inserts polling into a rich, even disputed, policy context. Rather than dazzle naive respondents with alluring government assistance programs, we insist that citizens navigate some of the same difficulties faced by legislators. Extracting hard choice data needs concrete, reasonably current legislative proposals or enactments—the bricks in the social welfare edifice, not the edifice itself. This task is far more involved than tinkering with prevailing poll questions, and we confess that these efforts here are undoubtedly incomplete. Many public opinion practitioners also will find our approach excessively cumbersome in today's rush to uncover public thought. We happily agree, and insist that this shortcoming only confirms our basic argument—the instant poll snapshots of public policy desires are the wrong tool. This chapter outlines in depth the two policy controversies that citizens will be quizzed about and then displays our questionnaire strategy. Chapter Five takes up the actual data, basically, what happens if respondents confront harder choices than the cost-free fantasies encountered in conventional polls. We hypothesize that enthusiasm for entitlements wilt when respondents confront constraints similar to those faced by decision makers.

Policy Domains

Analysis will center on government subsidies for local education and childcare. This first-cut policy sampling obviously does not define "the modern welfare state," although both ventures exemplify liberal attempts to expand the federal government into territory once outside Washington's grasp. Within each of these expansive fields, we zeroed in on one legislative proposal enactment offered by President Clinton ostensibly promising government-created progress: assistance to reduce classroom size by hiring more teachers and a multifaceted childcare assistance plan, respectively. Both possess an easy-to-grasp meaning and entail billion dollar, Washington-directed expenditures. That these propositions gained entrance to the legislative arena plus extensive media coverage attests to their popular allure. Lest our aim be misunderstood, we are not attempting to refute a scholarly consensus by focusing on two policy initiatives. Our examples cannot "stand for" the multitude of other enterprises though, to be frank, we suspect that our findings are generalizable. We can only contribute an analytical alternative to the extremely general (and misdirected) approach that now dominates.

Education Policy. The federal government has become an immense financial benefactor of public education at all levels. Since the 1950s, hundreds of billions have been lavished on everything from new school construction to assisting the disadvantaged enterprises. This legal and financial role grows larger each year—interventions now tackle handicap accessibility, school safety, and substance abuse training. As of February 1999, some 759 separate federal educational aid programs were in place (cited in Roman 1999). Surveyed opinion consistently endorses this proliferating top-down benevolence. Page and Shapiro's historical overview (1992, 132) notes the "overwhelming consensus" on educational aid transcending untold ups and downs of economic and political conditions. Hochschild and Scott's synopsis of dozens of polls over two decades depicts clear majorities endorsing greater federal education assistance. The "more aid" alternative is *always* the first choice (Hochschild and Scott 1998). Possible qualms over expanding centralization and polls indicating a link between intrusive federal aid and deterioration of the national educational system are apparently nonexistent.

Given the easy political rewards attached to being "proeducation," President Clinton's January 27, 1998, State of the Union address predictably announced another "helpful" initiative. Washington, said the president, would serve as a national school board to fund the hiring of one hundred thousand new teachers to reduce early primary school class size (refurbishing schools was also mentioned, but this element soon disappeared). Five months later, Congress received the "Class-Size Reduction and Teacher Quality Act of 1998" proposal. It claimed as "a scientific fact" that small classes (an average of 18 students in grades 1–3) are casually related to increased learning (notably reading skills) among poor, inner-city minorities. The tentative fiscal commitment was to be $20.8 billion guaranteed for the ten-year period. State allocation formulae provided every needy district its "fair share." Funds would also be available to augment teacher proficiency, while school "Report Cards" tying class size with test performance would guarantee accountability. Schools that fail following these remedies would be subject to Department of Education intervention.

This proposal promised something for nearly everyone nearly regardless of ideology. This alleged cure was a public relations masterstroke. Newspaper accounts showed comparable state-based proposals to be virtual "motherhood and apple pie" election issues. Five *U.S. News and World Report* polls between 1984 and 1997 consistently told of the public's clamor for smaller classes (cited in Hochschild and Scott 1998, 114). A February 1998 *Los Angeles Times* poll (without any cost figures or other "negative" information) using Clinton's proposal language confirmed this allure: 79 percent in favor versus 18 percent opposed (*Los Angeles Times* poll, January 1998). The National Education Association, the dominant national teacher's union and a major Democratic financial supporter, was naturally thrilled by the prospect of one hundred thousand fresh hires. Big government liberals gained federal aid to address an enduring problem (education deficiency) of a favored target group (the urban poor), while conservatives might have relished promised opportunities for state/local discretion, accountability provisions, higher teacher standards, and, surprisingly, private school participation (the proposal's section 12).

Nevertheless, dexterity at coalition-building and attractive rhetoric aside, Clinton's initial grand plan received a cool congressional reception. A few House and Senate Democrats quickly introduced it, but Republican majorities promptly disregarded the measure. Still, as part of the October 1998 omnibus budget bill, $1.2 billion was allocated to hire thirty thousand teachers in grades 1–3 for the school year 1999–2000 (kindergarten teachers could also be hired provided class sizes in grades 1–3 had already been reduced). A seven-year, $12 billion program was also specified but left unfunded. Monetary allocations followed past educational assistance efforts to direct subsidies to high poverty areas. Up to 15 percent of these allocations could be used by states to upgrade teacher competence. To be sure, in the overall context of the federal government's bountiful schoolhouse fiscal intervention, this gesture is inconsequential. It is, however, unequivocally typical of modern government's accepted efforts to redirect tax money toward centrally directed social welfare.

The seductiveness of the approach is self-evident, and the *Los Angeles Times* poll finding of overwhelming public support echoes the prevailing "profederal aid" pattern. Secretary of Education Richard W. Riley characterized the initiative as "common sense," while heaping scorn on congressional critics who bickered over "illusory" administrative issues. He further announced in reference to these qualms: "The American people have made clear that they neither need nor want that kind of bluster" (Riley 1999). Unfortunately, multiple real, not invented, problems bedevil this enticing "surefire" educational tonic. So that our hard-choice survey data will not appear "unfair," consider various shortcomings (and none of these are hypothetical or mere technical glitches). About half the nation's states have already experimented widely with comparable state-run programs, and respectable research on the subject is widely available. California alone has spent $3.7 billion on this type of aid since 1996. Offering citizens "the other side" in a questionnaire is not a scare tactic invented by penny-pinching, mean-spirited conservative education foes.

Consider the proposal's core premise—the "scientifically proven" tie between class size and early, enduring educational attainment. This association is constantly proclaimed in government pronouncements. Unfortunately, the harsh reality is less conclusive though advocates on all sides advance their favorite studies to bolster their case. If this link were undeniable how is one to explain Japanese or Korean children's proficiency when their class size is often nearly twice the U.S. average figure? Moreover, student–teacher ratios have fallen for decades while educational attainment declined, not improved. In 1960, the teacher–student ratio in public elementary schools was 28.4; by the late 1990s, this had dropped to around 19, a decline of about one third (*Statistical Abstract of the US, 1998,* Table 269).

More devastating is the unsettled scientific support despite Clinton's glib assertions. Statistical evidence from experimental studies is exceedingly ambiguous, and while glimmers of hope for improvement exist, impacts tend to be modest and disputable (Grissmer 1999 summarizes these technical quandaries). Erick A. Hanushek (1998) of the University of Rochester concluded from his extensive overview that reduced student–teacher ratios do *not* increase student achievement; they did, however, raise costs dramatically. Other studies of class size impact similarly find small to zero benefits (summarized in Hruz 1998, 31). The often repeated and heralded "scientific fact" is on the other side is usually the evidence from a single Tennessee study, not a research consensus, and even in that one study, the evidence is ambiguous (only smaller kindergarten classes had any impact, and this was modest).[1] Honest confusion also abounds regarding the appropriateness of research measurement strategies and definitions. Experts are uncertain *why* smaller classes might improve learning.[2] The intervention's long-term impact also remains unsettled (a "falling off" of early improvement often afflicts interventions). More generally, class size is intimately linked with innumerable causal factors such as teacher skill or student language background. It may be imprudent to expect a single element to work wonders apart from the total mix.

Clinton's recommendation also underestimated future costs.[3] States already carrying out similar programs (notably California, Maryland, and Florida) find that schools often lack adequate space for smaller classes. Adding required physical facilities—which necessitate everything from new furniture to extra support personnel—is hardly cheap, and building expenses are excluded from Washington's generosity. In urban areas, these construction outlays can be enormous, and states receiving "free money" are now pressed to issue expensive school construction bonds or boost taxes.[4] Nor is hiring new teachers a snap, and nobility of purpose hardly invalidates the law of supply and demand. When California in 1996 sought twenty thousand new teachers, administrators conscripted substitutes, raided private academies, enticed out-of-state recruits, or awarded uncertified instructors "emergency" credentials. The lure of fewer students even, ironically, led to teachers abandoning upper-level classes so that class size soared. A similar exodus transpired among inner-city teachers as thousands fled to newly created suburban positions (Ross 1999). In early 1998, Massachusetts' smaller classes campaign resulted in $20,000 signing bonuses to top education school graduates! Maryland favored paying tuition for future teachers, incentives to entice teachers out of retirement plus other financial benefits (Argetsinger 1999). A national large-scale teacher recruitment effort would certainly drive salaries upward, notably in science and mathematics, where demand already outstrips supply. And, rest assured, veteran teachers would demand equity raises (and union contracts might require across-the-board adjustments).

A particularly troubling aspect of this issue is that different strategies for lowering student–teacher ratios generate distinct price estimates under unpredictable circumstances (Brewer, Krop, Gill, and Reichardt 1999 cover this topic in detail). How these key details are to be decided remains uncertain, especially given state and local discretion. For example, the tab for smaller ratios in *every* class is far larger than if mere *average* ratios are to be reduced. Uncertainty also surrounds just who exactly is to be targeted for this reduction—all students or just those "at risk." If the "at risk" students are the exclusive beneficiaries, defining this category is critical, and this is not always self-evident. The "correct" ratio is of the utmost importance, as well. One cost appraisal found that reducing student–teacher ratios to 1 : 20 in 1999/2000 would require some 42,225 new classes; going to a 1 : 15 ratio bumps this figure to 101,337! Expected financial outlays (many of which are excluded in federal munificence) often heavily rest on problematic assumptions regarding future student enrollments, teacher recruitment and retirement, and numerous other uncertainties, all of which have multibillion dollar consequences (Brewer, Krop, Gill, and Reichardt 1999). All in all, the public is being asked to buy a product of exceedingly uncertain expense.[5]

Moreover, thirty thousand teachers are but a drop in the proverbial bucket (in 1997 there were a total of 817,104 public school teachers in grades 1–3). Despite the seemingly impressive numbers, not much would change. For example, Washington State received money to hire 275 new teachers, an average of less than one new teacher per school district. Bringing class size into line with the national average would, however, require hiring nine thousand new recruits statewide (Houtz 1998). Even the hoped-for one hundred thousand fresh recruits would barely be noticed in our expansive educational system. In short, Clinton's hefty billion dollar estimates may be far too small to secure the promised impact.

The nonmonetary costs are similarly emerging. Far removed from the debate reported by the mass media are the problems associated with further shifting education control away from communities and toward Washington. Surely it is hard to argue that this long-term transfer has proven bountiful other than financially. Tales of local school boards stifled by disruptive federal bureaucratic directives in racial balancing, gender equality, and mainstreaming the handicapped (among other areas) have become clichés. Shortly after Clinton's national address, Rep. John R. Kasick (R-Ohio) sarcastically commented, "Bill Clinton made a very good case tonight for eliminating state and local government and school boards" (cited in Hoff 1998). Ironically, while federal assistance advocates herald favorable poll data, surveys also repeatedly announce a widespread aversion to federal influence (cited in Hochschild and Scott 1998, 97).

Furthermore, supplying brand new federal funds to acquire warm bodies scarcely guarantees qualified instructors; it may even exacerbate an already difficult pedagogical situation. Recall pressures to staff classroom with untrained amateurs.[6] A decade might pass before colleges of education can fill demand and yet another decade before these novices acquire proficiency. There are also intraschool tradeoffs. In California, libraries, computer labs, music and art rooms, and special education facilities are often converted into conventional classrooms (Schevitz 1999). The smaller classes/inadequate building space dilemma is sometimes "solved" by split shifts and all-year schools, tactics disruptive to many parents (Gittelsohn 1997). Contrary to the proposal's intent, affluent districts—not poor urban schools—best compete in this artificially inflated market. Inner-city teachers are abandoning their troubled schools in droves for newly created, better-paying, safer suburban positions. Red tape also draws new energy from this initiative. As the Minnesota legislature has discovered, funding smaller classes need not accomplish this goal, despite administrative reassurances to the contrary (Hotakainen 1996). Teacher–student ratios are notoriously susceptible to manipulation and enforcing this legislative aim has instigated demands for yet more regulatory supervision.[7]

Lastly, significant opportunity costs surround Washington's generosity. These billions might be more productive if spent elsewhere. One can stridently reject this classroom reduction plan and still be "proeducation." In fact, a day after Clinton's State of the Union address, Senate Republicans offered a counterproposal stressing tax-free savings accounts for private schools, expanded federal block grant programs, and more special education spending. Despite promised support of the Senate leadership, this proposal vanished. Competing tactics for boosting academic performance among troubled youngsters exist. Unfortunately, the craze to utilize this "free money" may crowd out possibly superior solutions. Lowered taxes to free up discretionary income available for charter schools or vouchers are obvious rivals to this top-down, highly directed scheme. One Gallop poll found majorities endorsing partial tuition vouchers, government-funded school choice, plus various tax-credit schemes (cited in "Poll," *School Reform News,* October 1999, p. 8). One might surmise from overall poll data that the public gladly (almost desperately) welcomes *any* scheme promising relief from incompetent education.

Even if centralized generosity were accepted, education experts propose more suitable funding applications. Typical is Eric Hanushak, Professor of Economics and Public Policy at the University of Rochester, who recommends that improving teacher quality would be more effective and less disruptive than reducing classroom size ("The Evidence on Class Size" http://www.edexcellence.net/library/size.html). Researchers at Texas A&M University similarly argue that special reading programs, enhanced learning material and intensified teacher training might prove a more efficient and reliable solution (cited in O'Connor 1999). For decades educators have advanced a "return to basics" as the most effect step toward improvement. The list of proven superior possibilities is substantial. The value of smaller classrooms is not the central issue; the real choice is that singular option vis-à-vis alternatives, many of which are undoubtedly cheaper, less disruptive, and more efficacious. To assume from poll data that class size reduction is *the* educational enhancement preference is true only if one postulates that this represents the overwhelmingly superior solution. Conceivably, if supplied the full array of options and their respective drawbacks, citizens might find Clinton's plan only marginally appealing.[8]

Federal Childcare Assistance. Like promising more aid to education, guaranteeing government generosity for childcare is a political "no brainer." Being "antichild" is less popular than being "antieducation." Even public image-conscious fiscal conservatives typically accept an ample federal role in childcare, often under the "profamily" guise. Although the Founding Fathers would have forbidden this "nanny" vocation, this responsibility has become an integral part of the national social welfare consensus. During the 1930s, federally sponsored daycare facilities were created primarily to provide jobs to unemployed (daycare itself was secondary). World War II saw a temporary national childcare program to assist wartime factory workers. Today, this role has virtually exploded. One 1994 compilation uncovered some ninety childcare-related programs across multiple agencies, though it should be noted that some of these are small and only incidentally furnish childcare ("Greenbook" 1998, 676). In 1998, the federal government itself (mainly in the military) administered some 1,014 childcare centers enrolling approximately 215,000 children ("Steps to Improve Federally Sponsored Childcare" Weekly Compilation of Presidential Documents, March 16, 1998). Federal efforts in seemingly unrelated areas, for example, job training or antifamily violence intervention often contain child assistance features. Educational interventions such as Head Start are also childcare programs, although normally classified otherwise.

Critics anxious over government bureaucracies dictating childrearing practices can only silently disagree. For these disbelievers, the battle seems hopeless. Economic necessity provides a sizable standing constituency to welcome this facilitation. Between 1947 and 1996, the proportion of women with children in the working force soared from 12 percent to 62 percent. More telling, the number of single mothers (never married, separated, and divorced) has likewise climbed since the 1970s ("Greenbook" 1998, 660). What family might reject "free" quality babysitting? Government assistance advocates can make a powerfully seductive (and artfully exaggerated) socio-economic case. According to the Children's Defense Fund among poor families, childcare can consume between a quarter and 40 percent of family income (cited in Martin 1995). This "between a quarter and forty percent" figure probably exaggerates, but it does usefully capture the rhetoric surrounding this controversy.[9] These economic factors combined with grim statistics on single impoverished mothers shackled by unaffordable childcare costs, soaring crime among unsupervised children, and similar troubling tales make heartfelt pressures to "do more" virtually endless.

Given this permissive sociopolitical context, a Clinton administration initiative to assist childcare was hardly surprising. A facile public relations gesture would once more obscure a complex reality. On January 7, 1998, the president announced a $21.7 billion legislative package for federally funded quality, affordable, and accessible childcare for a million more children. Both quantity and quality were central. This five-year plan incorporated extensive state participation plus provisions to move aid recipients from welfare to work. Washington would now impose tougher health and safety standards on daycare facilities. Proposal sections sought to attract Republican support by granting business tax relief and after-school programs helpful for expanding the labor force. The admired Head Start would be expanded financially and now would include an "Early Head Start" infant program. Existing state block grants would be augmented together with fresh tax deductions for low- and middle-income families, tax breaks for company-run daycare facilities, and scholarships for childcare providers. In the president's words, this plan was "the single largest national commitment to child care in the history of the United States" (cited in "An Initiative's Fading Fortunes," CIS Congressional Universe, 1998).

The proposal quickly gathered vocal support across multiple key constituencies. A similar (although smaller) program had been enacted under the Bush administration with strong bi-partisan help. The Child Care Action Campaign's leader announced, "Women's voices have to be heard, and those voices have to be angry and compelling" (cited in "An Initiative's Fading Fortunes," CIS Congressional Universe, 1998). Ringing endorsement came from the Congressional Caucus for Women's Issues. Defenders could point to a February 1998 *Los Angeles Times* survey revealing 82 percent of respondents supporting Clinton's recommendation (and, as before, the question presented no costs or possible downside). Professional daycare and church-related providers—a presence in virtually every congressional district—also stood to gain substantially from this financial infusion. Advocates linked this measure to recently imposed welfare cuts—those mothers pushed off welfare into the labor force would undoubtedly desperately need low-cost daycare. Improved children's healthcare arguments were similarly advanced in a burgeoning bandwagon of endorsements.

Still, like the class reduction initiative, this captivating proposal turned out to be a tough congressional sell. Doubts abounded regarding how this ample generosity could be financed within existing budgetary limits without cutting other popular assistance programs. Originally, a huge tobacco settlement windfall was expected to provide the money, but this gift from heaven soon evaporated. Republicans, in particular, objected that Clinton's plan only favored those in the workforce, not stay-at-home parents. Washington's deepening involvement in micromanaging childcare alarmed other Republicans. Conflicts erupted over key tax provisions—for example, whether to make childcare tax credits refundable (if not refundable, its benefit to poor families would be about nil).

Less prominent than congressional squabbling, however, are disconcerting facts surrounding this ostensibly compassionate "prochild" federal outreach. Public opinion polls (or at least questionnaire writers) unfortunately shun this part of the story. In a nutshell, this promised relief is, in all likelihood, a hugely expensive solution to an exaggerated problem. According to some informed skeptics people are crying wolf.[10] Most plainly, an array of amply funded federal and, especially, state daycare assistance programs already exist. The Clinton initiative is not *the* response to a pressing need;

it comprises yet one more outlay on top of numerous other expensive efforts. The previous Congress passed a $20 billion children's health initiative. Analyses of welfare reform do not foresee an explosive and unmeetable demand for new assistance. The Department of Health and Human Services' own 1996 study on the daycare "crisis" concluded that the market already had adjusted to thriving demand (cited in Olsen 1997). Even low-income families are overwhelmingly satisfied with their daycare arrangements— a mere 3 percent of those surveyed sought to change providers due to cost (Brayfield et al. 1993, 95). If shortages were rampant, prices would have soared, and this had not happened since the 1970s (Kisker and Ross 1997).[11] Most damaging to this so-called crisis is that a recent government survey of parental satisfaction with childcare reported that 96 percent of parents were "satisfied" or "highly satisfied" with present arrangements (cited in Olsen 1997). Appraisal was unaffected by mother's employment status, type of care, family income, age of child, or race. Safe to say, prior to Clinton's $21.7 billion plan, existing arrangements seemed effective, although any enterprising journalist could assuredly uncover a daycare "horror story."

"Quality" national universal childcare may well be Utopian, as well. To intimate that every family should have free access to deluxe facilities (as interpreted by middle-class professionals) such as libraries and computers invites national bankruptcy. Tales of distraught parents unable to cope with unruly children are inescapable, not national emergencies demanding prompt government-directed remediation. Listening to childcare authorities conveys the impression that adequacy is insatiable and that every insufficiency is a "national crisis." Early enrichment programs in particular may be financial "black holes" if measured by boosted academic attainment or reduced delinquency.

Compounding this disconnection between the alleged childcare crisis and a less alarming reality is an ambiguous, culture-laden interpretation of "quality." For Clinton and like-minded advocates, "quality" denotes accreditation, generous staff salaries, positive psychological development endeavors, up-to-date instructional resources, and related educated middle-class requirements. By contrast, low-income parents (the proposal's targeted group) commonly stress the caregiver's personal warmth, his or her practical child rearing experience, and reliability (Olsen 1997). These modest requirements can easily and cheaply be satisfied by friends, relatives, and the neighborhood "grandmothers-for-hire."[12]

The "quality" component highlights many predicaments obscured in Clinton's seductive rhetoric. Present arrangements permit ample choice, and many mothers and fathers might not possess these options if government further intruded, regardless of financial bribery.[13] Untold facilities will be driven from the market by this mandated "upgrading." For example, church-sponsored childcare typically entails religious instruction, and this may be forbidden as Washington's financial role intensifies. This dilemma is especially likely in poor black neighborhoods, where sectarian instruction is popular.[14] Will an Orthodox Jewish organization hiring only observant Jews violate federal antidiscrimination laws by accepting Washington's money? What are disadvantaged mothers to do if their babysitting aunt cannot satisfy tough professional certification or workplace safety rules? Ironically, but hardly surprising, both government studies and journalistic reports find that daycare centers dependent on handsome public subsidies ignore strict safety and health regulations; free market providers, by contrast, toe the line to satisfy paying customers (cited in Olsen 1997). Contrary to the proposal's spirit, federal munificence may well reduce parental choice and artificially burden taxpayers by imposing luxuries on those desiring just the basics.

Government imposed "upgrading" may further degrade services by preventing natural market adjustments. Faced with new tough standards, a popular facility may be forced to reject applicants. While parents might accept imperfection in exchange for their child's admission, the facility's accommodation risks defunding. Decreed small staff–client ratios coupled with strict hiring rules are especially critical for undermining adaptability.[15] This situation resembles our class-size reduction initiative account—possessing funds scarcely guarantees finding competent personnel, and acceptable space may be scarce. Ironically, the incentive to hire only the properly certified may be a boon to wealthier suburban providers while hurting inner-city enterprises.

The Clinton proposal also conspicuously ignores dramatic increases in private sector-supplied daycare apart from any government mandates. A booming economy has generated employee shortages and, as resourceful capitalists, thousands of companies today facilitate low cost or free childcare. Crass self-interest has triumphed, not high-minded government paternalism. In 1990, for example, half of all families reported that their employer supplied some assistance in this area (Hofferth et al. 1990). Today, this benefit has become virtually standard in corporate America. Companies vie with each other to be rated "employee friendly," and this includes subsidized daycare. Moreover, private firms—unlike rule-bound state subsidized entities—often ingeniously meet specialized employee needs, for example, flextime, vouchers, referral services for local providers, onsite drop-off facilities, and even corporate donations to local child welfare agencies (these are described in Olsen 1997).

Finally, and perhaps a bit speculatively, the long-term murky social consequences of encouraging mothers (and fathers) to trade their childcare duties for workforce responsibilities might be troublesome. Research on daycare's impact on children is exceptionally controversial and ideologically tinged in the extreme. Still, that their biological parents—not hired help—best raise children—is plausible. This argument seems wholly forgotten in the rush to bestow yet one more "free" government benefit.[16] Financially enticing families to dispatch their offspring elsewhere may ultimately engender psychological harm plus the substantial taxpayer cost. At a minimum, government subsidized daycare can be made an option, not an economic necessity. It is certainly arguable that by scaling back "the nanny state" families will have sufficient after-tax income to facilitate one parent comfortably staying at home.[17]

This analysis is hardly intended to bash liberal welfare nostrums; only those questionnaire writers unaccustomed to peeking beyond superficial rhetoric may find this hard-nosed treatment "excessive." We merely insert balance in an enterprise in which survey items reflecting blank check acceptance of promised rewards is *de rigueur.* Nor is this a continuation of the methodological debate over question language, for example, using "welfare mother" instead of "poor working mother." Our challenge is more fundamental—we wish to present the full pictures warts-and-all to survey respondents, not just employ neutral language. Accounts of dubious results despite contrary assurances, unintentional negative outcomes and similar policy shortfalls are not manufactures diatribes. Survey respondents are not children to be shielded from an awkward reality. Nor are we arguing against hiring teachers to reduce class size or providing more federal assistance for daycare. After all, the benefits may outweigh the costs. These perplexing decisions should be left to public officials and/or expert judgment. Our aim is to impose "Truth in Polling" by insisting that respondents "read the fine print" before signing up for that free gift.

Data

Data collection for this research posed special problems given the design's complexity. Fully probing hard choices entails multiple, often intricate, questions likely to befuddle respondents. Moreover, since multiple items are closely interrelated, only fully completed interviews would suffice. The issue of cost required a telephone poll, though, ideally, a lengthy face-to-face instrument would have been more appropriate given complexity. Finally, to partially anticipate the charge that our instrument was biased to uncover widespread citizen inadequacy, the sample was expressly tilted toward better-educated respondents. For example, 14 percent of our respondents had post-graduate college degrees compared to 7 percent of the general population. By contrast, a mere 5 percent of those interviewed have some high school or less versus 18 percent of the general population. Beyond this overrepresentation of the highly educated, however, the sample is a virtual mirror image of the population with regard to sex, race, age, and region. The sample is an entirely national one. Questionnaire data on political leanings—partisan affiliation, 1996 vote, and ideological viewpoint—also display a close similarity to standard accounts. All interviews were conducted between March 9 and the end of March 2000 by Angus Reid Associates of Winnipeg, Manitoba, Canada.[18]

The sheer number of queries necessitated not asking everyone identical questions. The upshot, predictably, is an occasional smallish N and a data subset sometimes less than ideal. This strategy may be likened to experiments within experiments. But, the alternative was a more burdensome interview (and even higher costs). As it were, obtaining these data required a Herculean effort. The education and daycare items were asked in two separate samples of 550 respondents each. The arduousness of our task was considerable. Securing 1,100 completed interviews necessitated 9,374 telephone calls! Keep this in mind for a subsequent discussion of "hard choice" *vox populi* governance feasibility. The sampling initially divided the United States into the nine main census regions, and within these regions, respondents were drawn in a single-stage probability sample of all possible telephone numbers.

Beyond this sampling attentiveness was a near obsessive refining of the instrument. These measures scarcely resemble the familiar off-the-shelf National Opinion Research Center (NORC) or the University of Michigan's Survey Research Center questions. The contrast between these items and Gallup-style poll queries is also immense. Multiple versions were therefore tediously checked and rechecked, both by survey experts role-playing as "respondents" and in ample trial runs. Items underwent untold revisions, and even the final product was subject to recorded interviewer commentary to assess potential deficiencies. Especially troublesome was separating instrument deficiency from respondent inadequacy. This quandary is inescapable given this research's novelty, but here this matter raises its own special uncertainties. Repeatedly, interviewees stumbled when attempting to navigate the puzzles we posed. Was this instrument or respondent inadequacy? Or perhaps fault lay a bit in both? This is no small philosophical issue, but it is one better resolved elsewhere. For the present we must be satisfied with merely presenting the outcomes.

It is absolutely presumptuous for us to advance these data as definitive regarding public desires on these two policies. We merely inject greater realism and balance. This study falls well within the tradition of demonstrating how questionnaire vocabulary skews responses. We would hope, of course, that these experiments alter how public preferences are deciphered. We also confess that not every hard choice recovery requirement explicated in Chapter Two has been precisely attended to here. At least in some instances, the task seems beyond the reach of an already perplexing telephone interview.

Questionnaire Strategy

Recall the last chapter's stance on citizen policymaking competence: a huge gap separates venturing "an opinion" (or a wish) and providing informed counsel. While the latter might be worthy of being democratically heeded, only a fool would judge it to be a marching order. Upgrading poll musings to "public counsel" status imposes *exceedingly* strict requirements, and, contrary to fashionable contemporary scholarship, this certification cannot be awarded by the researcher's statistical razzle–dazzle. And, to repeat, even if every applicant failed this examination, this deficiency says absolutely nothing about democratic governance. Surely the appellation "democracy" cannot be withheld if leaders exercise discretion regarding citizen foolishness. Given our endeavor's novelty, it might be helpful to present this questionnaire sequence for one of the two issues areas, the classroom size reduction proposal (the childcare version is presented in the Appendix). Again, the aim is to impose realism and this inescapably inserts a degree of wordiness.

Our strategy insists upon would-be counselors *spontaneously* supplying relevant policy-specific information, if presented with a policy choice. Note well—this approach says *nothing* about citizen innate capacity or what might be accomplished via education or on-the-spot tutorials. If pollsters provided this vital information, it is possible citizen competence levels would soar. But, then again, if this were commonplace, our expansive portrait of public opinion might be radically different—citizens might respond more cautiously, if they grasped what they were "buying." The focus here is exclusively on the competence undergirding bare-bones conventional poll inquires. The overall hypothesis is that offering competent advice, not just wishful desires, on spending billions to reduce classroom size or to subsidize additional childcare is exceedingly rare.

The first assessed ingredient is an ability to make rough policy cost guesses. For the class size issue, this was accomplished with two open-ended questions, each randomly asked to half the sample. The first addressed total cost:

> President Clinton has called for the hiring of one hundred thousand new teachers in the next ten years to reduce class sizes in grades 1 to 3. The President claims that this would improve students' learning. How much you think hiring one hundred thousand teachers would cost?

The alternative formulates cost to a more personal level:

> President Clinton has called for the hiring of one hundred thousand new teachers in the next ten years to reduce class sizes in grades 1 to 3. The President claims that this would improve students' learning. How much do you think this would add to the bill of the average taxpayer each year?

A second competence element is being cognizant of drawbacks, even if unstated in the questionnaire. This capacity is a mental habit—when proffered a benefit, one intuitively conceives possible liabilities. For our purposes, imagining *some* reasonable deficiencies is critical. Without this inclination, gullibility is inevitable. We specifically excluded "too costly" as an objection since this is obvious. Again the format is open-ended:

> President Clinton's proposal has drawn some criticism. Can you think of any reasons, excluding financial reasons, why a person might be opposed to this plan?

Calculating tradeoffs across multiple domains is likewise integral to competence. Plainly, the "stand-alone" poll unrealistically permits respondents to escape painful choices. Resource limits are inescapable. This trading off among preferences can operate within a policy domain, for example, money for smaller classes versus modernizing facilities, and between issue areas— a dollar for education is a dollar less for fighting crime or reducing taxes. It is obviously impossible to present the federal budget to respondents in a telephone poll, and expect them to allocate a trillion plus dollars across hundreds of categories. Instead, a far simpler exercise was offered—allocating $20 billion across five general policy domains. Our focus was primarily on assessing the ease by which this "playing-at-policy-making" task was accomplished. In other words, could respondents without much interviewer aid even tackle this type of problem?

> As you know, there is only so much money to go around and choices have to be made on how best to spend taxpayer money. Suppose you were in

Congress and your task was to decide how to divide twenty billion dollars between several options: education, fighting crime, health care, national defense and cutting taxes.

How much would you spend on [ITEM]?
And how much would you spend on [ITEM]?

education
health care
fighting crime
national defense
cutting taxes

The willingness to pay (WTP) for one's choices, short of interviewer solicitation, is notoriously difficult to measure. Nevertheless, without some expressed generosity, the desire for greater spending, while refusing the bill, is *prima facia* evidence of opinion unworthiness. WTP has to be made as realistic as possible, for example, what policy adoption would mean for the respondent actual income or property tax bill or hikes in the sales tax. "Do you want government fixing the highways" is hardly the same item as "Would you be willing to pay fifty cents a gallon of gas more to improve roads." Here the choice was put in personal terms for a specific benefit.

Now imagine that you are a parent with a child in second grade. Your child has twenty classmates. How much extra would you, personally, be willing to pay—every year—on top of the taxes you now pay—to have the class size reduced to eighteen?

Preferring only legal, practical or fiscally feasible alternatives is a fourth competence ingredient. All bona fide policy menus are constrained legally and practically. This means both recognizing broad legal limitations (e.g., due process) and what is feasible, given current knowledge, technology, resources, and so on. Even if a poll entices utopianism, a competent respondent must *independently* impose these restraints. This assessment is accomplished by offering an eleven-point menu of "potentially helpful possibilities," some of which are patently out of bounds or highly unrealistic as viable policy remedies.

Smaller classes are one way many believe will improve student performance. I am now going to read you a list of other possibilities for improving performance. For each one of these, please tell me which ones you think should be tried. **Choose as many as you like.** Should we:

Punish poor teachers by reducing their salaries?
Give successful teachers a cash bonus?

Put the school under the Department of Education if it fails to meet objectives?

Pay students a bonus for passing national reading and math tests?

Permit private for-profit organizations to run schools?

Declare a "war" on bad education and spend whatever it takes to guarantee success?

Allow local communities to design the curriculum and hire all teachers?

Ban teacher unions?

Have a panel of government experts design teaching techniques and require all schools to use them?

Increase the length of the school year?

Increase the length of the school day?

Assessing Preferences Realistically

Our overall hypothesis is that social welfare spending appetites decline as survey questions impose real-world complications. Questionnaire items therefore insert levels of complexity well beyond what standard probes present. Nevertheless, at the outset, we admit that this "truth-in-polling" strategy can *never* mimic a true deliberative assembly, let alone information-rich legislative hearings and debate. Ours is a tiny step down a very long road. The opinion survey is fundamentally unsuited to this "truth-by-public-discourse" task, no matter how artfully conducted. There is just too much technical information to convey in a brief interview. Chapter Seven explores this foolish (and dangerous) conflation at length. We can only demonstrate that the barest inkling of policy realism shifts preferences away from statist enticements.

We used multiple follow-up questions to an initial polling question to bring four inescapable complications into the mix: (1) actual (or expertly estimated) costs; (2) tradeoffs across competing preferences; (3) demonstrated risks and drawbacks; (4) availability of nonoptimal choices, including private sector solutions. These factors infuse the questionnaire generally and are not treated individually. We began with two simple questions to assess preferences, the first is a "bare-bones" question similar to commonplace poll queries while the second includes the policy's rationale. These baseline questions are similar to others that confirm public support for expanding social welfare entitlements.

Eventually, legislation was passed to hire thirty thousand new teachers for grade 1 through grade 3. Do you strongly support, somewhat support, somewhat oppose or strongly oppose this legislation?

Supporters of the proposal to hire more teachers argue that it would reduce classroom sizes and help younger students. Do you still oppose the proposal to hire more teachers?

The next step was to introduce costs. This is far more complex than simple dollar amounts, especially since many burdens are as of yet unknown or uncontrollable. Indeed, the largest costs may be borne by state and local governments to secure this "free" federal largesse. There is also the well-known problem of enticing respondents with miniscule sounding "come-ons" that deceptively add billions in taxes, for example, a few pennies a day for a noble cause. Different types of questions were asked on a randomized basis. The simplest was just dollar amounts for the program's first year and specified (hoped for) duration:

> As eventually enacted by Congress, this $1.2 billion plan was for only one year. The plan also called for a seven-year program to hire more teachers at a total cost of $12 billion. Would you still support the program even if it cost $12 billion?

The second variation was to "individualize" this cost in terms of marginal tax increase on the average tax return:

> As eventually enacted by Congress, this $1.2 billion plan was for only one year. The plan also called for a seven-year program to hire more teachers at a total cost of $12 billion. This $12 billion program would cost the average taxpayer approximately $10 per year.

A third version stressed the marginal cost on top of the average tax burden:

> As eventually enacted by Congress, this $1.2 billion plan was for only one year. The plan also called for a seven-year program to hire more teachers at a total cost of $12 billion. The average American taxpayer now pays about $6,832 a year to the federal government. This $12 billion dollar program would raise the bill to $6,842 each year for seven years.

Some respondents were also presented with a cost-to-benefit ratio:

> Spending $1.2 billion per year would change the ratio of teachers to students in grades 1 to 3 from approximately 1 teacher to 17.8 students to 1 teacher per 17 students. Do you think that this $1.2 billion should be spent?

These respondents were then asked if they would be willing to pay the cost of this marginal improvement.

The final cost measure concerned the realistic possibility of the venture costing more than initially anticipated. We say "realistic," given that much of the burden will fall on states and localities. This possibility was in fact broached in the question itself.

> Some people have argued that $12 billion would not be the full cost of this program. Among other things, new classrooms would have to be built, new support staff would have to be hired, and teacher salaries might increase.
>
> Would you be willing to support the seven-year plan if the total cost exceeded $15 **billion**?
> And would you support the plan if the total cost exceeded $20 **billion**?
> And, finally, would you support the plan if the total cost exceeded $25 **billion**?

Related to costs is the odds-of-success issue. After all, even a cheap program is worthless if it is doomed to failure while a gigantic outlay may be a steal if it is immensely successful. Riskiness is central to this probe. This was assessed with:

> The proposal to hire more teachers is based on the belief that smaller classes improve student learning. [Some/other experts] believe that smaller class sizes improve a student's chance of learning. [Other/some experts] believe that smaller class sizes do not make much real difference to a student's chance of learning.
>
> Would you support the effort to reduce classroom sizes if:
> It was *mostly* successful in improving student performance?
> It was *somewhat* successful in improving student performance?
> It was *occasionally* successful in improving student performance?

The possibility of a downside to the president's initiative was further probed with questions that expressed mentioned risks and drawbacks.

> Some critics of the classroom-size reduction effort worry that schools would use the additional funds to hire unqualified teachers, especially in areas that already have problems attracting qualified teachers.
>
> Would you support the plan to hire thirty thousand new teachers even if **half or more** of the newly hired teachers were less qualified?
> Some critics of the classroom-size reduction effort worry that this financial assistance from the federal government will also give the Department of Education a greater say in local education decisions.

Would you support the plan to hire thirty thousand new teachers even if Washington insisted on greater control over local schools?

Of particular importance in this design is providing options to the presented item that might accomplish the same goal more efficaciously. Recall our earlier criticism of the standard probe that the implicit option was "do nothing." That is, someone who rejected Clinton's assistance plan might not relish the prospect of being "antieducation." Clearly, the choice of hiring more teachers is one approach versus other remediations.

Spending $12 billion to hire new teachers is only one of many possible alternatives to improve student performance. I am now going to read you a list of alternative possibilities for the education system. For each of these alternatives, please tell me whether you think it is better or worse than the proposal to hire new teachers. … Is this a better or worse idea than hiring thirty thousand new teachers?

Better
Worse
The same/no difference

Permitting parents tax-free savings accounts for their children's education in private schools
Giving the money to schools directly, with no strings attached
Funding improved teacher training
Giving the money to the states directly and allowing them to decide how to spend it
Using the money to set up a charter school program or a vouchers program
Letting schools solve their problems without more financial assistance

Finally, there are the opportunity costs associated with any particular venture. This is a point raised repeatedly by critics of the president's proposal, but absent in conventional questionnaires. This was asked in two versions capture two possible benefits forgone.

Some critics of the classroom-size reduction effort worry that hiring these additional teachers might shift valuable resources away from other needs. For example, local taxes will have to increase to build new classrooms. Would you still favor the plan to hire new teachers even if it meant more local taxes?
  Some critics of the classroom-size reduction effort worry that hiring these additional teachers might shift valuable resources away from other needs. For example, programs in art and music might be cut to pay for

needed facilities. Would you still favor the plan to hire new teachers even if it meant cutbacks in other education programs?

These competence and preference assessment questions were also supplemented with more standard demographic items, for example, age, sex, race, income, and so on. Political views were measured with a seven-point left/right self-anchoring ideology scale, partisan identification, and 1996 presidential vote.

Concluding Observations

Judging by what several highly respected polling organizations do, assessing public sentiment on reducing class size by hiring more teachers (and making childcare more available) is a straightforward, simple task. Polls on both topics appeared immediately after these initiatives were announced. Our own data extraction experiences are (obviously) quite different. Fleshing out the technical contexts of these two "simple" policies was a major undertaking. Not only were hundreds of hours of research necessary, but obtaining certain information required contacting government officials sometimes reluctant to release vital details. In those instances intelligent guesses and extrapolations were substituted. And some pertinent data—notably cost figures for state and local governments—may be incalculable for decades, if ever known.

Even when adequate background data were assembled, translating this richness into questionnaire items amenable to a brief telephone interview proved formidable. The education questionnaire necessitated five separate drafts plus ample (and often frustrating) pretesting. And, as we have previously confessed, it still remains inadequate for capturing critical nuances. Especially noteworthy is that lessons learned from one policy domain were not necessarily applicable to another. The daycare questionnaire posed its own unique challenges (e.g., establishing taxpayer costs for "government subsidized daycare" is perhaps impossible). This stands in sharp contrast to the familiar Survey Research Center or NORC strategy of using nearly identical wording while varying a policy.

This immense tedium suggests that our realism strategy is unlikely to be welcomed by those wedded to conventional policy preference extraction tactics. Simply put, this "upgrade" adds dramatically to costs while yielding results that are probably confusing and unwieldy to the typical poll consumer. Why should a researcher spend days devising custom-built, intricate items when the "Do you favor or oppose spending more money for X?" type questions are perfectly acceptable. The deeper issue here goes well beyond a technical dispute over questionnaire construction. What is of far greater importance is the relationship between garden-variety polling and the offering of "public counsel" when the pollster by necessity relies on faulty, inappropriate instruments. We shall have more to say on this vital point in our conclusion.

CHAPTER 5

Public Opinion II: Fervent Desires

> The most may err as grossly as the few.
> —John Dryden, *Absalom and Achitophel,* 1681

The American public's overwhelming endorsement of President Clinton's proposed teacher and daycare plans is incontrovertible. Recollect the January 1998 *Los Angeles Times* poll—82 percent agreed with his childcare proposal, while 79 percent favored federal money to reduce early grade classroom size. Both endorsement figures closely resemble past probes with virtually identical wording (and reaffirm the more general infatuation with the modern welfare state). Moreover, congressional foot-dragging regarding these initiatives, together with intermittent expert skepticism did not cool popular eagerness. A March 2000 Angus Reid national survey (two years after the proposals were initially broached) confirmed this abiding statist sentiment—both the hiring of new teachers and the federal government's daycare role remain highly popular.[1] No doubt, scholars interpreting "democracy" as close alignment between public sentiment and government action will chalk up yet one more "mismatch" between public desires and what government happily supplies. Bill Clinton also might have "reasonably" castigated tight-fisted congressional Republicans for being "out-of-tune" with this expertly ascertained public opinion.

That the public has pronounced often and unambiguously does not, however, certify these sentiments as wise counsel. Poll-supplied policy advice requires far more than dogged ebullience. For public opinion to reach enlightened mandate status requires both ample competence and continued endorsements in the face of unavoidable costs/risks. Ascertaining public sentiment should not be dangling fantasies before the naive, if it is to be accorded policymaking legitimacy. Here we demonstrate that this proentitlement public consensus, at least as embedded in these two specific proposals, is less authoritative than portrayed. Much of the clamor is, in fact, a mirage, the triumph of hope over knowledge. These overwhelming majorities hide a shaky respondent awareness of what both policies actually involve and obliviousness to their dangers. This is not to argue that these expressed desires are inauthentic—clear majorities *really* do want these educational and daycare enticements. In fact, as we shall see, majority endorsements continue even when costs and risks are announced. Chapter Two's hypothetical depiction of the "ideal automobile" that customers fervently long for should be recalled—something as cheap as a Yugo but as luxurious as a Rolls was the desired phantasm. Still, the central issue, as we relentlessly repeat, concerns the *fitness* of these opinions, not sincerity.

Reducing Class Size: Competency

Can the public pronounce *competently* on these two issues, at least when solicited by the garden-variety poll questions defining our entitlement "consensus"? If citizens were being interviewed for "citizen counselor" appointments here, what proportion would be hired? Judged by the gravity accorded these sentiments, the conventional rejoinder (at least the one publicly offered) would seem to be "nearly everyone." That the public speaks authoritatively is surely axiomatic among academics seeking democratic guidance via poll pronouncements. Our dissenting answer to the same questions is "barely any." Let's begin with their appetite to hire more teachers, in particular the public's appreciation of this endeavor's cost. We shall subsequently examine performance on other competence criteria, namely capacity to make trade-offs, aversion to pie-in-the sky nostrums, attentiveness to risk, and willingness to pay for desired policies.[2]

Conventional poll questions are typically deficient in this critical information. Conceivably, some policy supporters erroneously believe themselves to be receiving a great bargain, and if the heavy fiscal burden were accurately grasped, enthusiasm would wane. Others, might hanker after ruinous extravagances. Preferences offered by both bargain hunters and spendthrifts are unrealistic and thereby dismissable. Less obvious, but perhaps ultimately more consequential, the dollar figures associated with grandiose proposals might be meaningless to ordinary people. In fact, given other dreary accounts of popular political sophistication, whether terms like "billion" (let alone trillion) have *any* factual meaning to interviewees is debatable.

Analysis eventually adds these cost figures to the questionnaire, but the topic at hand concerns what interviewees freely imagine when quizzed about conscripting thousands of teachers to reduce class size.

Figure 5.1 depicts the public's perceived costs of this student–pupil ratio reduction enterprise among both supporters and for the entire sample. The original proposal, it will be recalled, was for ten years and requested $20.8 billion. And, as our prior analysis argued, this $20.8 billion undoubtedly underestimated likely future costs given labor market disruptions and other obligatory expenditures not explicitly authorized. The one hundred thousand new teacher figure also was the one informing the polls when this initiative burst upon the scene. What, pray tell, do respondents conceive this enticing policy option will cost? Clearly, and perfectly consistent with past similar policy cost estimation exercises, guesses range over extremes with few being even reasonably accurate. *Nearly every respondent grossly underestimates the proposal's cost.*

For the entire sample, 18 percent were unable to hazard even a guess, despite repeated interviewer encouragement. Twelve percent figured that one

Figure 5.1   Estimated Cost of Hiring One Hundred Thousand New Teachers—Total Sample, Supporters Only

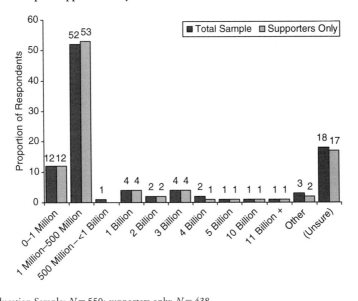

Education Sample: $N = 550$; supporters only: $N = 438$.

hundred thousand new teachers could be purchased at a million dollars or less! All told, some 79 percent guessed the cost figure at between zero and one billion (and even one billion comprised a mere 5 percent of the program's estimated minimal cost). Those within the most generous hailing distance of the correct figure—a guess of $10 or $11 billion—comprised a mere 2 percent of the sample. Not surprisingly, those lacking college did particularly ineptly here, seeing Clinton's scheme as an incredible bargain. The better educated, even those with postcollege degrees, were more accurate only by kindly comparison (most still guessed well below a billion!). Barely any of the well educated, like their less erudite compatriots, came even remotely close ($5 billion or more) to the true figure.

A second cost judging capacity tactic posed the question in terms of average taxpayer cost per year. This resembles house buying—a large, unaccustomed figure such as $135,000 is converted into something like "$785 per month over twenty years." Here, of course, the "mortgage is $20.8 billion over ten years." The approximate correct figure is $17.33 per taxpayer, per year.[3] Is the public better skilled when expenditures are calculated in smaller amounts? Table 5.1 reveals scant progress, though—unlike the previous cost-estimate exercise—the clear tendency is to wildly overestimate costs. Again, a quarter of the entire sample (24 percent) could not even offer a guess, despite interviewer prodding (a few even said "no cost"). Other answers were almost randomly distributed, a fair number at the bargain basement figure of $5 or less and an ample number—19 percent—at the high end of $200 per year or more. Taking $11 to $30 dollars per year range as being "somewhere

Table 5.1 Estimated Cost Per Taxpayer, Per Year for
Hiring One Hundred Thousand New Teachers

Dollar Amount	%	N
$0 to 1.00	4	11
$2 to 5.00	6	17
$6 to 10.00	4	12
$11 to 30.00	9	25
$31 to 50.00	7	20
$51 to 100.00	17	46
$101.00 to 200.00	10	27
$201.00 to 500.00	8	22
$501+	11	30
DK	24	65

in the ballpark," 9 percent fell into this very forgiving category. As before, those with more schooling did poorly, being only slightly closer to the truth than those with high school or less education.

Plainly, "buying" President Clinton's proposal is a far cry from supermarket excursions where items have predictable costs. This task undoubtedly reflects pure guesswork, not rough calculation. A skeptic might now depict the public's desires (unadorned by supplied information) to remediate our educational woes as wanting a Rolls Royce solution, Yugo-priced. Or, if the per taxpayer estimates are used, even gladly overpaying for a Rolls! More generally, this exercise recommends caution when interpreting entitlement poll results bereft of cost figures (and this omission is typical). As with untold marketplace lures, the getting "something on the cheap" optimism may powerfully cloud judgment and give the advantage to charlatans. One can only wonder whether today's public finance vocabulary—hundreds of billions, even trillions—possesses any concrete meaning to those who rarely buy anything costing more than $1,000.

Although already discouraging to popular sagacity fans, these figures mask an even grimmer picture. Unfortunately, citizen counsel devotees rarely see this confusion, much like meat shoppers are spared the sight of slaughtered animals. Interviewers themselves completed a questionnaire assessing overall respondent performance on these (and other) demanding probes. Of the forty-four interviewers, over a third said that over 75 percent of their respondents had *lots* of trouble completing cost estimation assignments. This is a far cry from, say, purchasing groceries or even buying a car where decent ballpark prices are surely known. By contrast, less than a quarter of interviewers reported that respondents generally breezed through this task. Overall, their sense was that *most* respondents were seriously perplexed.

Similar perplexity attends allocating funds across distinct policy areas. The assigned task is not to play-act at a "build-a-budget" task whereby multibillion dollar programs galore are adroitly integrated into an immensely intricate trillion plus national budget (complete with a matching revenue side). That standard is irrelevant, save for those blessed with supercomputer brains. More pertinent, to make a point whose centrality cannot be exaggerated, 550 telephone interviewees are not a collective assemble. Chapter Two's account of the pitfalls of exceedingly realistic tradeoff assignments—befuddlement was ubiquitous and many would-be "legislators" abandoned their "responsibilities"—should be kept in mind. Congress itself cannot perform that arduous task without relentless professional meddling (and critics often assert that this function is performed ineptly, even then). Still, when confronted with alluring novelties if solicited for advice, can respondents rapidly conceive, "Well, if I am generous here, what must be forgone elsewhere to satisfy budgetary constraints"? Put somewhat differently, can everyday purchasing skills be activated for gargantuan policy choices? What makes this exercise notable is its explicit constraint. Respondents must display a modicum of realism since they cannot allocate freely for every "good idea." Equally applicable, are these constrained allocations combinable into a "doable message"? That is, if the public speaks on splitting the pie, can leaders follow? Even accurately measured spending preferences must fail as democratic guidance, if the results cannot be summed into majorities. Noise galore is not necessarily a transparent message.

Judging by both interviewee and interviewer reactions, this exercise often proved troublesome for many respondents. One proficiency indicator concerns utilizing all five categories. Here, a mere 35 percent of the respondents completed the exercise exactly as required—reaching exactly $20 billion with all five domains allocated. Another 26 percent came reasonably close—successfully handling four of the five policy domains—although it should be noted that some (unknown) number of these respondents might be perfectly satisfied with a four-item "budget." A different success measure concerns the dollar figures reached. Again, difficulties were commonplace. Only 35 percent reached the precise $20 billion figure (regardless of number of allocation categories). Some 24 of the 550 respondents could not reach even a billion in this exercise; on the generosity side of the ledger, twenty-two got carried away and exceeded $40 billion (one respondent arrived at a $420 billion figure!). Such bewilderment is perfectly consistent with the dreary results derived from the slice-a-budget-pie endeavors illustrated in Chapter Two.

As with the cost estimation problem, cold statistics insufficiently capture the complete picture. Although a few interviewers usually found respondents up to navigating this task, anecdotal tales of befuddlement were commonplace. About 40 percent of interviewers reported that a majority, or more, of respondents encountered *lots* of difficulty. Descriptors such as "it was way over their heads," "they couldn't do the matter," "I had to make sure that that respondents knew that it was a 'B' [billion] not 'M' [million]" or "most couldn't absorb the categories" peppered interviewer assessments. Interviewers sensed that responses were often indifferent guesses or stabs in the dark. Both interviewer and interviewee often became exasperated the simple arithmetic problems in this exercise. Consider the following snippet in which a citizen play-acts as an "instant legislator."

Interviewer: As you know there is only so much money to go around, and choices … Suppose you were in Congress and your task was to decide how to divide $20 billion between several options: Education, fighting crime, health care, national defense, and cutting taxes...

Respondent: Am I helping the Democratic Party in doing this survey in any way?

Interviewer: I am unaware of the sources of this particular study.

Respondent: Ooookkay... uhhh... alright.

Interviewer: Out of the twenty billion how much would you use for cutting taxes?

Respondent: [Long pause] Uhhh, all of it because that would stimulate the economy.

Interviewer: And, so how much would that be?

Respondent: Uhhh... What did you say the full amount was?

Interviewer: Twenty billion.

Respondent: About half of it, I guess.

Interviewer: Half of it? Meaning how much?

Respondent: Ten billion.

Interviewer: And how much toward education?

Respondent: Five billion.

Interviewer: And how much toward fighting crime?

Respondent: Five billion.

Interviewer: And how much toward health care?

Respondent: [Pause, then laughing] Let's see there's nothing left for health care [laughing].

Interviewer: Just roughly...

Respondent: Okay, uh [pause] Let's go five billion on that.

Interviewer: And national defense?

Respondent: I just went over budget. [Laughing]

Interviewer: And national defense?

Respondent: Twenty billion.

It is critical to realize exactly what is (and is not) being demonstrated here. We are *not* proving citizens to be nitwits, incapable of allocating money across competing demands. This responsibility is definitely performed daily when shopping, paying bills, and similar humdrum chores. What *is* being revealed is that this task's performance is less than stellar when respondents are solicited via telephone about unfamiliar global policy under "snap quiz" conditions (as is done with the standard poll, it should be noted). Although most may eventually formulate a bona fide allocation recipe, ample coaching is often required, and many still fall by the wayside. No doubt, some training and practice could work wonders, and we invite polling experts to permit instant expertise on upcoming public solicitations. Indeed, a handful of respondents quite reasonably requested additional time and said that they could provide a better answer if given a pencil, paper, and a calculator. Our central point is that when quizzed, "Should we spend more on [some government benefit]?" those vital, institutionally imposed tradeoff mental habits are underdeveloped here. Choices are commonly made without regard to tradeoffs. And, to repeat, our dreary evaluation applies only to the respondent's answer, not his or her innate calculating capacity.

Just how this $20 billion "budget" was collectively carved up exposes the immense, and politically consequential, preference range across respondents. Remember our earlier criticism of the "more/same/less" format question— widely different defined sums could hide behind identical answers. Here we peek beyond this questionnaire terminology imposed gross categorization. And what do we discover? In a nutshell, these voices—although nominally constrained by the $20 billion limit—resemble a Tower of Babel. In every policy instance, desired spending stretches out from barely anything to $10 billion or more, or half the total budget (see Figures 5.2a–5.2e). Defense spending allocations are typical—8 percent allocated a million or less of this $20 billion pie, while 11 percent would award defense half or more of the

Figure 5.2a   How much of a $20 Billion Budget would You Spend on Education?

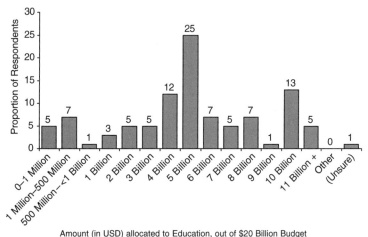

Amount (in USD) allocated to Education, out of $20 Billion Budget
Median = 5.00E + 9

Education Sample: $N = 550$.

Figure 5.2b   How much of a $20 Billion Budget would You Spend on Fighting Crime?

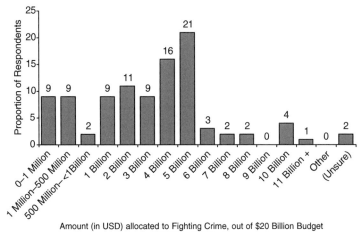

Amount (in USD) allocated to Fighting Crime, out of $20 Billion Budget
Median = 3.00E + 9

Education Sample: $N = 550$.

Figure 5.2c   How much of a $20 Billion Budget would You Spend on Health Care?

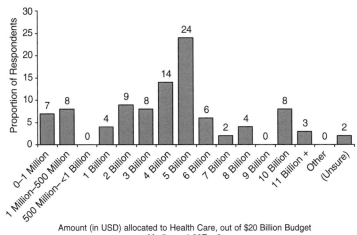

Amount (in USD) allocated to Health Care, out of $20 Billion Budget
Median = 4.00E + 9

Education Sample: $N = 550$.

Figure 5.2d How much of a $20 Billion Budget would You Spend on National Defense?

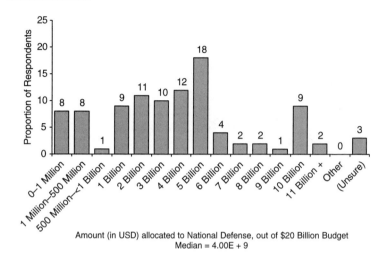

Amount (in USD) allocated to National Defense, out of $20 Billion Budget
Median = 4.00E + 9

Education Sample: $N = 550$.

Figure 5.2e How much of a $20 Billion Budget would You Spend on Cutting Taxes?

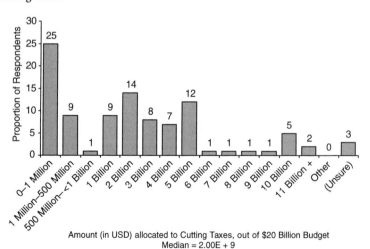

Amount (in USD) allocated to Cutting Taxes, out of $20 Billion Budget
Median = 2.00E + 9

Education Sample: $N = 550$.

hypothetical budget. Similarly, a quarter would barely cut taxes (if at all), while 7 percent would slash the entire budget in half via tax reductions. Clearly, even when obliged by an overall outer limit, the public advances wildly different policy priorities. This extreme variability is a far cry from legislative decision making where inertia-driven incrementalism (and statutory obligation) pushes budgetary changes only at the margins, for example, a "huge" shift may be 5 percent of last year's allocation. Also observe that when these allocations are averaged, even including tax cuts, this exercise in budgeting generated a $3.7 billion dollar "deficit," despite interviewer insistence on a "balanced budget."

These idiosyncratic preferences impose horrendous problems in transforming them into feasible instructions. This work in building-a-majority is conveniently swept under the rug when citizen poll-generated counsel is sought, but it is inescapable. If we assume that any consensus would begin at the mean, we can easily see that the immense variability entails serious jawboning to achieve 50 percent plus one. In each policy instance, rounding up a majority entails cobbling together skinflints willing to spend only a few million and benefactors favoring eight billion or more. This politically achieved consensus point *cannot* be uniquely and logically deduced from these poll data. A personal desire for "a million" or "ten billion" for a worthy cause is not a policy edict, regardless of authenticity; it is only an opening offer subject to future changes. Clever statistical calculations might *suggest* an expenditure point that *might* satisfy a minimal majority, but if the study of decision making across multiple issues teaches us anything, it is that "logical" outcomes are hardly guaranteed. Opinion intensity and flexibility virtually assures complex logrolling if these respondents were forced to decide collectively. And there is surely no guarantee that this can be accomplished or that the end product will be the statistically optimal solution. Why, for example, would those favoring allocating 25 percent to 50 percent of the budget to education surrender billions to those preferring to fight crime or enhance national defense? Budgetary paralysis is not, to say the least, exactly unknown. But, and this is key, a majority cannot be derives by asking one thousand people who cannot physically come to an agreement.

This last point brings up an argument of immense *political* significance if polls become guiding voices. Since polls of isolated individuals cannot substitute for institutional aggregation, pollsters themselves may have to carry out this process themselves. This can be innocuously done via questionnaire construction or by adroitly manipulating data, but it is indispensable if they are to determine majority messages. Although obvious, this point goes unmentioned by fans of plebiscitory democracy. Giving this power to those beyond pubic accountability is completely unavoidable save, maybe, putting all respondents on a conference call and letting nature take its course.

Furthermore, will poll-derived costs match revenue? Probably unlikely—these figures are abstractions divorced from taxation. In fact, polls soliciting public spending counsel seldom ask for corresponding tax advice. At best, poll takers are given opportunities to approve previously decided figures. For example, respondents might be asked, "Congress has decided to add $10 billion to the education budget, do you favor or oppose?" Now, thanks to legislative negotiations, those favoring unrealistic $100 billion increases are *forced* to be realistic. Even those who acquiesce may "really" want a tenth of this modest $10 billion figure can only grimly accept an inflexible reality. To expect citizen realism without offering a set figure is fantasy, even if respondents were eminently reasonable.

The ability to avoid tempting options that are not feasible is a third competence test. The public's craving for the unworkable or extralegal solutions can all too easily be obscured. Offering only legally attainable or financially affordable questionnaire items imparts a false civic reasonableness. It is conceivable, however, that stipulated choices mask dangerously foolish appetites. We confess to "tempting" people with seductive sounding, although inappropriate, solutions. We offer a "gullibility test," so to speak. The commercial equivalent is tolerating merchandise "too good to be true" such as "miracle diets" or cheap gadgets radically boosting gas mileage. One might also include astrology, lotteries, or TV psychic hotlines as "tests" of mass naivete. Admittedly, today's "unthinkable" solution or even shameless quackery may well evolve into tomorrow's status quo, but at any given moment, endorsing oddball or extralegal designs displays incapacity, no matter how sound in the abstract. In other words, vouchers and charter schools are currently realistic options, although they were once fantasy. It is likewise true that reasonable people can honestly disagree about short-term or medium-term practicality. Nevertheless, the constraints imposed by law and custom cannot be disregarded with the idea that "anything is possible."

The eleven possible solutions to our educational deficiencies are grouped into two broad categories: reasonable and unreasonable. Since it might be objected that *all* of these remedies are (in various degrees) politically feasible, a few words regarding "the incompetent" choices are necessary. Reducing teacher salaries clearly violates existing union contracts, and civil service laws. These constraints are exceptionally formidable—perhaps irreversible—legally and administratively. Firing incompetent teachers outright would surely be easier than partially voiding a binding contract—at least the former is legal. The same logic applies to banning unions—this step is both illegal and politically intolerable, although hypothetically enticing for some.

Awarding the Department of Education direct local control is equally off limits. The United States is not France where, evidently, Education Ministry clerks can instantly reckon what each pupil in every grade is reading. Allowing government experts to "solve" educational deficiencies (regardless of costs and legal impositions) and then compel the design's adoption is another unworkable option. Today's bitter national standards battle illustrates the colossal obstacles here. This "solution" also assumes, quite unrealistically in light of the historical record, that government-sponsored expertise can bring relief, if only sufficiently funded. The political costs of usurping traditional state-local authority spheres also would certainly provoke a firestorm of outrage. The "war on bad education" with "whatever it takes" feeds on naive hope. Surely proficient respondents realize that blank check, open-ended commitments that abandon legal and fiscal constraints invite wasteful disaster.[4] Finally, paying students piecework style for learning, although superficially alluring is justifiably on the edge of public debate. No evidence exists that such an approach would succeed. Even if one accepts the logic of incentives to accomplish miracles, this scheme inevitably invites corruption.

By contrast, other proffered alternatives have received serious discussion, even successful implementation. Financial incentives for superior teaching are already widespread, as are multiple versions of for-profit schools. Permitting local communities to control curricula and hire teachers is, of course, the former default (and once highly successful) option in U.S. education policy, and such decentralization still draws considerable support to counter deficient federal policies. Finally, plans to expand schooling, either by lengthening the school day or the school year are equally reasonable. To repeat, what is critical in this exercise is not to assess the popularity of these plausible options, but to see how many citizens will chase after the implausible ones.

Table 5.2 depicts an endorsement pattern roughly predictable from similar polls. That is, the public is generous in its welcomes to possible solutions. Still, and this is key, ample numbers elect schemes beyond reasonable practicality and/or legality. If government consumer protection agencies gained responsibility for monitoring dubious public policy proposals, our data suggest that here, too, enforcement would abound.[5] Perhaps most disquieting are the majorities favoring the two proposals that incorporate heavy-handed centralization—the "war" on deficient education and eliminating local control. Both approaches entail countless statutory (even constitutional)

Table 5.2   Support for Reasonable/Unreasonable Educational Alternatives

Alternative	%	N
1. Give teachers a cash bonus for improving student performance	73	402
2. Permit for-profit schools	35	195
3. Allow local communities to hire teachers and decide curriculum	57	313
4. Increase length of school year	44	243
5. Increase length of school day	26	144
6. Ban teachers' unions	20	111
7. Pay students a cash bonus to pass exams	20	108
8. Government experts design a nationally imposed teaching technique	28	152
9. Lower salaries of ineffective teachers	41	226
10. Declare "war" on bad education and spend whatever is necessary	54	295
11. Put failed schools directly under Department of Education control	61	334

changes, while subverting deeply ingrained habits. By contrast, requiring students to spend more time in school, a relatively easy policy to implement, drew less support. Also noteworthy is the 41 percent who expressed a desire to reduce teacher salaries for lackluster performance.

But, on the positive side, not all were taken in by pie-in-the-sky solutions. Three of the unfeasible options—paying students for performance, banning teachers' unions, and putting schools under expert supervision—received endorsements from a mere fifth to a quarter of the respondents. Particularly interesting is the role of the education level of the respondents played in who supported "expert" supervision as a choice. Fifty-nine percent of those with a high school education or less endorsed this option, compared to 14 percent of those with post-graduate degrees. Overall, then, substantial numbers (depending on the particular question) are enticed toward proposals beyond today's reasonable agenda, although, thankfully, not every scheme draws desperate majorities.

Do these numbers improve if we examine preferences among the better educated, people who should supposedly should "know better"? The answer is "generally yes," although the college-educated are hardly immune from some enticement. Of course, excluding the poorly educated from electing "solutions" is politically unthinkable (although perhaps warranted). In addition, this distaste for unfeasible solutions falls below a majority only among those with post-college training, which is hardly good news for those putting their faith in the college experience. Aversion among the better-educated to off-limits nostrums is most striking on the "solutions" calling for expert control, banning teacher unions, and paying students to pass tests. Still, placing local schools under direct supervision of Department of Education and declaring an all-out "war" on shoddy schooling did draw sizable endorsement from this group. Fondness for outrageous solutions, not unexpectedly, also follows ideological lines. For example, those on the political Left are disproportionally disposed toward greater centralized control and expert control. By contrast, those on the Right favor forbidding teachers' unions and paying students to pass tests (in fact, 50 percent of the self-identified Republicans would outlaw teachers' unions!). A proclivity for the unrealistic seems to be an equal opportunity employer.

Arguably, the embrace of these "unreasonable" options merely reflects exasperation with failed conventional approaches. Surely, some might argue that a solid case exists for the federal control of education (or any of the other off-limits nostrums) as potentially the most efficacious solution. Might a better label for these currently unfeasible options be "commendable desperation," not foolishness? Our rejoinder can only be that seeking the unobtainable, no matter how alluring or meritorious the motive, hardly certifies employment as "citizen counselor." The United States is not desperate for dictatorial guarantees of on-time trains. Imagine if one's tax accountant suggested fleeing the country to avoid taxes. Such advice is certainly "reasonable," although hardly persuasive, even if feasible. A prudent taxpayer might justifiably switch accountants after such "expert" opinion.

A fourth competence requirement is conceptualizing, however imperfectly, a policy proposal's drawbacks. An analogy with consumer behavior might again prove helpful. In shopping for cars encountering a bargain-priced exotic sports car might be tempting given superficial appeal—prestige, exhilarating performance, or the envious attention it attracts. Yet, a savvy purchaser *should* realize that this dazzling beauty likely demands exorbitant maintenance, requires costly insurance premiums, invites theft, and similar troubles. These features must all be weighed but, and this is key, no balancing is possible *unless* the buyer comes up with the drawbacks on his or her own. If polls routinely inserted these risks, this exercise would be unnecessary, but since they do not, we need respondents to supply these shortcomings independently. To be blunt, those contemplating proposals exclusively as benefits often display childlike cravings. Given that costs are an obvious liability in any proposal, and that the questionnaire repeatedly mentions

Table 5.3   Autonomously Stated Liabilities of Clinton Plan to
Hire One Hundred Thousand Teachers

Reason	Entire Sample
1. Federal control/involvement	11% (59)
2. Poor teacher qualifications	6 (28)
3. Classroom size unimportant	4 (23)
4. Parents should be more responsible	2 (12)
5. Money will not be used efficiently	2 (10)
6. Doesn't concern people without children	1 (8)
7. Various political reasons; for example, doesn't like Clinton	9 (51)
8. More power to teachers union	0 (2)
9. Should focus on all grades	1 (6)
10. Miscellaneous reasons	15 (84)
11. None/no reasons	47 (261)
12. DK	2 (12)

cost, respondents were explicitly instructed to formulate liabilities over and above financial drawbacks.

This exercise produced surprising results, even by our low expectations. Public reaction to Washington providing money for new teachers (Table 5.3) might best be described as near universal obliviousness to drawbacks beyond cost. Forty-seven percent were utterly dumbfounded when it came to supplying *any* possible drawback. When combined with the "Don't know" category, almost half the entire sample could not come up with a noncost liability on their own. A handful of others (4 percent) also mentioned, in one form or another, "too much money," although they had been specifically asked to avoid this.

Among those furnishing possible drawbacks, several fairly obvious objections were offered but their low frequency will disappoint fans of public wisdom. The most prominent objection—some 11 percent—mentioned too much Washington influence, while another 6 percent acknowledged insufficient teacher quality. Four percent echoed expert views that classroom size really didn't matter. Reservations often expressed in public debates—effective fund utilization, alternatives to hiring new teachers, or aggrandizing the teachers' unions—drew brief mentions. At best, between a fifth and a quarter could be deemed "competent" here. Many other "objections" were of dubious relevance, for example, a personal dislike of Clinton or extraneous commentary on declining disciplinary standards. This bafflement was hardly unique to the poorly educated—some 29 percent of those with some postgraduate education could imagine *zero* potential nonfinancial drawbacks (and here, too, prudent cautions such as burgeoning Washington control or the unproven merits of classroom size reductions, went almost entirely unstated).

Finally, there is the most daunting of competence measures, willingness to pay (WTP). Chapter Two's overview noted that appraising this decision making ingredient eludes untold ingenious questionnaire writers. Top-of-the-head verbal assurances without consequences still, alas, provide what must suffice as hard data. An immense paradox exists here. On the one hand, ample failed tax referenda plus vociferous opposition to tax levies strongly indicates public distaste for higher taxes. Yet, on the other hand, polls routinely elicit equally plain entitlement cries that virtually guarantee soaring costs. No doubt, the hypothetical nature of the poll encourages pseudogenerosity. Respondents are not being asked to put their money where their mouth is. Perhaps respondents believe that costs are personally escapable. Picture how differently things would be if the interviewer, like a bothersome charity fundraiser, forcefully solicited contributions from respondents. Further conjecture if would-be benefactors were threatened with legal action if "pledges" were dishonored.

At the onset we admit that uncovering what people are truly willing to pay for specific policy choices is not possible. Interviewers are not psychics predicting future reactions to candidates who endorse swelling the public till. The only true test would be creating something like a referendum with a legally binding vote to alter the tax code, a possibility beyond any poll, no matter how ingenious. Instead, we settle for asking respondents "what they would be willing to pay personally, if they had children in second grade, to reduce class size from twenty to eighteen" (the approximate impact of Clinton's proposal). This strategy mimics market research where a product's future demand is (partially) estimated by what potential consumers would spend for a specified benefit. Sincerity regarding future tax generosity is *not* being ascertained, although this would naturally be the ideal.

Matching policy desire with (hypothetical) largesse is central. If would-be shoppers insist on paying next to nothing for luxuries, we can rightly conclude that either the item is undeliverable (save some drastic price-reducing innovation) or that popular desires are misdirected. In consumer terms, imagine two prospective buyers for a new Honda Accord—one agreed to spend "as much as $1,000," while another would gladly pay $100,000. Both, we argue, are less than savvy potential customers given that the real price is roughly $20,000. Of course, if the interviewee rejected this car under any conditions, the competence answer would be "nothing" or maybe "a dollar."

How much, then, *should* a well-versed parent be willing to pay to pare class size down to eighteen? As the previous chapter explained, this cost rests on multiple calculation assumptions, whether the aim is eighteen students in every class versus an average of eighteen in each school district, and similar premises. Such number crunching procedures are not for the statistical faint-of-heart, but there *are* reputable, scientific ballpark estimations. Brewer, Knop, Gill, and Reichardt (1999, p. 183) calculate that for 1998–99, the national average per pupil cost of having every grade 1–3 student in a class of eighteen would be $448 per student. Thus, on average, every parent (not taxpayer) nationally would have to pay this amount to have their own children guaranteed a class of eighteen. Admittedly, other analysts might disagree, but $448 is a suitable rough baseline against which to judge what citizens think they might have to pay.

First the good news for those imputing *vox populi* wise counsel. If one averages all the estimates offered in Table 5.4, policy supporters and full sample alike, the average estimated tax cost is within generous hailing distance of the roughly accurate $448 figure. If one were calibrating public sagacity as manifested in some collective *Volkgeist* (spirit of the people) then, indeed, let us rejoice. But, a closer read of these data suggests a more

Table 5.4   Amount a Parent would Pay (Hypothetically) to have Child's Class Reduced from Twenty to Eighteen Students, Total Sample and Supporters Only

Amount	Entire Sample	Supporters Only
None	39% (212)	31% (137)
$1.00 to $20.00	4 (24)	5 (22)
$21.00 to 40.00	2 (12)	3 (11)
$41.00 to 60.00	3 (18)	4 (17)
$61.00 to 80.00	1 (3)	1 (3)
$81.00 to 100.00	9 (52)	10 (45)
$101 to 150.00	1 (4)	1 (4)
$151.00 to 200.00	7 (40)	8 (35)
$201.00 to 300.0	2 (12)	3 (12)
$301.00 to 400.00	1 (7)	2 (7)
$401.00 to 500.00	7 (41)	9 (39)
$501.00+	16 (88)	18 (17)
DK/NS	7 (37)	7 (29)
Mean	$562.70	$586.50

restrained inclination. Perhaps most notable is the huge dispersion of these data, from niggardliness to ample generosity. No doubt, pure guesswork is rampant. Among those who have *already* expressed support for the Clinton initiative, 31 percent answer "zero," when the initiative is framed in this "pay-up" language. Remarkably, the higher the education, the greater the willingness to pay "nothing" for this benefit. A third of college-educated supporters refused to pay anything versus to 22 percent of those with high school or less. So much for the accusation that only the ill-informed crave "free lunches." Moreover, having children under twelve in the household has only a slight impact, however (29 percent of that group of program supporters also would pay "nothing"). If we assume that $200 per child would be the average (plausible) minimum to achieve this goal, then about 30 percent of the respondents can be judged proficient future consumers. All in all, most of these proinitiative supporters are either willing to pay nothing or amounts well below what is financially necessary. In a phrase, these education consumers are largely unrealistic bargain hunters.

Reducing Class Size: Preferences

To assess fully the public's support for President Clinton's classroom size reduction initiative we posed multiple questions progressing from the "standard" questionnaire item to more complex variations that impose greater cost/risk realism. Once again, we acknowledge that no single format perfectly captures the ideal. Our attempt merely reveals how different questionnaire details elicit varying responses. The explicit attention to the political consequences of these "mere details" distances our analysis from customary survey-based experiments. From our perspective, the shallow stock questions commonly used engenders a misleading consensus regarding today's social welfare state. That devotion to that welfare state declines as questions become more balanced is the overarching hypothesis. Put sharply, the public is repeatedly seduced by the pollster, whereas presentations that reveal both positives and negatives find greater skepticism toward these entitlements.

We started by asking common polling questions of the respondent supported or opposed the legislation had been passed to hire thirty thousand new teachers in grades 1 through 3. Nothing negative was even hinted. Predictably, given past research in this area, nearly 80 percent favored the idea. To those who opposed the legislation, we asked a follow-up question mentioning that adding teachers would reduce classroom size and help younger students. This small bit of positive information was enough to get 22.6 percent of the "opposed" to support the initiative. These two "pro" groups were then combined to serve as the subsample favoring the proposal (84 percent of the total sample). Had analysis stopped here, as is customary, the likely conclusion would be that this policy was wildly popular, especially after its alleged "scientifically confirmed" benefits were explained.

We then introduced cost figures to randomly chosen respondents within this "propolicy" subsample. This last fact is critical—the question we pose concerns the possible erosion of support *after* the questionnaire item become more realistic. Note that those who already oppose the Clinton initiative are irrelevant, except where explicitly included. Introducing the costs and risks of this policy took several forms. In some instances, we specified gross dollar amounts applied for different time periods. Elsewhere, we personalized multibillion dollar figures in terms of average taxpayer payment, either as a net amount or as an incremental tax increase. Finally, we tied dollar figures to the marginal benefit expected from the classroom size reduction initiative. All of these formulations capture (in decidedly unique ways) the policy's substantial—and on occasion, unanticipated—monetary cost. Not surprisingly, support varied depending on how these fiscal burdens were portrayed.

An overview of these experiments appears in Table 5.5. Majorities in each variation still remain loyal to the classroom size reduction initiative, although occasionally at substantially reduced levels. In each instance, at least some advocates get "cold feet" at the very mention of cost. The strongest endorsement levels (94 percent and 90 percent, respectively) derive from two separate questions inserting the figure of $10. When the $10 figure was given

Table 5.5   Support for Hiring New Teachers Given Various Costs, Supporters Only

	Still Favor	N
Cost presentation, dollars		
1. $12 billion for 7 years	75%	108
2. $12 billion for 7 years, $10 per taxpayer per year	94	109
3. $12 billion, raise average tax bill from $6,832 to $6,842	87	104
4. $1.2 billion to lower average class from 17.8 to 17	57	117
5. Only $10 per year, per taxpayer to hire more teachers	90	67
Cost overruns		
1. If cost of $12 billion program exceeded $15 billion	69%	438
2. If cost of $12 billion program exceeded $20 billion	63	304
3. If cost of $12 billion program exceeded $25 billion	76	192

as a net, stand-alone figure—it would cost you 10 bucks a year to hire thirty thousand teachers—90 percent remained loyal. In the second alternate, the $10 figure was presented together with the $12 billion, seven-year cost. Again, nearly everyone remained true to his or her initial position (94 percent). A bit of a decline occurred when the average federal income tax burden was broached. With the tax burden going from $6,832 to $6,842, some 16 percent changed their minds. Overall, solving our educational woes for "a mere ten bucks" is apparently an irresistible bargain.

At the other extreme is the precipitous drop in support of the benefit of the policy posed in the language of the marginal (and rather tiny) change in classroom size. Arguably, this formulation may be the most honest in the sense that potential policy consumers are informed of their investment's return. Here, only 57 percent of those initially in favor still approve the plan after learning that fresh hires will drop teacher–student ratios from 17.8 to 17.0. Put differently, some 43 percent of the policy's fans decided the .8 ratio change was not worth the cost. And, note well, this more honest variant still remains silent on nonmonetary costs, surely a critical ingredient if "truth in advertising" were mandated for questionnaires. We shall have more to say on this point below.

A series of questions that broach soaring, unexpected costs further illuminates the unstable support for this policy (also Table 5.5). Recall from the previous chapter how this cure-all could easily exceed initial expenditure projections (e.g., labor market distortions in teacher salaries or expensive new school construction). Certainly ample precedent exists for programs doubling or even tripling their costs beyond initial expert estimations. Our experiment here assessed how support levels would be shaped by burgeoning costs. We hypothesized that endorsements would plummet with program overruns. This did occur, though not as systematically as one might predict. Employing separate, randomly selected subsamples, if the seven-year program were to cost $15 billion (a 25 percent cost overrun), support fell to 69 percent. If expenses climbed to $20 billion, enthusiasm among plan advocates dropped to 63 percent. Yet at the $25 billion figure—a program cost overrun exceeding 100 percent—76 percent of initial supporters continued their support. This nonlinear relationship in particular hints that ordinary citizens may find these figures meaningless—escalating from $12 billion to $25 billion is accepted with far greater equanimity than, say, gasoline prices jumping to $2.00 a gallon from $1.25.

A different picture emerges when we focus on the nonmonetary costs of this apparently "good thing." Adding these more nuanced risks is scarcely "bias" in the sense of attempting to discredit the welfare state. Hiring new teachers involves gambles, and these can interfere with the best of intentions, even if unmentioned in the usual survey (and recall how few respondents could spontaneously imagine these). The most notable is opportunity cost. There also are, as noted, problems of hiring inexperienced teachers, unwelcome federal intrusion into local affairs, the cannibalization of school facilities, and fresh paperwork demands, among many other likely dangers. Once more we hypothesized that this alluring proposal would find less enthusiasm as potential problems were brought closer to the surface.

Announcing risk was executed in two separate ways. The first simply proposed the general possibility of less-than-perfect success (hardly an unreasonable supposition given past federally initiated school accomplishments). After all, even optimistic state-based field trials report only minor improvements (recall the controversy surrounding the STAR program's ambiguous accomplishment), and certain hard evidence predicts zero improvement. Perhaps questionnaire writers should have included this pessimistic caveat, just as medical ethics require patients to be informed that certain surgeries invite serious danger.

What happens when we mention less-than-hoped-for success? Not surprisingly, enthusiasm cools (Table 5.6). When chances of success for the policy drop from "mostly successful" to "somewhat successful" public enthusiasm falls by 15 percent, from 95 percent still in favor of 80 percent. If the project were only "occasionally successful," however, only 63 percent of the original supporter group stayed. This sober finding—attachment depends on

Table 5.6 Continued Support for Hiring New Teachers Given Drawbacks, Proposal Supporters Only

	Still Favor	N
Support Given Likelihood of Success		
Would continue support if program were		
Mostly successful in improving student performance	95%	438
Somewhat successful in improving student performance	80	438
Occasionally successful in improving student performance	63	438
Support for New Teachers Given Liabilities		
1. Cutbacks in other programs, for example, art and music	29%	220
2. Half or more new teachers were unqualified	15	438
3. Washington insisted on more local control	48	438
4. Hiring teachers would raise local taxes	72	218

expected payoff—may be "obvious," but it is remarkable that past classroom size reduction polls conveniently neglect this point.

Stronger questions made potential downsides more explicit (Table 5.6). One mentioned the realistic likelihood of half of the newly hired teachers being less than adequately qualified. Among those already voicing approval of Clinton's plan, a mere 15 percent continued with their endorsement in the face of this potential liability! Another probe raised the specter of cutbacks in music and art as necessary to afford additional teachers—only 29 percent of the original support group remained steadfast. These are major shifts in support, and both perils are quite plausible. A third brought up Washington's generosity inviting heightened Department of Education intrusion into local affairs. Once more, support fell below majority levels—only 48 percent now welcomed the hiring of new teachers. Somewhat surprisingly, the possibility that the policy could increase local taxes drawback did not transform majority into minority support, although 28 percent of these proinitiative respondents changed their minds. One can only speculate possible support levels if surveys were legally required to list possible negatives or combine them into one single grand terrifying warning.

The upshot of this exercise is unmistakable—if prudently warned about dangers, respondents grow cautious, even adverse. This conclusion is hardly unexpected, but—to reiterate yet once more—its absence from conventionally polling is remarkable. Especially notable is the contrast between the poll takers responses monetary costs items verses their reaction to the liability questions. This divergence between the two was, frankly, unexpected. Dollar costs impose relatively modest impacts on devotion to hiring more teachers, an inclination roughly consistent with previously noted willingness to "do whatever it takes to solve the problem." Judged by these findings, crass office seekers would be advised to advocate lavish and expensive solutions to problems but avoid any intimations that such approaches may pose risks, or even make matters worse.[6]

The final insight concerns the attractiveness of the Clinton initiative vis-à-vis equally viable alternatives. The topic here is of momentous political importance given that several competing feasible remedies are available for any predicament, and priorities may vary among those seeking improvements. To furnish the public with a single option without mentioning rivals readily invites the mistaken conclusion that a majority pick is *the* most popular prescription. That nearly everyone endorses adding more teachers can never prove that "more teachers" sits atop the list of cures. Conceivably, this choice could reside at the bottom of the list and owes its popularity solely to being the only solution publicized.

Public choice devotees will surely grasp the immense complexities inherent in deciphering an accurate portrait of public preferences. More relevant for our purposes, however, is devising a way of determining what people want that does not require ordinary citizens to exhibit some statistically "general will." To demand citizens rank a dozen items in order of preference is an invitation to disappointment for those who seek popular guidance. We likewise want to avoid the "pick as many options as you want" format, since this often yields a jumble of desires with dubious policy relevance. In assessing how Clinton's initiative stacks up against comparable available options, we simply asked respondents (including those opposed to the initiative) how various alternatives compared to hiring thirty thousand new teachers.

Not unexpectedly, despite the immense popularity of adding 30,000 new teachers, other solutions were sometimes *more* popular (Table 5.7). First consider the entire sample, supporters and opponents alike. Eighty-three percent said that funding improved teacher training would be *better* than hiring fresh recruits (a view shared by numerous experts). A clear majority (57 percent) also preferred tax-free savings accounts. In the other instances, the option of hiring more teachers still remained the most popular pick, but the proportions were nowhere close to the overwhelming support recorded in stand-alone surveys. In fact, many of these rivals—vouchers/charter schools or increased fiscal discretion by the states—draw substantial endorsement compared to adding new teachers. Forty-three percent, for example, remarked that vouchers/charter schools would be a *better* choice than hiring more teachers. This is not to argue that these represent superior, "more competent" choices. Each may be as dubious or as risky in its impact as the Clinton

Table 5.7   Popularity of Hiring More Teachers vis-à-vis Other Options, by Initiative's Supporters and Entire Sample

Other Options	Supporters Only	Entire Sample
1. Tax free savings accounts for private schools	54%	57%
2. Giving money to local schools without restriction	28	31
3. Fund improved teacher training	83	83
4. Return money to states and permit them to spend it	40	43
5. Use money for vouchers/charter schools	40	43
6. Let schools solve problems without more financial aid	22	30
	N = 438	550

proposal is. Nor is there any guarantee that these other designs are properly understood. Everything may be a garble of desperate hope. The key point is merely that proclaiming that majorities favor a particular policy prescription hardly means that the offering is the most preferred pick no matter how overwhelming the numbers.

Perhaps even more telling is the popularity of alternatives among those already announcing their support of adding more teachers. "Better teacher training" was ranked ahead of "more teachers" by 83 percent of *those who supported the Clinton initiative.* A tax-free savings account likewise outshined hiring more teachers while vouchers/charter schools and giving money directly to the state each drew 40 percent as the superior choice. Ironically, among these endorsing hiring more teachers, 22 percent actually preferred that schools should solve their problems without any additional financial assistance.

Providing Federal Daycare Assistance: Competence

When assessing citizen competence for hiring more teachers we asked respondents to estimate costs. This tactic was justifiable since this initiative was fairly concrete and teacher salaries can be roughly estimated. However, the daycare issue does not lend itself to such specific dollar figure. Possible cost estimations here are exceptionally daunting since helpfulness can be provided in many, often-hazy ways. Childcare assistance might be secured via tax credits of indeterminate value or as educational or antiviolence interventions not labeled as "daycare." Nutritional programs are likewise partially daycare outreach. Many might not even define these interventions as "daycare."

Respondents were instead presented with the proposed cost of $22 billion over five years and asked to guess the yearly cost per taxpayer. Again, this exercise is analogous to breaking down large expenditures to concrete, "meaningful" figures. The correct answer is approximately $37 per year. We admit that this is an extremely vexing task, but our now familiar rejoinder is that this relevant information should have been pollster provided. Perchance questionnaire writers assume this erudition. The underlying logic is identical to the previous exercise—a competent buyer should possess a reasonable idea of what a desired product costs *personally.*

Guesses regarding this personal fiscal obligation covered a wide range, including—hardly surprisingly—grossly unrealistic answers (Table 5.8). Once more, about a third (34 percent) could supply *no* calculation whatsoever, regardless of interviewer prodding. Among those with a high school education or less, 45 percent were dumbfounded (and a third of those with

Table 5.8 Estimated Cost Per Taxpayer per Year of
$22 Billion, Five-Year Daycare Proposal

Estimated Cost	%	N
None to $1.00	2	11
$2.00 to 10.00	8	41
$11.00 to 25.00	5	27
$26.00 to 50.00	5	28
$51.00 to 100.00	11	60
$101 to 500.00	24	90
$600+	19	105
DK	34	189

postgraduate degrees also were unable to venture a guess). Overall, the amounts guessed far exceeded true costs. Some 19 percent put the cost at over $600 per year; forty respondents (7 percent) guessed the nice round figure of $1,000 per year.[7] Only a tiny fraction were somewhere in the ballpark near $37 a year. When these estimates are examined within groups conceivably having some insight, for example, families with children under twelve or the college educated, one can reasonably conclude that *everybody* is guessing without the foggiest idea of the correct answer. Again, this task is very difficult, but this reasonable excuse does not diminish the simple fact that when this proposal is presented for public approval, only a handful of respondents grasp the cost of their "purchase." Even then, most of the answers that come close are probably lucky guesses. This point will resurface when respondents are actually given the rough cost of this program.

Our daycare tradeoff exercise, not surprisingly, yields an overall outcome quite similar to what transpired with the education exercise. Most notable, when all the figures (presented in Figures 5.3a–5.3e) were summed, the aggregate "budget" was still $2.5 billion in the red (perhaps uncontrolled spending by Congress is more understandable based on these results). Again, less than a majority (43 percent) could arrive at the $20 billion figure. Nearly 10 percent could not get halfway to $20 billion, while another 12 percent soared beyond $25 billion (the highest figure reached was $68 billion). A recurring problem was separating millions from billions. A respondent might begin his or her allocation with millions only to discover that after going through a few categories, the total was still a tiny faction of the desired $20 billion goal. Similarly, respondents often experienced difficulty using all five categories, although, a few genuinely desired a more "limited government."

Figure 5.3a   How much of a $20 Billion Budget would You Spend on Daycare?

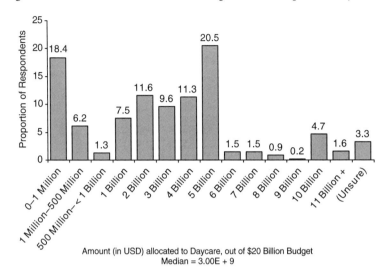

Daycare Sample: $N = 550$.

Figure 5.3b   How much of a $20 Billion Budget would You Spend on Education?

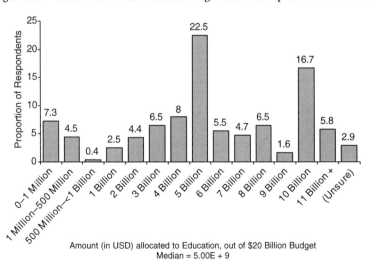

Daycare Sample: $N = 550$.

Figure 5.3c How much of a $20 Billion Budget would You Spend on Fighting Crime?

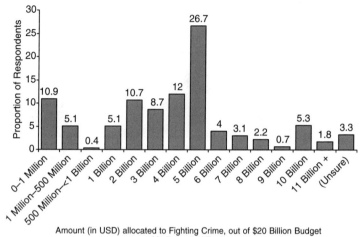

Amount (in USD) allocated to Fighting Crime, out of $20 Billion Budget
Median = 4.00E + 9

Daycare Sample: $N = 550$.

Figure 5.3d How much of a $20 Billion Budget would You Spend on National Defense?

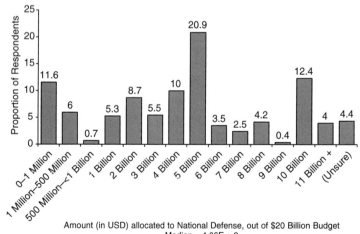

Amount (in USD) allocated to National Defense, out of $20 Billion Budget
Median = 4.00E + 9

Daycare Sample: $N = 550$.

Figure 5.3e How much of a $20 Billion Budget would You Spend on Cutting Taxes?

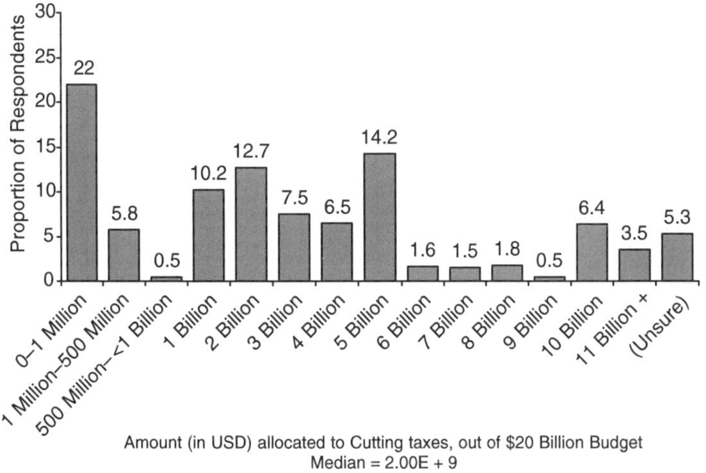

Amount (in USD) allocated to Cutting taxes, out of $20 Billion Budget
Median = 2.00E + 9

Daycare Sample: $N = 550$.

In fact, only 57 percent utilized all five categories while 10 percent used two or fewer policy choices.

Anecdotal interviewer feedback again confirms the difficulty of this "balancing" via the telephone survey. Comments such as "respondents were overwhelmed by the amount of money that they had to work with ..." or "respondents had a hard time remembering how many categories there was [sic]" or "some people were frustrated by this point ... could hear it in their voice," and so on. To repeat once more, the task's purpose is not to discredit the public's mathematical ability. We merely show that the talent for making tradeoffs—a dollar for education *requires* one less dollar for health care—is imperfectly displayed in the snap quiz telephone interview. It is not something that arises "naturally" and even those respondents who nominally satisfy all requirements—reaching $20 billion with precisely five categories—often need coaching. Alhough we are not psychics, these troubles do suggest that when policy A is "bought" via the conventional poll, no thought is given to what that support may cost elsewhere. The typical poll's long menu of separate questions thus (in all likelihood) invites rapacious appetites. Few respondents will spontaneously interject "Wait a minute, young man, since

I favored both upping health care and education just a few moments ago, I'll have to forgo fighting poverty since I'm probably going broke. Let me go back and balance my budget, please."

And, as was true in the education exercise, the desired amounts are scattered every which way. Bear in mind that obtaining reasonable dollar amounts is not the aim (that is impossible given question constraints and options). Rather, we simply illustrate the obvious fact that people differ greatly in slicing a budget pie, and discerning a majority consensus is hardly self-evident. For example, about 18 percent would allocate a million or less in their imaginary $20 billion budget for daycare. On the other end of the continuum, 31 percent would commit a fifth or more ($5 billion) to this purpose. When it came time to cut taxes, 28 percent were willing to slice off a billion or less, while a third agreeably slashed a quarter of the entire $20 billion budget. We hypothesize that such diversity of preference is commonplace in standard, highly simplified polls. We merely make explicit immensely troubling issues disguised by simplistic probes.

Imagine if all 550 respondents were assembled and told to negotiate a budget. Quite likely, the ultimate outcome would be statistically unpredictable and discussions might well go beyond the imposed constraints. Conceivably, the five-item budget would expand exponentially as the search for majority consensus sought side-payments, devious enticements, and intricate win–win solutions. Perhaps this citizen assembly would issue bonds, or pressure Treasury to inflate the currency. Lyndon Johnson's legendary arm-twisting skills to hammer out deals might be essential. What is most relevant, however, is not concocting hypothetical scenarios, but acknowledging the tentative nature of this fiscal advice. Wanting to spend, say, $3 billion on daycare is only one voice in a noisy chorus, not a majority mandate, and who can authoritatively judge where "true majorities" lie? These budgetary calls are, at best, initially offers, not directives.

The third competence test checks whether respondents can withstand the allure of unrealistic solutions. A "competent citizen" must grasp limits imposed by law, custom, or practicality for state-assisted child rearing. As before, respondents received a randomly rotated list of potential solutions to supposed daycare shortages. Can respondents separate the reasonable from seductively foolish propositions? A few "solutions" are patently bizarre while others have long-standing acceptance. Plainly impermissible—at least in the present-day U.S. context—were three totalitarian-like proposals: daycare centers for everyone run by the federal government, a national parent training program, and a federally formulated set of standards for raising children. Also included here were options for having Washington pay all daycare providers directly (in other words, nationalizing the childcare industry) and making "quality daycare" a constitutionally protected right.

The more realistic options we offered were lowering taxes to augment discretionary income, public school supplied daycare, and tax deductions for childcare associated expenses. Falling between these extremes were two picks that might be characterized as "feasible but seldom connected to the daycare debate." These were having government agencies enforce laws regarding home daycare and making it easier for state agencies to remove children from their home if parental care were inadequate. All alternatives can be roughly arrayed in terms of how extensively respondents would permit state interventions in family life. The important matter at hand, however, is not some debate over incipient popular totalitarianism, but whether or not respondents desire solutions beyond current acceptability.

As we saw with results from the hiring more teachers initiative, the overall pattern of public desires is mixed (Table 5.9). In several instances, majorities *do* approve possibilities of dubious propriety (at best) under our system of limited, decentralized government. Perhaps most disturbing (at least for devotees of family autonomy) was that 54 percent favored a national parent-training program. Fifty-eight percent also endorsed the rather meaningless constitutionally protected right to "quality daycare" (and recall past discussions regarding ambiguity of the word "quality").

Table 5.9   Preferences for Reasonable/Unreasonable Solutions to Daycare Problem, Entire Sample

	% Favor	N
Unreasonable Options		
1. Make daycare a constitutionally protected right	58	319
2. Create a national parent training program	54	294
3. Have federal government pay all daycare directly	34	185
4. Establish national, government-run daycare for all	28	155
5. Create national standards for how parents raise children	23	128
Reasonable Options		
1. Larger tax deductions for daycare	82	450
2. Lower taxes to increase discretionary income	73	401
3. Expand public school daycare offerings	65	356
Mixed Options		
1. Have government agencies enforce home daycare rules	62	339
2. Make it easier to remove children from inadequate homes	52	287

These centralization options were especially alluring to African Americans, for example, 59 percent of the black respondents endorsed a national daycare system for all children versus 23 percent for whites. However, there is some solace for those who champion popular wisdom. National standards for childrearing (surely a political nightmare of the first order), putting all daycare providers on the federal payroll, and mandatory nationally administered daycare centers all failed to gain majority endorsement, although these nostrums drew ample endorsements.

Enforcing laws regarding home care and easier child removal received majorities, although here many respondents also had their doubts. Perhaps the strongest evidence for the public's desire for government "assistance at a distance" is the overwhelming backing for the two measures involving the tax code. Interestingly, these drew prodigious enthusiasm among the lowest family income group ($30,000 and below), although these tax-based schemes are most advantageous to the wealthy (these proposals were also highly popular among African Americans, despite their simultaneous attachment to more centralized government intervention). All in all, the report card here is satisfactory but needs improvement.

The fourth competence test concerns spontaneous awareness of costs over and above financial burdens. If citizens are to be more than childlike consumers, conjuring up drawbacks without being specifically prompted is critical. How else are alluring nostrums resistible? Being aware of potential costs is not necessarily synonymous with opposing this initiative—a respondent can remain a fervent daycare supporter and still have grim reservations. Nor do we insist that objections be entirely reasonable. On the whole, we expected a better public performance here than with the hiring teachers issue. Daycare is less abstract than hiring thirty thousand new teachers, so awareness of potential liabilities should be more pronounced. Moreover, the issue of government involvement in family matters or regulating mundane babysitting have long permeated public debate.

Compared to the dismal performance of respondents during the poll regarding hiring more teachers, independently voiced objections were more plentiful. Still, as Table 5.10 reveals, the phrase "federally assisted daycare" does not seem to raise as many concerns as one might assume. Over a quarter of program supporters (26 percent) could offer *no* conceivable nonfiscal disadvantage to expanding government's role here. Another 9 percent could only repeat slight variants that it would "cost too much" leaving about two thirds to suggest other objections (about 10 percent said that those without children shouldn't pay for daycare). Of those remaining offering some noncost aversion, 20 percent proffered (in one form other another) the notion

Table 5.10 Perceived Drawbacks to Federal Daycare Initiative, Supporters Only

Reasons	%	N
1. None/Nothing	26	140
2. Families should look after own expenses	14	75
3. Doesn't concern people without children	10	57
4. No reason but cost, debt	9	50
5. Government has other priorities	7	38
6. Government would have too much influence	6	35
7. Up to state, not federal government	6	31
8. Would increase taxes	3	18
9. Eligibility issues	3	18
10. People don't like Clinton, other political reasons	5	27
11. People are selfish, don't want to help others	2	11
12. Abuse/fraud	2	11
13. Government already too big	2	10
14. Only benefit poor people	1	7
15. Other	10	52
16. DK	2	11

that government should restrict its involvement in family/daycare matters. Evidently, conservative fears about government interference in family life have not penetrated widely into public consciousness. A scattering of respondents also noted possible administrative headaches such as deciding eligibility or opportunities for fraud. Here again, an often mentioned fear of clumsy management by a bloated bureaucracy has failed to resonate widely. Oddly enough, comparisons between those with children under twelve and those without children evidenced no systematic differences.

Finally, there is the unavoidable willingness to pay for one's largesse. In the case of hiring additional teachers, this willingness to pay was relatively straightforward. The imagined parent was asked how much they would pay for the benefit of having one's child in a slightly smaller class. A federally assisted program aimed at lower income parents is a different matter. Asking people to imagine that they are poor and then asking "how much they are willing to pay ..." is nonsensical given their hypothetical situation. The logical answer would be "barely anything since I'm poor." Asking "How much would you *personally* pay to help an impoverished stranger with daycare?" does not work either. Obviously, the latter situation occurs—the affluent subsidize many benefits bestowed on the poor and, judging compliance with the IRS, they "gladly" make this transfer (and the wealthy also may make charitable contributions, too).

Under such circumstances our strategy was to keep it simple, stressing both agreeableness to pay *anything* if they supported Clinton's proposal and, if generosity was forthcoming, was this amount "reasonable?" By "reasonable," we mean that the dollar figure offered would translate into amounts consistent with what the Clinton proposal required. Recall from Chapter Two how hypothetical figures provided by the researcher could imply inadvertently quadruple agency budgets or otherwise result in bizarre outlays. The task here concerns a person's capacity to align his or her good heartedness with proficient political decision making. A respondent proclaiming: "Give the poor a million bucks each and get this childhood poverty thing over with" would certainly be classified as "benevolent." However, he or she would *not* be judged a "wise counselor."

At its most basic, we hope to discover whether supporters agree to pay or not. The answer is that most do, but many do not. Specifically, when daycare supporters (actually a subsample given the need to reduce questionnaire length) were asked if they would be willing to pay $40 per year for federally subsidized daycare versus having the money to spend anyway they wished, 61 percent said yes. By contrast, 36 percent said "no" (the rest either didn't know or offered some other opinion). In other words, more than a third of those in favor of the proposal were disinclined to pay, at least when stated in this form. Perhaps the mere mentioning of having the $40 to spend freely enticed some boosters to jump ship. Predictably, this fiscal consistency was most pronounced among the better educated and the more affluent. Perhaps these supporters believed that they could better spend the $40 themselves rather than rely on government designs.

A more open-ended probe on this issue offers a more complex picture. Here, again due to limited time resources analysis focused exclusively on supporters without children under twelve. In a sense, this could be seen as altruistic benevolence—agreeing to fund a favored measure lacking a personal payoff. In any case, what is central to this exercise is how abstract generosity—"the government should help families with daycare"—translates into dollar figures. Note well, there is no "correct" answer to this question. A taxpayer willing to add an extra dollar for daycare to his or her 1040 is, technically, "helpful," although not as generous as one throwing in an extra $500. The emphasis is on *aligning* abstract endorsement with tax money. Competency hinges on the congruence between already expressed support and agreeing to appropriate amounts.

Not surprisingly the personal generosity among those initially agreeable to the Clinton proposals covers a huge range. The Clinton initiative gave the figure of $22 billion costing roughly $151 to $200 per taxpayer. To put these offerings into a richer political context, we have provided a rough estimation of how much money these personalized figures would yield (Table 5.11). To be frank, these data offer a "peculiar" portrait of generosity among the initiative's faithful. Again, a fair number of fans would pay zero or tiny amounts to fund what they had previously endorsed. Another group—14 percent—didn't know what they would pay, a perfectly reasonable response given the task's obscure complexity, but this highlights that about one in seven of these supporters are buying an item of uncertain cost. An almost bizarre feature of this "generosity" is the immense spread between the mean and the median—$642.6 versus $98.1. Obviously, given an unrestricted opportunity to secure a benefit supplied from above, at least some respondents go whole hog in their bigheartedness, though most (judged by the median) stay closer to reasonableness.

Table 5.11 Personal Willingness to Pay for Expanding Daycare for Families with Children, Clinton Proposal Supporters Only with No Children Under 12

Amount	% (N)	Money Generated*
None	12% (29)	Nothing
$1 to $20	8 (21)	$120 million to $2.4 billion
$21 to $40	2 (4)	$2.52 billion to $4.8 billion
$41 to $60	4 (10)	$4.92 billion to $7.2 billion
$61 to $80	1 (2)	$7.32 billion to $9.6 billion
$81 to $100	18 (46)	$9.72 billion to $12.0 billion
$101 to $150	1 (2)	$12.12 billion to $18.0 billion
$151 to $200	9 (23)	$18.12 billion to $24.0 billion
$201 to $300	3 (8)	$25.8 billion to $36.0 billion
$301 to $400	2 (4)	$36.12 billion to $48.0 billion
$401 to $500	8 (19)	$48.12 billion to $60.0 billion
$501+	19 (49)	$60.12 billion plus
DK/NS	14 (32)	
Mean	$642.60	
Median	$$98.1	

*These cost figures are based on an estimated 120,000,000 individual taxpayers in 2000, the year when the question was asked.

With this in mind, might we settle regarding public willingness to shoulder more federally subsidized daycare? If these figures are judged as "hard" commitments—and there are multiple reasons *not* to do so—it is evident that gaps divide what people covet and what they will pay for. When presented a personal "bill" for the Clinton proposal, sizable numbers—a third, 20 percent depending on the item—demur or behave miserly. Others, by contrast, are excessively lavish, willing to spend $60 billion or more. Only if these data are taken as a whole, and subject to statistical interpretation, might one conclude that public generosity and fiscal requirements are roughly in the same ballpark (the median of $98 would be about two thirds of the program's estimated cost). A more sensible assessment is that cost estimates reflect great uncertainty regarding what "more federally assisted daycare" personally means. A savvy consumer who said, "KinderCare's charge of $120 per week is outrageous! I can get the same care at *La Petite Academy* for $98, plus they have longer hours" is justifiably clueless when confronted with enormous federal ventures. Consumer competence per se is not the issue; it is asking people to venture into murky policy issues about which they have no experience, and then interpreting their responses as judicious counsel.

Providing Federal Daycare Assistance: Preferences

Like having Uncle Sam cure our education woes by adding teachers, plentiful daycare has also been long welcome. Federally financed family assistance programs exist in dozens of legislative enactments; even avowed conservatives strongly endorse assisting families. This is unquestionably part of our national welfare consensus. When we asked whether the federal government should spend more, the same or less to assist working and poor families with daycare, the results we got were not surprising. Not unexpectedly, a modest majority (54 percent) said, "spend more," while about 18 percent responded with "the same." Opposition was small—4 percent said "less," while 22 percent rejected any federal role for the federal government in childrearing.

When we presented the Clinton daycare proposal with all the relevant details minus possible drawbacks but with information that the proposal's $22 billion cost over five years would benefit up to eight million families about two thirds of the respondents favored the initiative with only a small portion (3 percent) unsure or saying it "would depend." Sixty-five percent of those *without* children under twelve likewise joined those in favor of this entitlement. Endorsement predictably varied by ideology and partisan affiliation, but even among conservatives, assistance was generally welcomed (e.g., 53 percent of self-identified conservatives favored the measure). For the second time, then, the welfare state's popularity was reaffirmed.

Table 5.12   Impact of Costs/Risks on Support for Federal Daycare Program,
Supports Only (Percentage Favoring Proposal)

Cost/Drawback	Percent Still Favor
1. Program would cost $36 per taxpayer annually	91 (115)
2. Average tax bill would go from $6,832 to $6,868	88 (133)
3. Government already has many daycare programs for poor and disadvantaged parents	80 (90)
4. Plan would reduce parental daycare options	26 (96)
5. Make neighborhood daycare more difficult	29 (109)
6. Reduce parental control over daycare	29 (108)
7. Encourage nonworking parents to take jobs	82 (306)
8. Limit religious activities in daycare	31(115)
9. Give Washington more power over the states	33 (124)

What happens when we introduce reasonable risks and liabilities in this poll? Does supporter enthusiasm plummet, or is generosity impervious to warnings? The overall results (Table 5.12) are often erratic although they roughly mimic what emerged in the education questions. Most evidently, costs do not substantially cool endorsements among those already in favor. When large aggregate figures are "personalized" at $36 dollars a year per taxpayer, only 9 percent of the supporters "defect." Not much shifts when costs are displayed as raising the average tax payment from $6,832 to $6,868—overwhelming support still continues (12 percent alter their position). Nor does informing proposal supporters that "both the national government and the states have multibillion dollar programs, especially for the poor and disadvantaged" drastically alter the outcome. These different formats lower the percent in favor to 80 percent, still an overwhelming majority. Financial reality, apparently, only nibbles away at this popularity.

Nevertheless, when the downside is presented in nonmonetary terms the drop in support is remarkable. Again, we reiterate that these liabilities are reasonable considerations, not a mean-spirited, dogmatic assault on child-friendly welfare spending. Merely by raising the possibility that this federal assistance could reduce parental daycare options, the fraction of respondents still sticking with the proposal fall dramatically—just 26 percent of one-time advocates now favor it. Only 29 percent remain loyal if the Clinton assistance effort reduces parental control over daycare. Comparable erosion surfaces if respondents are alerted to reducing neighborhood daycare or restricting religious instruction. In both instances, 60 percent of those once in favor now *oppose* this federal helpfulness. And, contrary to the procentralization inclinations displayed in the education question, a mere 33 percent would still favor federally assisted daycare if it gave Washington even greater power over the states. The sole risk that does not encourage reduced popularity is the possibility that it would encourage employment among nonworking parents.

Especially notable about these results is that they occur in those population groups ostensibly targeted by the Clinton proposal. Small differences between likely beneficiaries and nonbeneficiaries are present, but these are far overshadowed by similarities. For example, only between a fifth and a quarter of families with incomes below $30,000 still supported federal assistance when faced with the possibility of reduced parental options, fewer neighborhood facilities, less administrative control, and cutbacks in religious instruction. Divergences between men and women are virtually zero as were differences between those with or without children under age twelve. The sharpest gap between subgroup occurs when the possibility of encouraging non-working parents into the workplace is broached. Here, predictably, enthusiasm still remains relatively high among the poor, the unemployed, and African Americans, although fall-off is still substantial.

One can readily see that a few reasonable caveats inserted into the standard poll questionnaire can have remarkable impacts. What if the *Los Angeles Times* pollsters added the following to their poll: "President Clinton has called for more federal daycare funding. However, while program advocates insist that this assistance is necessary, this effort might limit parental daycare options or even prohibit religious observances." Table 5.12 suggests that public enthusiasm would now be between a third or less, not the three quarters majorities routinely encountered. It is not that Clinton's proposal is "truly" unpopular; rather, its attractiveness is partially a function of what happens when respondents receive "the fine print."

Our final experiment is to test the popularity of this one solution vis-à-vis alternatives. Implicit in any evaluation is always "compared to what?" That a specific proposal elicits overwhelming majorities does *not* confirm its standing as the most preferred choice. This point is obvious even to public choice theory novices, but, again, conventional "stand alone" polls seldom acknowledge it. How, then, does this federal aid stack up against other equally viable remedies? The answer is that competing solutions often receive *more* ardent support, including rivals of a profoundly different ideological character.

Table 5.13 summarizes these results for both the entire sample and daycare initiative supporters only. As was true with educational assistance, tax code based assistances are better received than direct Washington involvement. Within the general sample, 81 percent of interviewees favor larger tax

Table 5.13 Preferences for Other Daycare Options vis-à-vis Federal Subsidized Solutions, Overall Sample and Clinton Plan Supporters Only (Percentage Favoring Proposal)

Proposal	All Respondents	Plan Advocates
1. Cut taxes to give people more money	62% (341)	53% (197)
2. Give parents larger daycare tax deduction	81 (447)	83 (309)
3. Reduce government rules regarding daycare	54 (292)	52 (195)
4. Give businesses incentives to provide daycare	85 (468)	88 (328)
5. Allow parents to hire overseas daycare help	18 (98)	12 (46)

deductions over the Clinton initiative, while 62 percent prefer tax cuts (even a bare majority of proposal advocates believe tax cuts to be a superior choice). Alhough both tax-based solutions are objectively more beneficial to the wealthy, the poor and rich are nearly indistinguishable in their enthusiasm (actually, the poor expressed even greater support for the tax deduction option—the most beneficial for the rich). Even among the unemployed, tax-based assistance is preferred over direct government action. Admittedly, this infatuation with relief via the IRS may be inept foolishness (particularly for those without sufficient income to make tax deductions economically worth-while). Still, to state that popular majorities "want" the Clinton scheme as *the* remediation is a bit misleading in light of more preferred options.

Granting businesses various worker assistance incentives is, alas, more popular—85 percent overall would prefer this "private" solution to Clinton's plan. The business-based alternative is even *more* popular among direct federal assistance advocates. And, again, support in both groups is virtually uniform across all income, age, racial, and ethnic groups (African Americans, in particular, fervently prefer this option). Cutting government red tape related to daycare is likewise a preferred pick among 54 percent of the full sample, particularly among those with a high school education or less. The only selection not receiving a superior rating was permitting parents to hire daycare from overseas (18 percent overall felt this was a better idea).

If one announced these findings as public counsel, the message might be: while President Clinton's proposal is, indeed, quite popular, the *vox populi* solicited in the conventional poll is not the final word. If the dialogue were to continue, the pollster would discover that of five alternatives, four receive more support vis-à-vis the initial proposal. Given that our five-item menu hardly exhausts the possibilities, one could speculate that a dozen or more competitors may outrank the original proposal. Hence, to encourage

Congress to heed this distorts reality. This single item "take-it-or-leave-it" style is also, we should add, virtually unknown in legislatures where remediations elicit multiple bills and amendments, all claiming excellence. Imagine if restaurants catered to public tastes with a single selection menu. Not even McDonald's is so foolish.

Conclusions

Analysis began with two baseline facts: the public's heartfelt desire for hiring more teachers to reduce class size and for providing the poor greater daycare assistance. These policies are typical popular government service efforts defining our social welfare state. This imposing, survey-created consensus entails more than social science or poll-driven journalism. The robust statistics constitute an inescapable reality affirming triumph of modern-day New Deal liberalism. Challengers contesting this "obvious" fact, confirmed scientifically, are branded as being disengaged from a plain-to-see truth or perhaps mentally unwell. A maverick pronouncing that the public is mistaken in its craving for more big government would be bombarded with poll findings proving him wrong much like bad actors were once driven from the stage with rotten vegetables.

This "welfare consensus" is less solid than announced. The public *really does* hunger for improved education and daycare as well as other benefits. This is predictable for few Americans cherish overcrowded grade school classes or want to push the indigent into exorbitant market-driven daycare. Nor are we a nation of misers reluctantly bestowing taxpayer generosity. Judged by willingness to endure tax burdens, Americans *do* gladly shoulder these entitlements. Yet, enthusiasm is far more moderate than what is glibly portrayed in this revered, poll-manufactured consensus. The typical survey exaggerates the positives of government policy, while suggesting that the choice is between government action and doing nothing. What we hope our two examples have demonstrated is that the public's appetites are (1) often extremely inexpert and (2) often a consequence of a grossly one-sided "factual" presentation. When competence and balance filter into poll taking, the entitlement consensus more closely resembles a list of uncertain, misdirected desires. They are definitely not clear guidelines for democratic decision-making.

Judged by our competence criteria, even fervent populists should be pessimistic regarding this advice. If consumer education instructors heard this clamor, the "we-need-better-training" outcry would be deafening. Whether the huge sums involved in policy discussions—often hundreds of billions of

dollars—have *any* concrete meaning to citizens better acquainted with gaso-
line prices or monthly utility bills is surely debatable. Moreover, we repeatedly saw that attempts to make these colossal figures manageable bring their
own problems. This confirms why the Federal Trade Commission (FTC)
wages a seemingly endless battle against widespread consumer fraud—
chicanery works. The public's incapacity to conceive of policy drawbacks is
also extremely important. This confusion is a standing invitation to electoral
pandering. The popularity of unrealistic solutions makes our warning regarding miracle cures quite real, not hypothetical.

Two competence criteria pose special problems in assigning a policymaking role to ordinary citizens. These are calculating tradeoffs among
competing demands and willingness to pay. Built-in defects in survey
methodology reinforce substantive confusion among respondents. Sad to say,
assessing these capacities successfully via polls may be impossible. Recall that
earlier measurement attempts, for example, budget pies, have nearly disappeared from research. Still, aside from this technical insufficiency, it seems
likely that respondents generally cannot reach levels of competency necessary
to offer wise counsel. To appreciate the difficulty of this task, even Congress
often cannot easily execute this assignment. Congressional travails in balancing the budget are notorious. Enormous resources, legal pressures and non-
negotiable deadlines are required for experienced lawmakers to execute what
we demand from citizens in inconsequential twenty-minute telephone
surveys. Perhaps these respondents would embrace sly backdoor spending
if they, too, had the chance. Profound implications for soliciting public
advice exist if these capabilities are beyond the poll's reach.

This fairly dismal picture will sure draw rebuke. Two accusations in particular can be anticipated. The first is that our criteria are so excessive that
they guarantee "failure." Are we being unreasonable? Perhaps. In one sense,
this draconian set of criteria is indefensible much in the same way that any
tough ability standard—whether for the medical board or bar exam—can
always be attacked as "arbitrary." We admit to extreme toughness, and further confess that this strictness is unusual when calibrating public policy proficiency. Chapter Three reviewed several alternative (and far more generous)
approaches, based on researchers statistically manipulating simplistic poll
responses. Our version hardly invalidates these rival tests, and it would be
preposterous for us to state that our "test" enjoys official accreditation from
some imaginary National Academy of Civic Standards. Plausible appropriateness is our only defense.

Central is the explicit tie between our uncovered data and requirements
for wise counsel (in scientific terms face validity). The benchmark is high

because the job of public counselor itself is exceedingly tough. Public policy text-books take this arduousness for granted; why should citizens be excused from these obligations, particularly given the consequences for grievous error? To make an extreme comparison, would patients awaiting brain surgery argue that medical care should made more affordable by lowering proficiency standards? The opposite is more likely, given the consequences of a botched job. Not even desperate patients would accept surgery performed by a randomly selected "citizen operating team." And who would insist that such "surgeons" could gain expertise with an on-the-spot crash course in brain anatomy? Insisting upon skillfully estimating costs, juggling tradeoffs, and so on *is* eminently sensible *if* one were to hire a personal public policy advisor. Imagine the reaction if this job applicant confessed that he or she was totally baffled by sums exceeding a million? And, as we shall soon argue, *no* compelling reason exists why this counselor should be hired. "Democracy" certainly does not require it.

Critics surely will further charge that knowing per pupil cost of reducing class size to eighteen or deriving average taxpayer outlays from huge budgetary figures is absurd. Experts would be baffled, too. We unequivocally agree! This arcane knowledge is *not* to be expected. But, unlike conventional defenders of public adequacy, our inference is not that the competency standard should be lowered, but that the public's advice is therefore discountable. Assessments cannot be adjusted as teachers "curve" abysmal test scores to guarantee ample "As" and "Bs." This may suffice for pollsters trying to get citizens to pick up their phones, but it has no place in making hard choices. If the goal is sound advice, the guiding standard must be absolute.

This stipulation is totally realistic. Popular proficiency is regularly—although often somewhat imperfectly—achieved in legislative bodies. Here, citizens transformed into lawmakers can request esoteric information of the type informing our questionnaire. If insufficient, they can hire specialists, demand hearings, subpoena records, and otherwise gain workable mastery over hugely complex dilemmas. Even doltish legislators cannot effortlessly spend trillions on imagined woes or enact laws apt to be declared unconstitutional. We do not indict citizen talent *per se*. We suspect that if our "clueless" respondents entered Congress, their civic competency would soar. Such is the underappreciated beauty of institutions. Alas, the pollster cannot work this magic.

Nor do we argue against soliciting public opinion or even treating it seriously. The *vox populi* assuredly has much to pronounce politically, and present-day polling mechanisms can certainly capture these sentiments accurately. Even a bewildered public can legitimately assert their fears, economic satisfaction, reactions to events, and untold other readily grasped items. And who would say that such musings are unimportant? Commercial pollsters have long assessed popular tastes, and such assessments assuredly have their political equivalents. Rendering a moral judgment on President Clinton's escapades with Monica Lewinsky hardly required a crash course in public finance. But, to repeat yet one more time, to proclaim a wish is not to render legitimate counsel on matters beyond one's ken. Transforming "one's two cents" into "wise advice" cannot be done by decree, even if that "decree" displays a prodigious talent for statistical manipulation.

A second criticism of our pessimism might address its permanence. Surely, better schooling or media attention to policy expenditures and the like might improve citizen competence. Additionally, these deficiencies might be partially fixed by instrument redesign. The questionnaire itself could serve as a learning device enlightening citizens about public policy. Then, happily, subsequent responses would be more authoritative. Taken together, competence—even by our austere standard—is reachable. Populist democracy devotees are thus not misguided in their aspirations; underestimating the amount of work needed to reach this exalted goal is the culprit.

This approach makes wonderful rhetoric but it is just that, glittering bombast. Even the college educated performed feebly in our exercises. Since these individuals undoubtedly possess the necessary intelligence, their dismal accomplishment suggests that shortcomings must lie elsewhere. We'd hazard a guess that the irrelevance of hard choice policymaking to everyday life, not its inherent difficulty, produces inadequacy. After all, as we just acknowledged, ordinary folk thrust into legislatures often rise to the occasion. But, leaving aside deputizing citizens as legislators-at-large, *why* should respondents monitor policy costs and liabilities (plus even more vexing aspects) when their views count for nothing? Even if the survey were legally binding, the odds of being personally polled on a "researched question" are infinitesimal. Lotteries offer better investments. Similarly, commanding a nongovernment controlled mass media to insert more public affairs aimed at unreceptive audiences is fantasy. Compelling pollsters to alter the polls drastically to enhance "informed populist democracy" is likewise futile, a waste of money. The costs would be gigantic, and no financial reason exists to offer this upgraded product. Those still unconvinced are advised to wait until Chapter Six, when these "citizen upgrade" fantasies will be given their proper *coup de grâce*.

The ultimate response to this seductive "more education, better polls" approach is that this remediation is *absolutely unnecessary*. Popular power over government—the very essence of democracy—hardly demands proficient polling. Why wage monumental education campaigns needlessly? We already enjoy a mechanism that robustly conveys the public will: elections. This democratic accomplishment is indisputable, warts and all. If the pollsters confessed, "We surrender—securing wise public counsel via polls is totally hopeless," democratic vigor would not diminish one iota. Imagine the opposite—canceled elections and replacing them with polling. Chapter Six will develop this key argument at much greater length.

What can be said regarding the public's "true" preferences on the hiring of more teachers and federal daycare assistance proposals? From one perspective we can merely reaffirm a bit of conventional insight: ask a different question, get a different answer. Our experiments mesh nicely with comparable studies in which shifting vocabulary, different phraseology, and other questionnaire details yield substantially different respondent outcomes. In other words, manipulating surveys or using "loaded" questions is not inconceivable. Most likely, those who disapprove of our antientitlement message will dismiss our data with precisely these "methodological" qualms. For these survey champions, our approach is easily defeated by sheer convention—we are but a lonely voice in the wilderness.

Might these explorations suggest *some* worthy public advice? To conclude that "the public 'really' is less statist than once believed" is undeniably tempting. Surely devotees of free-market solutions will be emboldened by our findings. Nevertheless, just as we reject statist urges as inexpert counsel, so must the opposite interpretation be forsaken. The public's embrace of tax deductions for schooling or business-provided daycare incentives are probably as dubious as their support for federally provided benefits. Our analysis is not intended to be a libertarian polemic. If we had used conservative, market-based policies as our examples instead of the two big government propositions, our analysis would have (no doubt) reached roughly the same conclusions—public desires are shaky. In principle, whether the questionnaire is slanted toward "liberals" or "conservatives" is irrelevant. To state that, "the people are more skilled when presented with laissez-faire proposals and inept when confronting Big Government enticements" is preposterous. Skepticism rightfully applies to all responses equally. Recall how poor people strongly preferred tax deductions even though these are virtually useless for them personally. The abiding moral of our investigation is that superior ways exist to choose policy than by soliciting public advice via hurried telephone conversations.

CHAPTER 6

Bestowing the Democratic Mantle

Don't live in a city run by scholars.
—Akiba, from the Talmud, *Pesahim,* 112a

In a society that reflexively venerates "democracy," it is a great prize to appropriate this term successfully to a specific political arrangement. Immense legitimacy and prestige are instantly granted in a feat of lexical magic. After all, who wants to be labeled as antidemocratic? Every faction seeks to ride the democratic bandwagon. Those who dub egalitarian-minded governments that bestow countless welfare entitlements to appease popular clamor as "true democracy" are absolutely blameless in their determination. That terminological trophy should immediately be conceded; stripping anything of alleged democratic authenticity is pointless. Politics is not physics, in which basic terms have precise definitions. Those who insist that voice of the people certifies "real democracy" are no less correct than their opponents.

If banishment from the "democracy club" is pointless, why object if governance via public opinion polling asserts its claims, as well? Our argument over the democratic character of this professed populism is straightforward: *bestowing democracy's mantle on unrestrained popular cravings, regardless of content, does not fortify democracy.* Little is gained by this labeling, and simplemindedness is only the most transparent flaw. We strongly believe that it is specious to argue because (a) democracy means heeding public wishes and (b) the people according to the polls desire more state welfare generosity, it must be true that (c) anything expediting these desires enhances democracy. To be frank, such selective veneration of "democracy" does more to enhance statism than expand citizen rule. These populist supporters would respond quite differently if, for example, citizens were to clamor for abrogating black civil rights or incarcerating homosexuals. Moreover, only a particular (and somewhat eccentric) meaning of democracy is being advanced, and it is wrong to declare that one definition as *the* superior embodiment. Polls that reveal a citizenry anxious to participate in making policy may honor the democratic spirit but they do not enhance democracy.

We contend that this quest for "more democracy" is less practical than claimed, and these weaknesses are pervasive, far beyond repairing. In addition, imbedded in this alluring egalitarian, statist siren song are forces antithetical to this—or for that matter, any—democratic prescription. Madison's fear of popular passions remains valid. Although anticipating cloudy futures is always risky, we submit that populist governance, whether by public opinion polls or more directly, may evolve quite different than advertised. It certainly will not flatten socioeconomic inequalities. The chance for incessant bad advice suggested by previous analyses only begins the list of woeful possibilities.

The Many Odd Faces of Inclusive Democracy

Advocates of egalitarian democracy are a divergent lot and what they propound is wide-ranging. Some favor surveys as the central democratic mechanism, a sort of continuous initiative, subordinating all else before its pronouncements. Others would like to see polls incorporated into multiple mechanisms (e.g., electronic assemblies) authorizing encompassing, although more personal, *vox populi* sovereignty. From one perspective, supporters of polling and devotees of "town meeting" democracy occupy antithetical positions. The latter see polls as perniciously usurping face-to-face politics and allowing citizens to escape their serious political responsibilities (see, for example, Abramson, Arterton, and Orren 1988, 165).

Emphasis and terminology aside, the common thread is that "the people" have something useful to contribute to policymaking that is not captured by traditional influence avenues (e.g., elections), and that treating these additional musings rejuvenates authentic democracy. As Benjamin Barber, the unofficial guru of this approach intones, "We suffer, in the face of our era's manifest crises, not from too much but from too little democracy . . . . There is little wrong with liberal institutions that a strong dose of political participation and reactivated citizenship cannot cure" (1984, xi). Barber further ads that without this participation in common life, women and men cannot become individuals and freedom, justice and equality will melt away (xv). And for what grand purpose is this participation carries out? In an essay aptly entitled "The Second American Revolution" (1982), the aim is to equalize the rich and the poor, the powerful and the powerless (62).

We begin by exploring murky issues surrounding the implementations of a government based upon opinion polls. This dream will most likely never materialize, but one can never be certain, and if our explication assists this failure, we insist on due credit. We then analyze various embodiments ranging from initiatives through small-scale applications of this plebiscitory spirit, modern utopianism with an electronic bent to enhance "democracy." Our concluding section argues that these egalitarian crusades will *undermine* political leveling, the common, though often hidden, goal informing these pleas for "more democracy." A peculiar paradox awaits us: the social welfare policy outcomes so desired by fans of expanded politics, often alleged to be available only with increased mass participation, may be feasible *only* under through hierarchy and exclusion.

The Wages of Government by Plebiscite Writ Large

Popular wisdom reminds us that fantasies always outshine reality or, to invoke that familiar cliché, the grass is always greener on the other side. This definitely applies to grand poll-centered plebiscitory visions. A wonderful, "true democracy," in which problems are resolved by the assembled multitude "telling" the attentive pollster is a powerful draw.

However, consider the most obvious flaw—controlling the authoritative poll. Existing political arrangements, consistent with limited government, carefully keep government power in check. At its most basic everything rests on popular consent. Statutes precisely spell out what office is elected, candidate eligibility, voter qualifications, term lengths, campaign finance legalities, and so on. Control over nonelected positions, for example, federal judges, the military, civil servants, is likewise dictated by statute. It has taken centuries of trial and error to achieve this popular supremacy.

For contemporary polling, however, the possibilities for antidemocratic mischief abound. Most plainly, while we now enjoy a single legitimate constitutional system, which of the hundreds of respectable polling organizations deserves similar affirmation? "The people" have not spoken on this point, nor has any polling organization sought or received certification as "Official Peoples' Purveyor of Poll Data." When the survey pronounces, it acts as a *private* entity. The questionnaire is not a legislative agenda proposed by public servants beholden to the public. Moreover, today's polling industry truly embodies *laissez-faire* principles. Literally *anybody*—regardless of talent, training, or integrity—can quiz willing strangers to pronounce "public opinion." Giving superior political authority to privately administered, self-certified polls violates popular sovereignty.

Anarchy—not democracy—may more aptly describe this cacophony and, as survey related technology grows more commercially accessible, proliferation is almost assured. One 1987 estimate of privately run opinion polls was "in the thousands" in addition to the approximately fifty in university settings (Sudman and Bradburn 1987). Another late 1980s study reported that 82 percent of large circulation newspapers and 56 percent of TV stations were substantially involved in polling. Significantly, these organizations over time increased question frequency (Ladd and Benson 1992, 22). The questions will undoubtedly multiply as technological costs shrink, further exacerbating the confusion of authority. To appreciate this dilemma fully, picture self-designated private citizen groups by the hundreds establishing "legislatures" and asserting binding authority? Yet, this roughly transpires among those extracting survey guidance—a sort of political radical Protestantism run amok. Nobody would challenge the House's legal power to initiate revenue bills; but, how are we to select among, say, the Gallop Poll or National Opinion Research Center (NORC) or endless other claimants supplying public tax "mandates"? Legally, all are illegitimate. Furthermore, what prevents the dissatisfied from sponsoring alternative queries rigged to yield more agreeable results?

Survey inaccuracies take on a fresh significance in this context. Even the best surveys can vary enormously in the choices they offer respondents on the identical issue. In one famous instance, polls carried out at roughly the same time reported wildly divergent prescriptions on the Strategic Arms Limitation Treaty (SALT), everything from overwhelming approval to near total rejection (Robinson and Meadow 1982, ch. 4). A comparable Tower of Babel ensued when public views on pornography were ascertained (Tom Smith 1987). Michael Kagay, a longtime polling industry observer, contends that this divergence is unavoidable given the commercial necessity of product differentiation (Kagay 1992, 96). Timing can be highly consequential—public sentiment can shift dramatically following declarations of war or ecological catastrophes. What should happen when popular advice points every which way or seems highly volatile? Are the results to be pooled and the grand average accepted as the "authentic" voice of the people? Only banning competing "unofficial" polls may solve these problems.

These multiple polls, each lacking supreme authority, point to a particular difficulty fundamental to all democratic claims: public accountability. Presently, foolhardy public officials are readily punishable. They are known, periodically judged and, critically, their stipulated responsibilities are legally enforceable. This is the essence of democracy. By contrast, pollsters labor beyond public control. As in sausage making, who knows what transpires in obscure corners? What remedies are available if pollsters misspeak? Can they be found "guilty" of unsuitable sampling, inept question drafting, and misguided statistical analysis? Will the "offending," hapless interviewers be disciplined for their incompetence?

Even more important, what if pollsters ignore certain topics since they, not public officials, deem them "too controversial"? To be sure, compelling Congress to address neglected issues is daunting, but this is a snap compared to directing nameless private pollsters. *Quis custodiet ipsos custodes?* (Who will guard the guardians?) Only those affording poll sponsorship—hardly an accountable, cross-sectional group, either—enjoy this civic luxury.[1] Survey research experts do not campaign for office and are thus unmotivated to exploit unarticulated desires. Sponsorship—money—dictates the question-naire direction.

Far more burdensome is fashioning authoritative, enforceable technical standards in an enterprise rife with serious disputes. Accountability would require writing (somebody's) methodological strictures into law. This is no sim-ple enterprise—professed experts routinely offer methodological critiques of existing practices, and this quibbling appears incurable. Relevant research design is comparatively far more intricate and exceedingly more contentious than election law. What, for example, might be the standard questionnaire item probing entitlement preferences? Who decides if potentially inflammatory terminology, for example, "welfare mother," is illegal as biased?[2] Imagine ensur-ing that only citizens, not illegal aliens, respond in faceless telephone polls. Such obstacles are easily swept under the rug when seeking public opinion.

Increasing the power of the *vox populi* also increases mass media power vis-à-vis elected officials. Currently, the media can only put pressure on government. For example, outrageous crime stories might push handgun legislation to the forefront, but public frenzy can never be legislatively deci-sive. Officials correctly grasp that vehement citizen outpourings eventually dissipate. If—as Madison greatly feared—aroused sentiment now ruled, power now flows *away* from elected officials toward those insulated from public retribution. Thanks to public opinion supremacy, unelected, unac-countable, and typically obscure private individuals now assume prodigious power, not mere influence. Even the infamous "faceless bureaucrat" is more accountable. The possibility for "political ventriloquism" is obvious. The power to excite through publicity becomes, via the poll, the power to rule. How this immense privatization of power enhances democracy is unclear, to say the least.

This shift involves far more than mass media empowerment. Subsequent ripples touch on almost every feature of popular control. Established political parties—those organizations long applauded as indispensable democratic auxiliaries—may now find themselves downgraded in this new plebiscitory political order. Of what value is control over nominations or the ability to mobilize voters if policy is dictated via the random telephone interview? Bereft of this aggregating agency, parties may well degenerate into amorphous factionalism, squabbling over questionnaire wording or interviewer demography. Similarly, the president, by virtue of occupying the "Bully Pulpit," can now dominate Congress and the courts in ways once unimaginable. Whether or not this weakening of traditional checks and balances (and untold other intergovernmental relationships) would somehow enhance democracy is hardly self-evident.

Balancing public versus private control to insure accountability poses an even greater problem than achieving narrow technical consensus. Presently, privately run organizations dominate, although several notable university affiliated bodies, for example, the University of Michigan's Survey Research Center, rely on periodic federal grants and employees are nominally "state workers." Public agencies also commission private or university run polling organizations. This private, largely for-profit (or at least financial survival) status is deceptively consequential if polls are awarded this democratic responsibility. Without doubt, insufficient resources constrain accuracy and, it is highly unlikely that *any* existing polling organization possesses sufficiently deep pockets to fund needed improvements. It is cost-ineffective, for example, to translate questions into multiple languages, ask key items monthly, locate reclusive respondents, or conduct time-consuming face-to-face interviews. To appreciate the political implications of this insufficiency, imagine if states slashed their election administrative budgets—fewer election judges, fewer supervised vote tallies, and barely any registration verification. Outrage over "subverting democracy" would surely ensue. The poll's technical faults are notorious, though, again, this is quietly ignored by those attributing guidance to its numbers.[3]

Can accuracy be improved so that political legitimacy also rises? Upgrading existing arrangements both financially and legally is one possibility. Congress might, for instance, generously commission NORC to ascertain sentiment on Social Security and then, as per statute, follow accordingly. Now, for example, hard-to-find or reluctant respondents can be relentlessly tracked down and queried in obscure Laotian dialects. This fresh benevolence would, predictably, also entail heightened state supervision. Polling organizations, like the food industry, might suffer draconian regulations to guarantee product "purity." Inspectors could unannounced descend on NORC to audit the data processing. A lavish, quality-controlled national opinion referendum, if you will.[4]

However, this effort only offers a partial solution. Still left unresolved is deciding between disputes endemic to survey research, such as question wording, interview format, item sequence, the number of alternatives, or filter use. Bountiful resources cannot guarantee resolution, and the political consequence of favoring one seemingly innocent technical choice over another cannot be over-estimated. Who is sufficiently trustworthy, particularly (as is likely) if inflammatory topics like abortion or school prayer are probed? These squabbles are well beyond "mere technicalities." Even if outsourced to faceless academic experts at the most renowned academic survey organizations (e.g., University of Chicago's NORC) nothing guarantees that these guardians might surreptitiously impose their own preferences. It is presumptuous to insist that these experts—like Caesar's wife—be above suspicion. Again, *Quis custodiet ipsos custodes?* Furthermore, are elected office holders capable of distinguishing between truly neutral items and those subtly biased toward preselected outcomes? Most likely not—it is reasonable to assume that they would leave that up to the experts.

The *vox populi* enhancement is not free of political meddling, either. Jacobs and Shapiro (1995) recount incidents of ostensibly "objective" polls exploiting partisan advantage in their well-documented history of presidential polling. Everyday tactics included leaking polls to the mass media to cultivate favorable publicity or using polls as feedback in manipulative public relations ventures. President Nixon in particular cultivated personal contacts with leading polling organizations to, in his words, "… keep the published polls honest" (cited in Jacobs and Shapiro 1995, 190). Congress also may seek to "play the polls via well placed budgetary allocations—a Republican controlled Congress will assuredly finance different "good" questions than their Democratic colleagues.

A different approach would be to establish a quasi-public body, an assembly of political appointees (and technically trained staff) that would decide opinion referendums as the Federal Reserve now nimbly guides interest rates. The independent regulatory commission arrangement also might be an appropriate model—ample polling freedom within statutory guidelines. For example, polls might be strictly advisory, executed only at the bequest of Congress, and not publicly released without a majority legislative approval. An even more constrained version would be an agency under tight congressional control, similar to the General Accounting Office.

Although sufficient resources would be guaranteed and questions could zero in on pressing public issues, this "cure" may be worse than the disease.

Authorizing government agencies to monitor citizen preferences most likely collides with laws regarding confidentiality. Unease already exists over gathering innocuous personal census information. Do we want intrusiveness extended to opinions on pornography, abortion, or similar moral viewpoints? No assurances may be adequate to those fearing that their responses might be permanently recorded and put into the wrong hands. Nonparticipation and false responses to "controversial" views could quickly sabotage government run polling.

Also consider the unexplored legal nature of this relationship. Who possess superior authority—an elected legislative body or appointed custodians of a national poll organization? The nightmarish constitutional issues are immense. What if Congress disbelieved poll findings, and decided to resolve the conflict by firing the chief pollster for alleged malfeasance? The legal squabbles associated with successful initiatives offer a parallel. On repeated occasions, both courts and legislatures have comfortably "overruled" the *vox populi* as expressed via initiatives. Witness the recent bizarre confrontations in California in which factions normally associated with liberal, populist causes denounced the conservative inspired Propositions 187 (denying state benefits to illegal immigrants) and 209 (banning racial preferences in state actions) as "undemocratic." Can the verdict uncovered by the pollsters be legally appealed? Who knows?

Fusing "real-world" politics with the technical detail of the survey is beside the point where polls are just curiosities. However, if plebiscitory democracy prophets gain ascendancy, this will inevitably change. Disputes engulfing binding polls will differ profoundly from altercations limited to Ivory Tower *aficionados*. Those bitter and extremely expensive battles over citizen initiatives, for example, California's Propositions 187 and 209, are the appropriate standard. Elected officials' inclination to meddle in polling details has already been mentioned, and this tendency will unfold dramatically as polls become authoritative (Wheeler 1976, ch. 1, offers some gory details that can occur). Political claimants will pressure pollsters for special treatment or eliminating "biased" terminology. More important, to anticipate a point explored below, those forces dominating "regular" politics will inevitably forcefully intrude into poll-driven politics. That inconspicuous technicians now freely settle key survey details can only be explained by poll inconsequentiality. As stakes escalated, insulation would diminish. Should the NORC become the "official" Polling Agency, its supervisor would surely rank among the most powerful political appointees, and perhaps subject to Senate confirmation.

As the public opinion poll gained enlarged authority, its control would, more than likely, flow toward elected officials. The two might ultimately become indistinguishable, and this shift would hardly contravene democratic governance. Presuming that elected officials would voluntarily surrender their legal powers, particularly control over the public agenda, mocks reality. A constitutional amendment would be indispensable and it is unlikely that Congress would endorse such an act. At best, Congress would take poll numbers into account and even then, this acknowledgment would be made subject to legislative supervision. This is not what academic fans of the *vox populi* envision, but subjection to elected authority is inescapable.

This convergence between the idealized government by public opinion poll and the pedestrian electoral process is deceptively important for supporters of poll-driven democracy. Major "players" in one arena will be vigorous competitors in the other. Options offered in campaigns may closely resemble poll question options as appointed poll curators prudently follow shifting political winds emanating from those in power. Today's inconspicuous poll custodians will find their hoped-for "real-world" capacities gravely pared down. Those currently disadvantaged by conventional, election-based politics—the poor, certain racial minorities, among others—will likely suffer comparable exclusions when this *vox populi* government arrives. The marginalized will, as before, complain of politics "being dominated by the rich and powerful."

It is this troubled political baggage hidden by the drive toward plebiscitory democracy that drives this inquiry. It is a *new* political system that is being advocated, not a mere proposal for "greater attentiveness to now banished voices." What is being advanced as "improved democracy" is, in fact, a scheme that redirects power away from elected officials into the hands of those beyond public accountability. At core, this venture is both duplicitous and impractical. The institutional/legal ramifications are colossal and cannot be overcome by a technically improved survey. Even if the public grants wise counsel, and our instruments proficiently report this sage advice, this does not end the project. It is wrong to believe somehow that faithfulness to the public will is "real" democracy's *sine qua non.* A million voices speaking with absolute clarity do not constitute governance.

The Quest for Participatory Inclusiveness

The quest to grant everyone "his or her say" in the political community of equals is a remarkably irrepressible urge. It has long dotted the American landscape—recall those fascinating early nineteenth-century agrarian communistic schemes with enticing names like "New Harmony." Early American socialism, especially its Christian variants, similarly partook of this leveling participatory spirit. One might even include the anarchistic 1960s hippie communes in this cabinet of egalitarian curiosities. The infatuation with plain clothing or collective ownership has now given way to greater technological attentiveness under expert scholarly direction. Nowadays, it is proclaimed that the twin evils of elitism and inequality are finally conquerable. Impressive technical advances aside, this egalitarian dream in which the people themselves, not far distant leaders, rule remains utopian. It is no more viable today than when the true believers intoxicated with the preachings of Robert Owen or Edward Bellamy disappeared into the wilderness.

Traditional Direct Democracy

A useful place to begin is with the tried and true. The initiative—citizen proposed legislation—and the referendum—legislative proposals placed on the ballot for citizen judgment—have thrived for nearly one hundred years. Since South Dakota first adopted it in 1898, initiatives have burgeoned, largely in the west where Progressive influences were strongest (Donovan and Bowler 1998a). From the onset, this cause was championed by the "have-not's" (smaller farmers, labor groups) against the "have's" (trusts, railroads) who often dominated state legislatures. Moreover, and again to anticipate today's more electronically minded devotees, advocates celebrated the putative educational impact these procedures would have. It was surmised that these opportunities to decide public issues would inspire the once apathetic, thus raising civic virtue to lofty heights.

Although direct democracy processes have varied across states and during historical periods, their overall popularity is unquestionable. One estimate (Magleby cited in Donovan and Bowler 1998a) is that between 1898 and 1992, state voters decided some seventeen hundred issues. Contemporary politics has witnessed a virtual initiative explosion, many of which address high-profile issues such as affirmative action, treatment of illegal immigrants, gambling, taxes, homosexual rights, legalized marijuana, and assisted suicide. In 2000, some forty-two states placed 204 measures on the ballot for voter consideration (Verhovek 2000; Reed 1996). Spreading skill at getting propositions on the ballot (and the emergence of professional consultants) suggests even greater future popularity, especially as cautious elected officials shun "hot-button" moral and racial dilemmas.

Has more than one hundred years of initiative experience remedied "insufficient" democracy? The evidence is mixed.[5] Impact per se is not the issue; examples abound of citizen-sponsored initiatives profoundly altering politics. For example, the 1978 California initiative drastically cutting property taxes sparked a tax-cutting revolution nationwide. California and Washington State measures striking down state mandated racial preferences had a similar effect. More generally, their very existence may well potentially impede legislative excessiveness or prod lawmakers to brave divisive issues.

Still, impact cannot be automatically equated with successful implementation of this populist vision. The overall empirical evidence remains inconclusive. If proponents of direct democracy are correct in their praise, inclusive representation should be superior where the initiative flourishes. This is an exceedingly complex research question, but those brave souls tackling it are pessimistic regarding the initiative's capacity to implement the general will accurately (see especially Lascher, Hagen, and Rochlin 1996, as well as Donovan and Bowler 1998b).[6]

Several obvious features of initiative-based direct democracy suggest representational shortcomings. Most plainly, despite the allure of making policy on tangible, controversial topics, direct democracy turnout tends to be on the low side, almost always below already dismal turnout for elective office (Weissberg 1976, 69–71; Cronin 1989, 66–68). Of special relevance is that today's "have-not's" seldom deploy these devices as counterweights to elite dominated institutions. Those less likely to vote in general—African Americans, the less well-educated—are even less likely to participate in direct democracy (Cronin 1989, 76). In fact, analysts suggest that putting issues before the general public often *hinders* African Americans, recent immigrants, gays, and other supposed beneficiaries (Gamble 1997). Although hardly incontrovertible, it demonstrates the uncertain connection between "more democracy" and assisting the downtrodden.

A variety of other complications similarly undermine the "democracy" in direct democracy. Placing measures on the ballot is not reserved for the formerly excluded. In California well-healed industries such as insurance, trial lawyers, and casino gambling avail themselves of initiatives and, equally important, wealthy interests can often outspend and outcampaign their opponents. The image of the less fortunate vanquishing the plutocrats via the initiative is fantasy. Even the most rudimentary initiative now requires multimillion dollar war chests.[7] Direct democracy cannot abolish the preexisting advantages in standard electoral politics. In fact, the rising cost of all election contests plus signature requirements necessary to secure a spot on the ballot may well increase the edge enjoyed by the well-off. One in-depth examination of contemporary initiative efforts repeatedly applied the term "*faux* populist movement" to these enterprises (Smith 1998, esp. chs. 4–6).

According to this analysis, so-called spontaneous grassroots citizen uprisings were frequently underwritten by established economic interests and orchestrated by professional public relations firms.

Finally, and perhaps the most pertinent, doubts exist regarding voter capacity to interpret ballot issues (these are summarized in Donovan and Bowler 1998a, 12–13). To be sure, ardent fans (e.g., Cronin 1989, ch. 4) argue that these devices do not bring disaster and elected officials are often no more adroit in legislating. Occasional collective "reasonableness" aside, the research literature suggests a bounded citizen capacity to grasp the intricacies of an issue. This deficiency persists regardless of efforts to educate, including widely available information packets explaining each issue together with the pros and cons. Voter confusion will only grow as ballot issues proliferate and language becomes more legalistic.

A second traditional form of direct democracy is the New England-style town meeting. Here ordinary citizens assemble to govern. Indeed, this mechanism—which still flourishes in many New England towns (as well as in Switzerland)—is often the unmentioned ideal against which all modern contrivances are judged ("electronic town-meetings" and so on). It has inspired a plethora of government sponsored citizen involvement forums ranging from urban neighborhood advisory councils to awarding citizen control over local schools (Weissberg 1999, ch. 6 describes these schemes).[8] Alas, romantic idealizations often overpower humdrum reality.

Frank M. Bryan collected data on some 1,378 Vermont town meetings in 210 localities between 1974 and 1997 (1999). These gatherings were not mere discussion groups or advisory panels—they possessed ample legal (and financial) powers. Although they governed as advertised, this smooth functioning should not be equated with invigorated inclusiveness. Easy openness to town residents is one thing; actually showing up is another. While the participants may look formidable as a group (a mean of 139 people per meeting), this assemblage generally averaged to only to 14 percent of a town's eligible voters, and of those who attended, only about 40 percent spoke (200). Equally notable, participation was seldom inclusive. There is less participation in larger communities and men are more active than women. Interestingly, the socioeconomic character of the town did not, however, make any difference and, somewhat tentatively, the wealthy were often absent from these assembles. Bryan's overall assessment of this institution is generally favorable but he still notes, "It [the town meeting] holds *no promise* for mass democracy" (221, italics in original).

Joseph F. Zimmerman's (1999) comprehensive analysis of New England town meeting democracy confirms Bryan's findings. Once more, low turnout—usually in the 20 percent range—was the rule, although high-profile issues might occasion surges. And, despite all of today's talk of enhanced citizen involvement, participation is falling. Meeting "regulars" tended to be middle-aged and older, although differences across economic groups were minimal (as in Vermont, towns were relatively homogeneous racially and ethnically). As to whether these meetings are "packed" by special interests to subvert the overall public interest, the evidence is inconclusive. Ironically, having specialized official committees—not the citizen assemblies decide key issues, often solves this "packing" problem.

A pervasive theme in Zimmerman's account is that even under ideal conditions, citizen involvement is difficult. Just the problems involved in physically attending the meetings (e.g., inclement weather, busy schedules, etc.) are many. In addition, unwillingness to voice personal views in public was customary. A few feared retribution from their neighbors. Less obvious, but perhaps more telling, is the gradual centralization of power away from the community level. Decisions regarding education, land use, taxation, and policing are now made elsewhere. Overall, to advance the New England-style town meeting as the template for direct democracy is little more than an exercise in nostalgia.

Upgrading Direct Democracy

Direct democracy's uncertain success has not deterred others from enthusiastically launching increasingly novel and costly invigorating schemes. According to Laudon (1977, ch. 1), during the 1960s the federal government lavished nearly $50 million in grant money to "upgrade" democracy via technology (private outlays for the same purpose were even larger). Prominent politicians, notably Newt Gingrich and Ross Perot, have more recently reaffirmed this hope. Here, we take a quick overview of elaborate devices intended to accomplish similar aims, beginning in the early 1970s. These are the first tentative steps in the direction of electronic democracy. Our tour then samples contemporary high-tech versions including worldwide cyberspace politics. This section concludes by examining high-tech giant town meetings. The underlying question remains whether anything is to be gained from all this "new and improved" democracy.

The "Alternatives for Washington" program introduced in the early 1970s was typical of this quest to utilize modern technology to enhance popular input. Ironically, this was an essentially top-down effort, with an incumbent governor expending immense energy to develop programs soliciting citizen views on Washington State's long-term planning. Over its two-year lifespan, its organizers commissioned multiple polls, sponsored varied media presentations, and held countless meetings at all levels of government. Getting the right demographic mix in each component was paramount. Booths were even situated at state fairs and similar events to receive citizen counsel. TV programs invited the audience to call in and, eventually, overall opinion was ascertained via statewide survey entailing one million questionnaires. This popular input was supplemented by a variety of task forces, study groups and advisory panels. An estimated sixty thousand citizens participated in one way or another in this massive, expensive outreach effort.

The Alaskan Teleconferencing Network made similar attempts to enhance citizen political involvement via video transmission to scattered populations. It, too, was a state-sponsored system directly under elected official control, although a technical staff played a vital role. "Teleconference" centers were strategically located throughout the state. Through hookups under different administrative units, citizens "tuned in" to Alaska's governmental activities in real time. Opportunities for feedback abounded. Individual legislators could listen to citizens "in person," special interests (e.g., the fishing industry) could witness "live" legislative hearings, while an e-mail system permitted both constituent commentary and virtual legislative office hours. Lawmakers themselves used the system to communicate when the legislature was out of session. On the whole, at least during this study (and prior to the advent of direct satellite TV), Alaskans seemed quite taken with watching civic goings-on and offering their opinions.

Both efforts in Washington State and Alaska sought to supplement ongoing government decision making. Far more ambitious are "stand-alone" designs. These remain beyond government supervision and, supposedly, offer attractive citizen forums to invigorate civic democracy. An ambitious precursor of today's more high-tech innovations was MINERVA, a New York City apartment building project in the early 1970s and the brainchild of the sociologist Amitai Etzioni. Essentially, tenants could watch other building dwellers debate pertinent issues such as crime or escalating food prices via closed-circuit TV and radio. To encourage interactions, tenants were initially divided into small groups, although the entire building would assemble for final decisions. Reactions to these discussions were recorded and broadcast via closed-circuit TV to other apartment dwellers. Residents then voted by dialing one of two telephone numbers. This was supposed to be energetic, inclusive democracy for shut-ins.

An especially noteworthy experiment in this direction was the Qube "electronic town meeting" inaugurated in various Columbus, Ohio, suburbs. Privately run by the Warner-Amex cable company, subscribers (for a small fee) received two-way access to local political affairs (the city of Columbus also had its own TV studio and offered political programming to cable subscribers). The system's unique contribution consisted of two forms of citizen interaction. The first was a series of political shows (including actual town meetings) encouraging "real-time" citizen telephone call-in commentary. A five-button remote control device (one per subscriber) permitting watcher opinions to be expressed "live" on televised discussions was more innovative. These votes were automatically tallied and reported on TV screens every ten seconds. One button indicated a desire to speak directly to the ongoing televised discussion, and show staff would then telephone the intended speaker. Mailed questionnaires and broadcasts of special political events, for example, regional planning meetings, also were used. Relevant interest groups and ordinary citizens were relentlessly encouraged to participate via direct invitation and local newspaper ads.

The Televote and Electronic Town Meeting systems are two participatory ventures inspired by academics. In the former, citizens are randomly telephoned and solicited to join Televoting. If the response was "yes," they were mailed a brochure discussing select public issues. This printed material was to "jump-start" procuring new information plus stimulate discussions among friends and coworkers. Either the respondent or an interviewer would then call back to elicit opinions. This device has been used in Hawaii, New Zealand, and Los Angeles. In one instance (Hawaii), a local newspaper reported on the Televote together with the outcomes to generate further citizen awareness.

The Electronic Town Meeting (ETM) was actually a collection of citizen encounters, which transpired in Hawaii following the state's 1978 constitutional convention. Initially, convocation details were printed in the local newspaper and citizens were invited to participate. Demographic representation was not sought. Several TV programs were aired about this time on the issues being considered. In one instance, a local theatrical company dramatized conflicts in economic investing with a live stage show. These assemblies, although varying in duration and specific issue agendas, all sought to elevate citizen political awareness. In fact, although formal opportunities existed for citizen feedback from these ongoing discussions, tallying up votes was evidently subordinate to "stirring things up" on such issues as the nuclear freeze and Reaganomics. As with the Televote device, the ETM soon faded into oblivion despite initial enthusiasm and prodigious effort of its founders.

An especially notable plan for "enhanced democracy" is the deliberative poll promoted by James F. Fishkin (1995). We say notable not for its demonstrated impact, but for the gushing publicity it has generated. Basically,

Fishkin stridently rejects the traditional poll as superficial and excessively atomistic. The New England town meeting or the ancient Athenian Assembly of informed, face-to-face discussion is the appropriate model. Technology by itself, no matter how encompassing, cannot solicit popular sentiment unless ample opportunity exists for reasoned, informed discourse. According to Fishkin, citizens must be prepared to rule, and the standard poll or even other one-shot feedback mechanisms cannot perform this function (18).

The recipe is fairly straightforward and, indeed, several major experiments have already occurred. A national random sample was chosen and then assembled together for a few days. Discussions over contemporary issues utilizing counterbalanced information then transpire, often augmented by resident experts or politicians. In Manchester, England, 869 respondents, all selected to be as representative as possible, were surveyed prior to assembly. Of this group, three hundred actually arrived in Manchester (one nonfinancial participation inducement was a chance to visit a popular soap opera TV set). All were told in advance that their debates (the topic was crime) would be televised. This awareness apparently energized their political attentiveness even before arrival. As discussions progressed, expressed opinions (at least according to Fishkin) became more diverse, even sophisticated, though actual opinion did not always change direction (168). On the whole, these three hundred average English citizens became "... more sophisticated consumers of the competing policy prescriptions" (168).

A far more ambitious effort was an experiment carried out in Texas in 1996 costing nearly $4 million provided by private industry, foundations and government itself (these details are from Merkle 1996; Gastil and Dillard 1999). It attracted such political notables as Republican presidential contender Steve Forbes and Democratic vice presidential candidate Al Gore. Technical details were handled by top names in the survey industry and PBS devoted expansive airtime to the proceedings. A half-million dollar national survey by the prestigious NORC was also conducted. Discussions addressed family policy, the economy, and foreign affairs. Balanced materials were prepared by leading experts and scrutinized for fairness by two former members of Congress. All told, some 459 respondents gathered in Austin to offer what Fishkin would call the "real voice of the people" (Fishkin 1995, 49).

Significantly, these enterprises *never* seem to inquire whether the outcome is "good policy" (or even an improvement over the status quo). That is, does all the information and discussion add up to anything more than a vigorous bull session? Has the *vox populi* rendered *anything* of value on quandaries facing government? Recall our earlier warning about evaluating alleged public expertise—judgment is hard when the problem has *no* obvious answer. Where outcomes are examined, "attitude change" comprises the near exclusive focus, not superior counsel. The experiment's "success" also heavily stresses respondents' enjoyable experience, not expert contribution (Levine 2000, 131). Assessing whether attitudes shifted toward extremes or became more structured often distracts subsequent follow-up analyses. Again, possibilities of sound counsel are neglected. This oversight is endemic. One lengthy celebration of this mechanism depicts it as the way to save democracy, yet it is notably silent on concrete evidence (Bohman 1996). Conceivably, initial foolishness remains as fatuous as ever, although minimally more enlightened.[9]

While Deliberative Democracy is low-tech (simply broadcasting group discussions), a plethora of high-tech schemes also have been advanced to remediate our "antiquated" politics. These novelties seem to be gaining ever-new popularity as technology infuses daily life. Let us begin on the edge of the technological explosion with the electronic town meetings. An early model was the Alaska Department of Transportation's 1980 solicitation of opinion across the state concerning future policy options. This virtual meeting took ten days, occurred in ten urban centers, was accompanied by extensive multimedia informational advertising, and then was followed up with a public opinion poll. Additional feedback came through other arrangements (including face-to-face meetings), all entailing rapid computerized counting of citizen-initiated messages. Responses were quite high, although it should be noted that the college educated were overrepresented (Slaton 1992, 111–113).

Given recent technological advances, schemes to "improve" democracy via electronic means have become even more popular and are often proposed in offbeat publications catering to computer devotees. Even just to catalogue these designs would require a small treatise, so we will note a handful. *The Electronic Congress: A Blueprint for Participatory Democracy* (Wachtel 1992) exemplifies this new Utopianism. Here citizens would "vote" by pressing telephone buttons in a way similar to voice mail now used for customer service (i.e., "Thank you for calling Congress … Press "1" to declare war on Iraq, press "2" to begin negotiations …"). Indeed, technological globalization has encouraged an explosion of "cyberdemocracy" experiments worldwide (see, for example, Tsagararousianou, Tambini, and Bryan 1998). Predictably, these "e-schemes" are often marketed as "essential" to sustaining democracy in the face of untold economic and financial "crises" and other modern dysfunctions (e.g., Elgin 1993).

New and Improved?

For those still unconvinced, hope springs eternal, and no rejoinder is possible. One estimate counted twenty-four foundations working toward electronically enhanced democracy. A separate "Democracy channel" was at one time even in the works (Schwartz 1994). Nevertheless, this enthusiasm aside, several conclusions are warranted regarding whether these experiments actually repair the alleged shortcomings of traditional electoral politics. Whether something is intrinsically worthy is not the right question. By that low-bar standard, nearly any civic action, no matter how modest, might be judged "useful" or "democratically helpful" if the alternative is paralysis. The real question is: Are the alleged defects of conventional democracy significantly remedied by these complicated, sometimes expensive e-strategies? Unfortunately, the answer is that not much is accomplished beyond an occasional stirring of the polity's pot.

Dramatically expanded participation informs all these strategies, whether "old-fashioned" initiatives or contemporary technodemocracies. Apathy is the cardinal sin of today's crisis-ridden liberalism, so we expect citizens to flock to these new and improved polities. Moreover, we should expect these new strategies to bring those who feel excluded by the current system, notably the poor, disadvantaged minorities and all others historically relegated to the sidelines. It is not enough to provide yet more ways for current activists to discharge their democratic responsibilities. Without this more inclusive engagement, the goal of socioeconomic leveling is, alas, beyond reach.

The hard evidence reveals participation rates in these schemes to be comparable with conventional electoral participation on occasion, but almost always far less. This finding is common enough to be declared an "Iron Law." The comparatively low turnout for initiatives, despite the presence of attention-getting issues, has already been noted. Convenience seems immaterial. Even today's rapidly rising Internet figures are notable for spectacular growth, not absolute numbers. In the Qube experiment, for example, a mere half of political show audiences cast their electronic vote, though this required only pressing a handy button! To add insult to injury, only a tiny percentage of potential viewers ever tuned in, and attentiveness apparently fell as the shows lumbered on (Arterton 1987, 141). The MINERVA study also reported rapid declines in involvement after the initial rush. In the massive, well-funded Alternatives for Washington project, the return rate for ballots was a mere 4.5 percent of all ballots printed, a figure that translates into 1.8 percent of the voting age population (Arterton 1987, 157). In the

Hawaii Televote experiment, just about half of those initially contacted agreed to participate, and among these volunteers, about 15 percent returned their ballots as requested (only when prodded, or when opinions were solicited directly by phone, did participation exceed 50 percent). In Fishkin's English Deliberative Democracy experiment, even payment, free travel, and an opportunity to visit a famous TV set failed to elicit much involvement. In the Texas version, $325 payments, permission to take a guest to Austin plus assistance with babysitting, securing time off from work, and other helpful interventions still resulted in disappointing participation rates.

As to whether these strategies improve the quality of democracy, the answer is uncertain. Not every project carefully attended to this quality objective, and, even then, strict demographic proportionality (one conventional measure of "representation") was rarely achieved. Also, engagement itself may alter preferences, so those "inside" will always differ from their apathetic compatriots so producing a cross section of participants is not proof of representational quality. In many instances, for example, the Qube project or the Alaska Teleconferencing Network, the representation dilemma solves itself by being established in largely homogeneous communities. Elsewhere bits and pieces of evidence suggest that long-standing disparities in participation remain unimproved by easier access. In an early 1980s venture that saturated Des Moines, Iowa, with sophisticated information on rising health care costs, attentiveness came disproportionately from older, better-educated residents (Arterton 1987, 148). The same occurred in the Texas Deliberative Poll—the higher educated were overrepresented. In the Washington State program, higher status residents secured greater involvement despite conscious efforts to the contrary. A British TV show that closely resembled Fishkin's experiment similarly reports that participants were disproportionately higher status and middle aged (Denver, Hands, and Jones 1995). Recall that a $4 million budget could not bring demographic representation to Fishkin's Texas experiment. The failure of openness to generate microcosms is especially notable in electronic projects, hardly a surprise given required technical acumen (Hill and Hughes 1998, ch. 2). If some brilliant design has successfully enticed the hardcore apathetic into the political fray, it remains obscure. Achieving precise equity will, no doubt, demand a degree of coercion. We shall return to this important point below.

The relationship between the character of the mechanisms and heightened citizen input is noteworthy in grasping why recruiting some fresh faces may be far less than revolutionary.[10] Inviting a few outcast eccentrics to the Grand Ball of the Establishment does not make it any less a Grand Ball of the Establishment. Specifically, the fulsomeness of citizen contribution is most apparent when participation coexists with already established, elite-dominated political arrangements. This point is easily forgotten in the rush for what is "new and different." Citizen input, like water after a storm, flows through accustomed channels. This certainly transpired in the Alaska project, but it occurred equally well in North Carolina and Reading, Pennsylvania experiments with quite different procedures and populations (Arterton 1987, ch. 5) Graeme Browning's *Electronic Democracy* (1996) illustrates in detail that in terms of massive volume, the traditional humdrum issues—presidential elections, pork-barrel projects, and so on dominate this new computer-driven medium.

When offered access by those far removed from power (politically ambitious academics, business hungry cable companies), indifference ordinarily follows. At best, an initial gush of curious enthusiasm followed by lethargy. No matter how unsophisticated politically, people readily grasp that expressing one's views to a talk show host or pollster sponsored by a private foundation counts little. With time these experiment will resemble those desolate city council meetings broadcast over cable channels. Why watch neighbors babble on, no matter how improved their verbal performance? The catalogue of failed citizen "outreach" programs divorced from actual power is immense (Laudon 1977, ch. 2). Voter initiatives may disappoint their most optimistic fans, but they usually outperform all other direct democracy rivals. It is no wonder, then, that these "nonestablishment" mechanisms often resort to entertaining novelties to boost citizen involvement. In the Qube experiment, the cable company awarded prizes for activism to hype the endeavor. That all these schemes have long vanished speaks to their supposed popularity.[11] Consequentiality, not unexpectedly, excites participation although hardly of the massive variety so fervently desired.

This last point is noteworthy—this virtually dooms the endless parade of unofficial "countergovernments." Enterprising radicals who see the self-initiated forum as an alluring shortcut to societal upheaval and economic leveling will fail. The inescapable lesson from settings as diverse as Pennsylvania, North Carolina, and Alaska is that direct democracy can enhance, not fundamentally transform, politics, and then only at the margins *when directed by those already in power*. Moreover, in each of these setting feedback mechanisms were kept largely free of strident partisanship, let alone radicalism. The model was one of government directed information gathering plus citizen feedback through conventional channels, not raising mass consciousness as a prelude to drastic change. Interactive television *inter alia* helped get roads repaired in Pennsylvania and conveyed the fears of remote Alaska fisherman; it does not bring upheavals of the status quo departure. Success, to the extent that it occurs, happens under the aegis of elected officials and dutiful bureaucrats, hardly people inclined toward rapid changes. The inescapable conclusion is that to the extent that political innovations gain authority, they will fall under the already powerful's jurisdiction. Governments are disinterested in outsourcing their authority. A fascinating, unpredicted cycle repeats itself: those very plans so artfully advanced to supplant tired old liberalism may only serve to rejuvenate it.

A final point is more cautionary to those attracted by enticing visions of electronically invigorated democracy. It is all too easy to conflate electronically induced citizen agitation, even swelling political awareness, with the expectation of dispersing *power* to those currently locked out. The familiar "knowledge is power" adage is only a cliché. Let us not get carried away with heady visions— surely, other enhanced interaction devices such as faxes, toll free numbers, cheap long distance rates, call-in radio, or even overnight mail do not signal a true revolution. An electronically amplified Tower of Babel is not the template.

Santa Monica, California, created an easy-to-use computer-assisted system that permitted nearly every citizen (from home, office, or the library) to interact with each other, to access city records and to express views electronically to officialdom (Varley 1991). This arrangement energized and educated citizens. Fresh movements for various political causes rapidly ensued.[12] However, it is one thing to mobilize public opinion by the electronic grassroots to assist the homeless (as was done), but it is quite another to begin an electronic revolution from outside. The most enraged mob cannot print money to pay for projects if government is destitute. Obviously, those who are plugged in can be unplugged when the powerful are sufficiently aroused. In fact, private industry, not agitated citizens themselves, donated the $350,000 to get the Santa Monica system operating and the city maintains it. Even more telling, growing communication networks may subvert the cohesion necessary for effective radical politics (and the same information routes permit counter-mobilization). People habituated to watching TV screens or computer monitors may be disinclined to abandon this pleasure. One skeptic of this electronic democracy has forcefully argued that it merely gives more power to the well-established mass media (Schudson 1992). Greater access likely brings more voices, more discord, and endless fragmentation, not unity. In short, a powerful—and perhaps unresolvable—tension exists between politicizing the multitudes and empowerment.

Egalitarianism's False Hope: The Reality of Cognitive Talent

Expanding popular participation, whether via plebiscitory democracy or some town meeting arrangement, is seldom exclusively directed toward purely procedural goals. The objective is, primarily, leveling of socioeconomic disparities. It is assumed that incorporating current outsiders—the familiar list of the poor, racial minorities, women, and so on—into a vibrant civic discourse will redistribute societal resources. To hearken back to the original Greek meanings of "equality," it is thought that *isokratia* (equality of political influence) will necessarily bring *iskleria* (equality of possessions), or at least diminish material differences. This is not mere selfishness or Socialist expropriation of wealth to ameliorate human suffering. This destination, at least as expressed by academics, represents a move toward authentic, fairer democratic governance. In short, a moral aim—equality of the tangible variety—is to be accomplished via expanding the political universe.

Of course, this scenario is hypothetical and seems improbable given the insufficiencies already documented. Nevertheless, this idealistic vision powerfully seduces. Here, we add yet one more rejoinder to our catalogue of objections. We dwell briefly on the common arguments concerning the unleashing of popular passions. As for feasibility, our suspicion is that this egalitarian paradise would degenerate into the hierarchy depicted in George Orwell's *Animal Farm*. Though these two qualms remain as applicable as ever, analysis emphasizes less familiar territory conveniently neglected by devotees of expanded participation. Specifically, indirect evidence suggests that the outcomes desired by egalitarians are hardly preordained. As with so many failed revolutions, hope triumphs over a grim reality. This is not to claim that this quest subverts democracy; rather, what will ensue will be unlike the *egalitarian* democracy so fervently sought.

The place to begin is recognizing that devotees of expanded participation exclusively conceptualize political activity only in quantitative terms. This flows naturally from the methodological dictates of survey analysis. Gathering data on voting, campaign contributions, rally attendance, and so on is effortless—just ask: "Did you [some action] ... ?" This is the disciplinary fashion—every act counts exactly the same as every other comparable act. Some behaviors are "harder" (rarer) than others, but instrumentally no action is "better" or "worse." The results a predictable pattern: Society's "haves" politically participate more than the "have-nots," and this gap expands as one proceeds from easy to more demanding acts. Given government's potential for redistributing wealth, logic suggests that eliminating these activism disparities will reduce socioeconomic differences. In that case, to establish mechanisms that invite "outsiders" in—from mobilizing the nonvoters to permitting the homeless to confront landlords. Political inclusiveness, say the faithful, will bring socioeconomic equality.

This cosmology is woefully incomplete, even misleading, despite mountains of reputed corroborating data. Analyses conspicuously ignore *how* resources are utilized. As with marketplace decisions, foolishness and brilliance are possible with equal monetary sums. Surely no sensible person believes that consumers spend equally wisely—some cleverly invest in stocks, others accumulate lottery tickets. Why else promote "consumer education"? A letter mailed to the wrong official, filled with unintelligible rantings, is not the equivalent of an adroitly targeted, well-argued one. Contemporary politics positively demonstrates that some interests outperform others, even if outnumbered and outspent. Unfortunately, while astute political observers accept this distinction as self-evident, this transparent fact vanishes when political conflict is examined through crude survey research.

Simply equalizing political activity quantitatively will *not* banish ability differences and attendant accomplishments. Perfunctory participation, all things being equal, will not necessarily breed skill, let alone equalize civic performance. Ample evidence suggests limits on building policy-savvy citizens via the familiar remedies of education, intensive training, mentoring and other interventions. Trillion dollar educational failures speak to this point. The inarticulate do not spontaneously gain fluency if only provided a friendly forum. Obviously, education and the like can beget marvelous improvement, but there are limits to any regime; sufficient preexisting ability is essential (Gottfredson 1997). For those with nonexistent or weak talents in a given domain, betterment beyond some initial modest improvement is unlikely. If this pessimistic observation was offered on, say, nuclear engineering, it would be blatantly self-evident; only its political application is novel.

Flooding the environment with politically relevant information cannot bring about equalization either. This is a favorite solution of those who desire the flattening of participation differences (see, for example, Delli Carpini and Keeter 1996, 273–277). These well-intended idealists assume that by squeezing political content into community newspapers or televised entertainment, the once ignorant grow more sophisticated to compete better with the economic "haves." Delli Carpini and Keeter even herald the entry of rap stars like Ice-T and Sister Soulja into politics, since they stimulate political awareness among the once indifferent (277). It is argued that since knowledge is power redistributing knowledge will lead to economic leveling.

Leaving aside the totalitarian measures necessary to insert unappreciated media content into fluff entertainment, the result would likely the reverse. The egalitarian dream will become a nightmare. To anticipate a point developed below, since intelligent people process more information faster and more accurately, the greater the volume of information distributed (particularly complex information), the *greater* the advantage to those with a better intellect. If knowledge equality were our singular goal, abolishing *all* political information is the *only* viable strategy. No doubt, this idealized civic factual equality existed only in small preliterate societies where miniscule political "knowledge" could be verbally disseminated hastily to each tribe member.

Expanding information will likely *exacerbate* inequality. Compared to a century ago, everybody now enjoys far greater access to political information, at least abstractly. The current affairs "junkie" (along with everyone else, in principle) has newfound access to thousands of websites, electronic discussion groups, newsletters and tiny magazines, public affairs cable channels, and so on. "Overwhelmed" is the familiar complaint among those committed to following public affairs.

The politically uninterested seldom gain from this wealth, however. Potential is not actuality; hyperabundance breeds divisions and escapism. The person who dislikes television news programs is extremely unlikely to compensate by surfing the web or watching C-SPAN. One study of political use of the Internet reports that the better educated used the Net significantly more than those with less schooling (Hill and Hughes 1998, ch. 2). Nonpolitical distractions have similarly exploded, and thus the disinterested are permitted an even easier escape from their putative civic responsibilities. The information superhighway is fully accessible for personal pleasure via cell phones and beepers. A 1950s TV addict might have encountered occasional news programs since all three networks insisted on programming public affairs in identical time slots; today, dozens of news-free stations exist. Sex and entertainment, not politics, dominate the web (Hill and Hughes 1998, ch. 1). To suggest that information bottom dwellers will *disproportionately* seek political information as the grand total expands is ludicrous. The very opposite is more plausible.

If identical information packets were imposed on everyone, perhaps in some mandatory televised civics session, extraction would surely vary to the advantage of the "haves." The pertinent model is compulsory schooling—all pupils may receive the same mathematics instruction, but some students absorb more. Inserting below average pupils into advanced classes does not solve the initial deficiency. The reasons are self-evident: distinctions in attentiveness, tenacity, motivation, and, most critically, cognitive talent. It is inconceivable that, given the massive quantities of new complicated civic information to digest, assimilation levels will violate existing absorption patterns. Again, those already advantaged will sustain their position and, more than likely, use their superior learning skills to widen the gap. Abolish instruction in mathematics altogether, if strict mathematical equality is paramount.

Let us now venture further into hypothetical politics. Suppose that through some sort of magic transformation everyone transformed into a highly energetic political animal. Suddenly, monitoring current events, voting, contributing money or whatever was everywhere. All the familiar complaints regarding apathy evaporate along with every past participatory difference—black and white, rich and poor, men and women all are equally politically engaged. Further suppose that these energized political creatures no longer relied on others to do their bidding. After all, such passivity violates the dictates of this new energized citizenship. The urban poor now make their own decisions, express their own views, and, where necessary, take matters into their own hands. Elected representatives still occupy their positions and pursue careers, but these public servants no longer independently commanded.

Such politics would be, almost by definition, highly individualistic, entrepreneurial, and amateurish. People must still earn livings, raise children, or attend school, so one's civic responsibilities cannot be full-time. This new individualism entails far more than breaking down the classic leaders-followers division. Personal autonomy becomes supreme and, naturally, rival collective mechanisms of political clout would decline. Today's guardians would go into semiretirement. In jargonistic language, politics becomes disaggregated. Historic group-centered guiding arrangements—urban machines, politically active unions, and even interest groups with their dutiful followers—would be now obsolete or radically transformed. These forms may still persist but actual operation would be more open and membership responsive.

Would such energetic populism destroy socioeconomic hierarchies? Academic consensus notwithstanding, divergences would probably widen. Imagine giving every destitute person $100,000 to fight economic inequality. Eventually, previous patterns would reemerge as the economically inept squandered their newfound wealth. Understanding why this applies equally to political clout requires a brief detour into a very sensitive topic, individual and group differences in intelligence, measured by IQ. Our argument is that crude participatory populism will only empower the inept to their disadvantage. Foolishness is not transformed by amplifying its voice.

Although "intelligence" in general and its principal statistical measure—IQ—are steeped in bitter controversy, certain research findings are solidly established. It is their public awkwardness—for example, racial variability—that ostracizes these conclusions from political analysis. To begin, what is "intelligence"? To many the term is exceedingly contentious (see, for example, Jensen 1998, ch. 4). A few even deny its very existence or argue that so many types of "intelligence" exist (such as "physical intelligence") that applying it to social analysis is pointless, even dangerous. A particularly fashionable contemporary assault views "intelligence" as a mechanism for sustaining white "Eurocentric" economic privilege (see, for example, Gould 1996).

These attacks rarely emanate from professional researchers and belong more to larger political disputes unanchored in scientific research. Leaving aside the specialized debates over technical details, there is a consensual on what "intelligence" means (see Snyderman and Rothman 1988). A 1994 statement published in *The Wall Street Journal* (reprinted in Eysenck 1998, Appendix) and signed by fifty leading intelligence specialists stated:

> Intelligence is a very general mental capability that, among other things, involves the ability to reason, plan, solve problems, think abstractly, comprehend complex ideas, learn quickly and learn from experience.

This formal usage fits common verbal usage—everybody (save a few radical academics) grasps that surgeons are more intelligent than agricultural laborers given their job requirements. Moreover, intelligence is conventionally measured by IQ tests (of which several exist) and this, too, has been accepted by professionals, although matters are not 100 percent settled. Contrary to what is often asserted by some critics, IQ tests are not culturally biased—they predict well for all groups, even illiterates far removed from mainstream "white culture' (Jensen 1980).

How does intelligence matter? To quote further from the statement endorsed by the fifty experts, "It is not merely book learning, a narrow academic or test-taking smarts. Rather, it reflects a broader and deeper capability for comprehending our surroundings—'catching on,' 'making sense' of things, or 'figuring out what to do.' " It is not a narrow personal talent such as being a superb piano player. It powerfully molds academic accomplishment as well as occupational performance. Admittedly, statistical associations between IQ scores and various proficiencies are imperfect, but, overall, they tend to be moderate to high. Ample evidence also shows its impact on health, proneness to accidents, and even criminality, among other attributes (Herrnstein and Murray 1994, chs. 5–12).

A second critical point is that other traits—notably, personality, experience, formal education levels—are generally less pertinent than intelligence in accomplishment. If one had to guess future accomplishment across multiple situations, IQ is usually the best (though surely not the only) predictor.

Of utmost importance, intelligence's impact is causal, not a result of education or on-the-job training. Cognitive capacity is nonfungible—the U.S. military, for instance, has heavily invested in training marginal recruits to perform exacting tasks with typically dismal success (findings summarized in Gottfredson 1997). This has immense repercussions for those participatory schemes intended to upgrade public capacity via experience or education. Note well, intelligence imposes a ceiling on accomplishment and does not argue against the value of education. Research also shows the value of "character traits" in achievement. Conscientiousness in particular is especially weighty in certain vocations. And, no doubt, even the smartest person may fail if he or she possesses terrible work habits, is dishonest or is addicted to drugs. Intelligence never guarantees proficiency.

Still, critically, all other factors being comparable, the relevance of these other qualities wane as tasks grow cognitively intricate. Even practical experience cannot overcome intellectual deficiencies when "brain power" is at a premium. Eliminating the impact of intelligence entirely requires specifying virtually every task. This strict "by-the-book" option is seldom feasible. The average person cannot be a physicist no matter how diligent, how dexterous in the laboratory, or how much practice is offered at playing physicist. It is the same for politics—there is no simple formula or list of directions that produces success.

A third telling point concerns manipulating cognitive capacity. Everything up to now would be irrelevant if intelligence itself could be equalized. If it could life would be conducted on a level playing field and rewards would be far more equitable. Unfortunately for egalitarians, every shred of available evidence confirms the futility of this hope. We cannot foretell what scientific advances await, but for the moment things do not look good (Herrnstein and Murray 1994, ch. 17; Eysenck 1998, ch. 7). Even early childhood educational enrichment programs such as Head Start have failed to push intelligence upward.[13] Billion dollar educational innovations will not do the trick, either (these failures are summarized in Jensen 1998, 333–344). Solutions often reflexively offered to surmount cognitive differences, such as improved prenatal health, similarly fail though they may prevent more extreme forms of mental retardation. Outside of correcting specific nutritional deficiencies among infants, nothing works beyond tiny increases (and even then, relatively few people are assisted—see Eysenck 1998, ch. 7). Evidence from adoption studies confirms the tenacity of initial intelligence differences—children from parents with low IQ are not transformed when placed with highly intelligent adoptive parents. The difficulty of boosting intelligence is true even if the hereditary element is factored out—early environmental factors such as poor maternal health habits are hardly reversible and even then, the IQ augmentation is, at best, modest. As critics of intelligence are quick to note, IQ scores can be individually unstable, but this does not prove that systematic intervention can level differences.

Fourth, the intelligence and socioeconomic position are positively linked though, to be sure, all occupations display a range of cognitive ability and being smart scarcely guarantees wealth (Gottfredson 1997, 87–91 reviews several disparate statistical studies on this point). The affluent generally owe their top economic position to superior intellectual performance, not some ill-defined special privilege. Intelligence sets a minimum threshold for the most financially rewarding occupations. The empirical evidence here is overwhelming—the overall correlations between adult socio-economic status and IQ range from .5 to .7, remarkably high numbers for social science data (Jensen 1998, 491; also see Herrnstein and Murray, 1994, ch. 2; Murray 1997). Ample, though hardly absolutely conclusive evidence, strongly suggests that intelligence causes economic position not the opposite as some contend (Jensen 1998, 491–494). Prestigious, professional occupations such as medicine, law and engineering require higher levels of intelligence than lower status jobs and pay higher salaries. Additionally, within a job classification, intelligence matters. Compared to a dull waiter, a smarter one will accomplish more—it takes "brains" to keep orders straight, decide what tables demand immediate attention, and resolve crises. He or she will probably thus receive larger tips. Significantly, as one advances from menial jobs to positions demanding greater cognitive capacity, intelligence grows more significant. Gaps among truck drivers are relevant but less telling than differences among professors (Gottfredson 1997).

Most controversial, many (though not all) researchers argue that the disadvantaged who expect to advance via political mobilization tend, on average, to be on the low side of the cognitive ability distribution. Note well, IQ scores reflect a multitude of factors, including cultural and environmental factors, but the raw distribution of scores across different social strata has been long documented. While people from every demographic category occupy all cognitive levels, differences still remain (Herrnstein and Murray 1994, ch. 13; Jensen 1998, ch. 11). The familiar "nature versus nurture" debate that often surrounds these differences is essentially irrelevant to its existence (see Eysenck 1998, ch. 15 on this point). Even if 100 percent of these inequities were environmentally determined, nothing suggests they could be successfully minimized.

These facts powerfully impose themselves on egalitarian hopes for lifting up those at the bottom via political action. Proceeding from unexceptional political acts (e.g., voting) to more demanding responsibilities (e.g., calculating policy costs, organizing a campaign) increases the need for brainpower. The parallel with economic activity is inescapable—nearly everyone can be trained to cook, but only a tiny handful can be trained as physicists. To suppose that those who unable to excel occupationally will master complicated political assignments is bizarre. Recall Chapter Two's tales of respondents with little education struggling with rudimentary policy tradeoff exercises. This bodes poorly for visions of energetic mass participation. Debates among the intellectually challenged cannot be erudite public discussions. Piling on information cannot overcome deficiencies if participants cannot recollect facts, are unable to integrate abstract concepts, or are incapable of drawing accurate inferences. Nebulous casual links may well mutate into naive conspiracies or garble. This populist reverie—the once disadvantaged "rising up" politically if only invited to the Decision maker's Ball—is only attainable perhaps for those wholly ensconced at elite universities. Even those of average intelligence may require complicated issues to be "dumbed down." One only has to scan mass-market news programs or popular newspapers such as *USA Today* to appreciate the length of average attention spans. Woe to those who offering longwinded presentations if ordinary citizens are holding their remote controls.

Newfound accessibility to the levers of power will probably *exacerbate* political inequalities. Consumer economics provides some sturdy lessons. The consumer protection movement is directed largely toward shielding "have-not's" from endless ruses—deceptive advertising, one-sided legal contracts, mislabeled merchandise, and so on. Regulatory watchdogs such as the FTC justifiably assume gullibility among the poorly educated. To anoint the destitute as "King Consumer" invites calamity both economically and politically; only by *de*powering the cognitively unskilled does he or she escape ruin. The political parallel abounds. History affords countless examples of demagogic charlatans preying on those seduced by facile slogans and ridiculous promises. Though even the bright can be periodically victimized—for example, Marxism's odd allure among intellectuals or Ponzi schemes among greedy investors—the "have not's" seem particularly vulnerable to deception.

Where, then, does this lead in assessing egalitarian politics? If civic struggles entail nothing more than autonomous individual versus autonomous individual, divergences in cognitive capacity will occasion colossal mismatches. The wealthy will be superior fundraisers, more sophisticated voters, better communicators, and more skilled at whatever else winning requires. Gulfs now apparent in income distributions will assuredly surface in public quarrels. This is like a totally unregulated economic marketplace—the ambitious predators will triumph completely without government protection to shelter the less competitive.

There is some welcome news egalitarians: economic redistribution *can* be accomplished peacefully within the context of democratic politics, and without a totalitarian revolution. In fact, this solution is already at hand—rummaging through obscure historical dustbins or inventing Electronic communities is unnecessary. If ever an instance prevailed of the perfect dislodging the good, this is it. The flattening of economic inequalities will be far from complete, but substantial advancement is possible. What is required is a political process where the exercise of power is *unrelated* to cognitive differences. In technical shorthand: IQ-free politics.

The way to achieve this is through aggregations of interests, a return to hierarchy and command. In an ironic twist, surrendering one's voice is perhaps the surest path to advancement among those outgunned when politics is reduced to hyperindividualism. Subordination at one level yields triumph at another. Powerful interest groups—energetic pluralistic democracy, if you will—offer one sensible alternative. Cognitively talented individuals exist within all ethnic and racial groups. Equally decisive, extraordinary talent can often be "rented"—for example, the homeless may prudently hire smart lawyers to wage their battles. The minimization of cognitive advantages across contenders would result since leaders—not ordinary people—are equally smart. As in class action litigation, the unskilled cleverly pool meager resources and hire a brilliant champion. In turn, this cognitive heavyweight forges a bureaucratic organization to perform those analytical tasks incomprehensible to the clients. In an instant, as Max Weber promised, the playing field of expertise and sophistication is leveled. The pretense of grassroots vitality and input would now be sacrificed to tangible accomplishment. Gone are the endless survey consultations or intruding electronic solicitations. Ordinary citizens pay dues and obey orders.

Of all the mechanisms that counter cognitive talent-based politics, a strong political party system is undoubtedly the most potent. If the individualistic, entrepreneurial system is the homecourt advantage of the intellectually gifted, the centralized programmatic party system is the weapon of choice among the have-nots. The disciplined armylike model depicted in Michel's *Political Parties* is the template. Most critically, it is heavily weighted toward minimal mass intellectual dexterity—the top–down directed vote. It does not matter whether geniuses or idiots cast ballots, provided that the latter are properly directed. This is untrue of other participatory outlets to the extent that those options demand IQ-related skills. If politics is based on persuasive argument or inventive schemes, the less intelligent are doomed.

Nevertheless, if ballots reign supreme, and the inept far outnumber the capable (as is likely) as long as wiser heads instructs them, egalitarianism might well triumph. Rigid aggregation can surmount formidable average brainpower deficiencies. Unfortunately for those at the bottom, scholars infatuated with direct democracy seldom consider the impact of these novelties on traditional aggregation mechanisms (an insightful exception is Budge 1996).[14]

An unease exists between a system that graciously welcomes every voice, no matter how inept, and the benefits possible when the erudite benevolently direct the less capable. It is a ragtag mob versus a disciplined army. Either version justifiably claims democracy's lofty mantle. Each is but one interpretation of a notoriously ambiguous concept. Both heed the public will though in profoundly different ways; it is a matter of starting points and effective strategies. Advocates of plebiscitory democracy are infatuated with a particular process that will, supposedly, invigorate civic life and, subsequently, redress sociopolitical inequality. By contrast, those inclined toward supervised organizational aggregation focus on material outcomes independent of putative democratic inclusiveness. For the latter, effective power—not its theatric imposter—is exercised collectively, not individually, and only when expertly guided.

Conclusions

Our exploration has reviewed many designs and visions, all sharing a common theme: heighten democracy by infusing it with an energetic, vocal citizenry. The belief that democracy's problems are solved by yet more democracy continues to thrive. Implicit is a Darwinian-like progression—the elitist status quo is but a flawed precursor to some future populist Utopia. It is not the alluring spirit that offends; nor do we seek to repossess the democratic appellation. Rather, it is their application that is cause for unease, and this goes far beyond practicality. Let us not conflate a fad within an energetic academic coterie with real world progress.

What draws our attention is the abandonment of those sturdy alternatives briefly sketched in our concluding observations—interest groups and strong political parties, in particular. Supporters of populist enterprises are not offering their schemes as superior to traditional rivals; they are put forward *in vacuo.* Naturally, these ideals easily outshine today's humdrum, imperfect reality, especially when scant attention is paid to any potential flaws. To be frank, bad advice is being proscribed. Two such deficiencies are especially noteworthy—the first is the duplicity associated with empowering the inept;

the second concerns the coercive element awaiting those pursuing "enhanced democracy."

A prudent scholar must be aware that the intellectually deficient cannot single-handedly overcome their misfortune by controlling their own fate, democratic rhetoric aside. Recall the disturbing parallel with the consumer marketplace—bereft of government regulatory protection the deprived will seek folly, not excellence. Invoking the "more education, more information" mantra does not suffice as demonstrated by the failed multibillion dollar education campaigns.[15] Limits on human improvement are not easily overcome. What future miracle do these counselors recommend to reverse past failures?

If we had to speculate on this curious situation, our best guess is that all these populist nostrums permit the academic a powerful advising role not present in rival remedies. There is a well-disguised agenda—advance the social welfare state *and* anoint the academic counselor. This latter point appeared earlier in describing how scholarly experts, not elected officials, decide question wording, statistical interpretation, and similar matters when it comes to assessing the public will. This influence among assembled citizens ostensibly guiding their own destinies far outshines the position granted in the "real world" of interest groups and muscular centralized parties. In the latter, influential academics are exceedingly rare. In democratic arrangements resting on strong parties power is given to those who deliver tangible goods: money, votes, access, publicity, or deal brokering. Academic talents such as formulating policy positions or even conducting poll are merely lower status "technical tasks."

The forum, whether the mass media or some electronic town meeting, is the most agreeable format to academics because it bestows enormous influence to skilled data manipulators. Those witnessing scholars jockeying for worldly power have long appreciated this fact though guilty participants seldom confess. Consider, for example, J. S. Mill, the unquestioned champion of government as an open, nearly all-inclusive marketplace of ideas. This would not, however, be the expected populist heaven. Cowling (1990, ch. 2) observes that Mill passionately wanted the "higher minds," largely literary and professional minds, to dominate all public discourse. This clerisy, as Mill designated the intellectual elite, given their inability to secure power directly would operate behind the scenes, guiding the political elite. Aaron Director (1964) suggests that sophisticated public discourse favors the intellectuals just as the economic marketplace favors business people. Their embrace of truth by public argument is thus hardly accidental—it is self-interested, although not necessarily materially so. Ginsberg (1986), in his review of the intellectual marketplace's emergence, succinctly argues that: "The chief proponents of free communication can generally be found among the most powerful producers of ideas and among those groups that believe that they can increase or expand the popularity of their views" (104).

Of course, it is arguable that fabricating these schemes is just harmless academic wordplay. Chalk up another instance of the impotent (professors) seeking worldly influence. Perhaps, but recent history cautions otherwise. Repeatedly, outlandish classroom theory conveyed as "higher truths" unleash cadres of radicals convinced that the dreary status quo can be repaired. As Paul Johnson (1988) documents, if the force of ideas disappoints their intellectual creators, real—sometimes brutal—compulsion is the next step. The anarchism and nihilistic self-indulgence of the 1960s propagated in Marxist-flavored seminars at prestigious universities. Many of these "harmless" fabrications soon became violent. Such overblown idealism might be commendable, but it often makes people overlook the serviceable to secure unreachable perfection. Why settle for *mere* liberal democracy with its problems; instead, substitute the professor's egalitarian dream world. No matter that this old-maidish liberalism required hundreds of years to fashion and with immense cost. Needless to say, it is understandable why these university professors are unwelcome as worldly Philosopher Kings or Queens.

The second warning is more somber. The mechanisms promoting enhanced citizen participation disguise a potential totalitarianism. We have shown that even under ideal circumstances, citizen activism was spotty. This is not merely a matter of repairing bugs in the system. Save tumultuous times, politics is not our passion, and perhaps we should celebrate this freedom. Left alone, even the most civic-minded drift away from endless political discourse. Combining the Home Shopping Network with C-SPAN alienates both clienteles. The inevitable next step then is more vigorous mobilization. As ancient Athens paid its citizens to offer public counsel, so we must coerce the apathetic to enroll in the assembly. This push is essential lest this new politics degenerate into today's rule by the talented few. If "voluntary" attempts fall short, we may have to legally require this civic duty and herein lies the danger.

There is nothing undemocratic in assembling citizen to pronounce policy. It is the regular *coerced* assembling of those who prefer apathy that sounds the alarm. *1984*'s account of compulsory two-minute hate sessions captures our unease.[16] Historically, citizen mobilization has often provided governments a cheap, efficient device to control its subjects, not vice versa (Ginsberg 1982, esp. ch. 6 details this process). "Soviet" merely signifies council, and the former Soviet Union was justly infamous for forcibly mobilizing citizens in false "democratic" shows to ensure ideological faithfulness. Awarding the disenfranchised the vote was hardly a generous invitation to governance; it was a prudent response to possible violent uprisings. Participation "domesticated" the potentially unruly by channeling mayhem into routine, predictable, and peaceful forms. Contemporary elections continue this critical though obscure role (Ginsberg and Weissberg 1978). Compulsory mass political participation, from obligatory voting to "voluntary" political study groups, has almost always been the hallmark of dictatorships, not democracies.

The periodic, formalized citizen gathering provides a superb mechanism for the dominant to enlist the powerless to their hidden schemes. As Michael Sandel warned regarding electronic town meetings: "[this is] not electronic democracy, but electronic Bonapartism—a conception of personalist rule in the name of the masses, reinforced by the most advanced information technologies" (1992, 6). To insist that "the people" will shield their autonomous assemblies against abrogation by the powerful is fanciful. Haranguing public officials via the forum or interactive telecommunications is a two-way street: it also affords fresh access to citizens themselves. President Clinton's farcical "national dialogue on race" was a perfect example of a bogus "citizen assembly" to advance a party line. Many of "citizen outreach" designs depicted earlier consciously embodied this aim. Televised town meetings are perfect reelection stratagems. More generally, this is nothing but co-optation, a clever staple to manage the unruly. Co-optation is especially effective when applied to the naive, a category that is included in the currently politically excluded.

Ironically, then, "giving a voice" to the once voiceless may only compound the problem. Opportunities for "discussion" become chances to spread propaganda with options slanted to favor predetermined choices. Meanwhile, collective ratification gives this choice the appearance of being volitional (Ginsberg and Weissberg 1978 describe these mechanisms). If the outcome is unsure, the more intellectually talented can always pack the meeting, reinterpret rules, shift the agenda, exploit parliamentary procedures or pledge selective bribes for compliance. Marxist factions with their infamous "come early, stay late" tactics wrote the book on this infiltration. Keep in mind that heightened participation cannot provide the intellectual capacity to disentangle deceitful lures. In short, expecting ordinary citizens to defeat entrenched expertise flies in the face of reality.

Defeating such co-optive mobilization can only be accomplished by disengagement—voting with one's feet (or with the remote control or e-mail filters) to avoid these encounters altogether. Obliviousness is how Soviet citizens "tuned-out" political campaigns directed toward mobilizing citizens to absorb state-dictated lies. Similar "spontaneity" transpires in those ill-fated "enhanced democracy" schemes, although undoubtedly for profoundly distinct reasons. More to the point, whatever the impetus, disengagement critically sustains limited, free government. Provided daily calls for the faithful to congregate can be disregarded, so long as indoctrination lessons are directed toward empty chairs, tyranny can be thwarted.

CHAPTER 7

Conclusions

> I know of nothing grander, better exercise, better digestions, more positive proof of the past, the triumphant result of faith in human kind, than a well-contested American election.
> —Walt Whitman, "Democratic Vistas," 1871

We started by noting the public opinion poll's growing accomplishments. Whether judged by the amount of attention that the White House gives them or by the rapidity with which they can be carried out, progress is undeniable. Also, despite what might seem like constant carping over polling clumsiness, we generally applaud this advancement and welcome even greater headway. Our own limited efforts are certainly intended as a contribution to this march forward. To claim that this book is "antipolling" or disdainful of popular opinion is inaccurate. It also is not our purpose to reopen dimly remembered debates over the ability of polls can "really" assess some mysterious *Volkgeist*. Our inquiry centers on the poll's *political role,* not its technical validity.

This question of the "proper political role" for the most part has passed largely unnoticed among practitioners. To paraphrase (badly) from Lord Tennyson, for those launching surveys, "Their's not to reason why, Their's but to design the questionnaire and dissect the results." The mere existence of polling apparently certifies worthiness, and the very idea of restraining polls to some "proper" civic purpose seems impertinent. If asked about their political function, pollsters would most likely depict themselves as dutiful village criers ever willing to announce the daily news, albeit news uncovered by trained interviewers. Mike Kagay, the senior *New York Times* news editor, and longtime polling expert, aptly expressed this view in his 1999 American Association for Public Opinion Research (AAPOR) presidential address. Polling's primary purpose, pronounced Kagay, "... is to bring the views of typical Americans into the rooms where elites reside and decide" (1999, 463). What might this activity add? It "... can force elites to look beyond the Washington beltway, to look outside midtown Manhattan, to look more broadly than the usual news source" (463). In brief, polls—thanks to the publicly minded, disinterested survey experts—afford leaders a window on to opinions outside their immediate ken, and who could possibly be opposed to that?

This politically neutral justification is surely sincere, absolutely correct, and certainly the industry's official *raison d'être*. Nevertheless, a chasm separates the intentions of this enterprise intends and its actual consequences. To say that polling is "just supplying more data to leaders" is a bit like saying TV is merely radio, only with a picture. Matters are far more complicated than Kagay's rhetoric intimates. Obviously, this official justification does not indicate why polling should be a political necessity. Polling is not the *sine qua non* of democratic governance like the rule of law, competitive elections, or civil debate. One might assume that, if polls vanished tomorrow, democracy would continue undiminished. Lest we forget, vigorous democracy flourished in the United States for more than one hundred years before polling could "help" leaders. If our government's vital ingredients were ranked in descending order of importance, polling would assuredly be near the bottom. Elected officials might not even notice the disappearance of polls, given their already ample access to popular feedback. Frankly, the survival of public opinion polls seems to depend more on consumer habits and the power of the polling industry than its usefulness to democracy. The decision to ask about defense spending or health care is neither legally mandated nor central to government decision making. It might be more accurate to label these polls as "entertainment for the politically inclined."

Yet, as Chapter One argued, to view polls as nothing more than entertainment neglects their evolving political impact. A steady stream of front-page poll results, all roughly pointing in the same direction, all portrayed as the "true voice" of the people have an impact beyond just conveying information. It is the high-profile public proliferation of survey results, not the message details, that is critical. These repetitive announcements slowly, yet inescapably, seep into our collective consciousness. The phenomenon resembles TV's subterranean effect—even avoiders ultimately absorb its peculiar cosmology by living among others immersed in television. After a point, skeptics of polling actually repeat survey factoids as "truth," though unable to cite any source or even realize the origins of their wisdom. Poll findings thus become "everybody knows" public knowledge.

Nowhere is this poll-created consensus more apparent than with announcing the public's desires for enhanced federal entitlements. The announcements are so regular that technical analyses monitor only the proentitlement majority's magnitude and distribution, not its veracity. Sheaves of poll data, all collected by prestigious organizations, quickly silence the doubters. Whether the public authentically desires or not what the modern welfare state wants to deliver—low cost, effective health care, well-funded senior citizen programs, compassionate welfare entitlements, and so on—is seemingly settled. The reality of these desires is, as we have repeatedly admitted, incontestable.

Liberal statism is hardly intrinsic to polling. This relationship is merely an historical occurrence, a confluence of information gathering habits joined with ideological leanings, not some predetermined logical progression. Polling itself is blameless. If libertarians dominated public opinion polling the outcome might be wildly different. Survey after survey would show majorities "genuinely" adverse to expensive forays into potentially catastrophic social engineering when solutions that let people devise their own private fixes were so attractively portrayed by the interviewer. This reversal could be accomplished without using loaded terminology or data spinning. It is merely a matter of the ruling paradigm. Every technical choice would be broadly consistent with the identical methodological rules guiding today's polls which uncover a desire for bigger government.

And to be perfectly fair, the results of libertarian polling would be no closer to wise counsel than current results. To reiterate chapter five's final warning, free-market solutions such as educational tax breaks or business-supplied daycare can be just as misguided and personally foolish as uncontrolled federal spending. Worthiness must be empirically established one policy at a time, not deduced ideologically. The argument is against poll-driven government, not the welfare state per se. The controversy concerns the democratic *legitimacy* of public opinion polling results regardless of who carries out the poll.

Do polls offer sound democratic advice? Our view is that these desires expressed in the standard "Do you want more …" opinion poll questions are *not* instructions worth heeding. Note well—this qualm over social welfare polling hardly rejects social welfare policy *qua* policy; conceivably, every public entitlement longing is meritorious and should be implemented tomorrow. Program advocacy surely exists independently of securing poll majorities. It is how the directive is conveyed, not the proposal itself.

In Chapter Two's terminology, wishes and hard policy choices fundamentally differ. Citizen desires, no matter how beneficial, are seldom perfectly obtainable, and thus public requests cannot be equated with leadership obligation, even in the most accommodating democracy.

Those with some knowledge of economics clearly recognize the foregoing distinction. For these realists, our cost/risk data merely certify the obvious. The same goes for those charged with enacting legislation—certainly few trustworthy leaders feel obligated to enact the public's fantasies. Some disingenuous rhetoric might satisfy popular desires. Chapter Six recounted how elected officials often solicit public sentiment but refuse authority to rivals claiming a more technically adroit ear-to-the-ground. Those responsible for raising taxes generally know that polls are corrupted by "free lunchism"—the conflicting desire for more government spending coupled with lower taxes. Now, given this ability to act realistically among those making binding choices, are we not sounding a false alarm about some implausible power grab? Must we worry that today's pollsters, like some restless developing world military, will inappropriately meddle in politics?

A coup d'état by the gnomes of Ann Arbor's Survey Research Center to install their director as America's Grand Pooh-Bah is not our worry. That fear is clearly irrelevant. Our concern focuses on the fashioning of underlying "civic habits of mind," the unspoken consensus surrounding daily humdrum politics. To appreciate this psychological power, reflect on today's electorate. Two centuries ago, giving African Americans and women the right to vote, let alone seek office, was unthinkable. Today, it is similarly odd to imagine noncitizens legally voting, yet this was once permissible. Imagine a soapbox orator suggesting that women and blacks be disenfranchised, while noncitizens legally vote? These rantings are easily dismissable—neither idea fits with "obvious" reality. Examples of how what is considered "reasonable" can evolve are virtually endless.

We detect a comparable political evolution regarding polling's political role. What were once occasional curiosities reported in newspapers are now regularly heeded facts among political decision makers. The proliferation of polls that reduce complicated issues to false yes or no choices, are interpreted by unelected, self-appointed guardians, and are promoted as the superior embodiment of modern democracy, awakens unease. That these polls rarely dwell on costs or risks makes it worse. The contrast between the attention the press devotes to poll-driven plebiscite democracy compared to campaign finance is enlightening. While most pundits complain about financial contributions from hidden, unaccountable sources undermining democracy, virtually none ever discuss sponsorship or ulterior motives of polls. Apparently, money is somehow "tainted" while far-fetched poll pronouncements are "normal," if not commendable.[1] Chapter Six's warning deserves repeating—the privately sponsored poll passed off as the certified messenger of the public's voice is anathema to popular rule, not its modern enhancement.

When elections share the political stage with polls as the people's legitimate voice, the authority of the former is undermined. These two mechanisms are more different than they might seem and, critically, can collide as democratic instruments. The vote is plain to see, officially monitored and counted; the polls, by contrast, pass through multiple private filters prior to being announced to the public. Elections pose difficult choices between realistic alternatives; by contrast, polls welcome fantasies unhindered by the outcomes. Election fraud is a felony; falsifying survey data might—at worst—sully a researcher's reputation.[2] Those doubting the negative impact of polls on elections should remember mass media accounts in which poll supplied information turned an ostensible "victory" into a "defeat" or where office seekers became recognized "leaders" thanks to unrivalled poll standings.[3] Historically, elections have always played a vital role in our democratic self-definition. While it is easy to imagine democracy without polls this does not work with elections; they are quintessentially democratic.

More telling in this context, however, is that elections are proven and perfectly suitable for ordinary citizens. They permit balloters, however clumsily, to reward the good and to punish the wicked, while sparing them untenable civic obligations. Voting hardly requires skill at ordering priorities or detailed policy knowledge, yet elections—however crudely—can cower even the mighty and do so absolutely democratically. In 1932, for instance, citizens might not grasp macroeconomic theory, yet they knew that Hoover was misguided. To intimate that citizens could be democratically "upgraded," if afforded far more demanding governing instruments, when many are already challenged by the simple act of voting, is bizarre. The vote, like the sturdy Colt 45 of Western folklore, is the great equalizer in granting democratic power. Admittedly, our electoral deficiencies are legion—bartering votes, misrepresenting tallies, unfair exclusions, circuslike campaigns, low turnouts, and so on. Still, warts and all, they have served the Republic remarkably well, insuring a modicum of popular sovereignty, especially when judged against rivals. Jeopardizing this proven instrument in the hope of securing chancy progress is not an act lightly taken. That many poorer nations cannot sustain a tradition of free and open elections should be remembered when castigating this popular control.

Formulating alternative histories is always risky, but imagine what it would have been like if opinion polling was unknown when President

Clinton sought some solution for faltering public education. Chapter four showed that the number of potential remedies is huge, and without polls who can predict what he might have chosen. With polling presidential advisors enjoy a great advantage in hunting for instantly alluring panaceas: poll after poll offered up the beguiling "smaller classes" cure without considering any costs or drawbacks, and the naive public overwhelmingly embraced it. No matter that the supporting scientific evidence was weak (at best), or that the liabilities possibly outweighed the slight gains. The pollster (who probably lacked any familiarity with this complex issue) ever on the lookout for trendy items framed the issue; Clinton saw his opportunity and took it. Today's apprehensive officials might hire poll scanners much like the Air Force assigns soldiers to watch radar screens every minute of the year to detect missile launches.[4]

Unusual in this push for poll legitimacy is its distinctly *un*populist nature. Expanding political access has traditionally entailed sizable bottom-up pressure, if not boisterous mass movements. Referenda and initiatives, for example, resulted from Progressive agitation, as did nearly every expansion of suffrage. Contemporary campaign finance reform efforts attract noisy high-profile adherents. The same goes for instant citizenship for prospective voters or same-day registration. By contrast, the thrust to enhance the poll's political legitimacy is stealthy and nearly totally outside public debate. Would-be office seekers may be quizzed relentlessly, but "How authoritative do you regard public opinion poll messages?' escapes the interrogation list.[5] Even critics ridiculing President Clinton's poll-driven pandering never ventured beyond superficialities. That the President of the United States may take action rooted in uncertainties of questionnaire design, sampling, fortuitous timing, and statistical extraction, passed unnoticed. Polling and pollsters are unchallenged here; only how the *vox populi* is opportunistically manipulated draws rebuke.

The impetus for this shift comes from pollsters themselves and, most critically, their academic colleagues. This assembly is hardly a group of obscure campus-based radicals communicating to each other in coded language. If anything, this drive comes from the best and the brightest at the most prestigious polling firms and universities. Judged by the pervasive support among younger academics milling survey data, it will probably proliferate as skeptics of polling fade into obscurity. If this domination is not believed, merely recall all the expert statements and well-funded designs to build future plebiscitory democracy scattered about previous chapters. Those few agnostics remain silent in the scholarly debate. Disputes are intramural events concerning technique, not larger political purpose. Although these plebiscitory schemes may currently fall short, internal deficiencies are judged the culprit, not resistance from those rejecting the underlying populist ideology. The future, it would seem, belongs to these driven supporters.

Let us offer one last effort to put an end to this nascent "new and improved" democracy. Reduced to its essentials, this plebiscitory vision embodies four grand (though sometimes well hidden) propositions. None of them are especially reasonable or empirically supportable; survival rests far more on repetition than hard evidence. The first is that ordinary citizens can competently render judgments on the esoteric, hugely expensive dilemmas faced by government. Their zeal for more (or less) defense spending, health care, etc. is real in the same sense that marketplace consumer purchases are proficient. At a minimum, citizens grasp what they are acquiring, realize approximate costs, and accept potential drawbacks. More exacting, but no less indispensable, citizens comprehend policy limits and accept the inescapability of tradeoffs.

Second, these articulated wants are sufficiently genuine so pollster packaging cannot alter their fundamental character. Translated into polling terms, questionnaire vocabulary, phraseology, interviewer traits, and similar factors should not substantially mold expressed preferences. If selection stability is *not* evident, the *vox populi* is nothing more than a pollster creation. This is no trivial matter, for who would concede democratic governance to nameless, unaccountable technicians possibly possessing their own agendas?

Third, if some public policy desire exists, the survey instrument itself should be capable of fully and accurately extracting this preference. For example, when respondents volunteer a willingness to shoulder financial burdens, some certainty must exist that this is sincere. If citizens have nuanced opinions, this complexity should be recoverable, if it bears on policy. These instrument virtues are routinely displayed in the marketplace—sales figures authentically portray what consumers "really" want. Capturing only the rough, or even inaccurate, approximations should be avoided at all costs. We want to see reality itself, not the murky shadows on the cave's wall, and computer-enhanced renderings of these shadows will not suffice.[6]

Finally, the polling information must advance democracy, plausibly understood. More is expected than an empty logical statement that proposes because democratic discourse requires facts, and polls provide more information, polls must strengthen democracy. By this low standard, nearly anything, even sleazy tabloids, enhances democracy. For decades poll defenders have repeated the benefits that polling bring democracy. We take this claimed association seriously. No doubt, if this assertion concerned a vaccine, the federal government would have conducted an investigation into safety and effectiveness long ago. Even if we momentarily accept the simplistic definition of democracy as giving the people what they want, might polls permit leaders to do this? What if the survey asked for the impossible? More telling, can survey instruments be used by citizens to hold leaders accountable?

Citizen Competence

That citizens can actually solve the complex issues confronting government by themselves must be a reality if survey results are to become anything more than a form of entertainment. This is not something that can be demonstrated though statistical manipulation. Historically, claims regarding popular wisdom were rhetorical flourishes suitable for civic occasions, not actual assessments. Granting the franchise was initially offered to solidify citizen loyalty; soliciting sage counsel was incidental given voter shortcomings. Our antipopulist Constitution clearly takes a pessimistic view toward heeding the voice of the masses. Devices long used to exclude would-be voters—property requirements, literacy tests, and residency—can all be interpreted as efforts to impede the less-qualified hoards from meddling in politics. Given the amount of voter error uncovered in Florida's 2000 presidential election (e.g., voters repeating their presidential choice in the "write in candidate" space), this historic unease may still be applicable.

While Progressives relied on optimism, today's academic populists conclude that competency already exists; the task is merely divining it from bountiful survey. This is a momentous shift in appreciating the public's political role. The acrobatics that advocates of this position must go through to defend the claim are staggering. Chapter Three displayed an impressive wordplay matched only by statistical ingenuity. "Proof" of civic competence abounded, typically linked to data notable solely for its convenience, and when such capacity did not initially surface, no statistical trick was spared. In one case, epidemic public ignorance was casually brushed aside as irrelevant to assessing citizen proficiency; in fact, this deficiency "proved" that the system not citizens themselves, was insufficient (Della Carpini and Keeter 1996). Elsewhere public talent for making difficult calculations was asserted without any plausible documentation (e.g., finding no contradiction between the public's craving the expensive social welfare entitlements while rejecting tax hikes) (Page and Shapiro 1992).

There also are many conceptual shortcomings. "Competence" was often conflated with some refurbished status quo, not a superior capacity to manage today's political challenges. A predilection for formulating "competency traits" based on a haphazard disciplinary consensus was common.

More serious, however, was a disjuncture between competency and the ability to deal capably with a specific policy. Adequacy was conceptualized as omnipresent. Good scores on a current events quiz scores might be used to "prove" respondent skill at navigating everything from Social Security to solving education shortcomings. That policy proficiency was not a generalizable trait was unthinkable. Nor were respondents asked to accomplish anything concrete. The upshot of this tactic was that finding capacity (however oddly defined and calibrated) *anywhere* announced respondent authority *everywhere* without any predictive validity. This approach is sensible only if the goal is to make public competence appear widespread in the face of ample contrary evidence.

Our strategy was to link civic capacity narrowly to a particular policy. We assume that a respondent expertly able to grasp the impact of class size on student achievement might be a dunce regarding federal daycare subsidies. This merely applies the familiar division of labor to the job of citizen lawmaker. Even in legislative bodies, the tax code genius may be baffled by agricultural policy. This approach is laborious, but it is routine when hiring prospective employees for most tasks in the real world. Of course, this effort is unnecessary if the poll's aim is merely to extract wishes, and this is certainly a legitimate survey purpose.

Our results paint a vastly different picture than what is proclaimed by these supporters of citizen competence. We found much public misinformation regarding policy costs. In one experiment many respondents believed that they could "buy" a $20.8 billion education program for a few million dollars or less annually. Using a different questionnaire format (cost per taxpayer), we discovered that public cost estimation was grossly inaccurate in the opposite direction. A large number of respondents were often incapable of even offering guesses at a policy cost, despite interviewer reassurances that only a rough number was needed. Twenty-four percent could not imagine what the Clinton education initiative would cost an average taxpayer per year. Overall, these results suggest that fiscal terminology—hundreds of billions and or even trillions—has scant concrete meaning to most citizens. This assessment was reinforced by other contexts where public enthusiasm gushed forth when cost figures where presented in manageable terms like "just $10."

Other competency indicators likewise gave dismal results. When asked to make fairly simple tradeoffs across a few policy domains, many respondents encountered trouble, judged by their totals reached and the number of categories employed. To be sure, this task is well performed in daily life, so we are not exposing some grave cognitive deficiency. Our point is the far more modest one that this vital mental habit unlikely colors poll solicitations—respondents freely feed at the "all-you-can-eat" policy bar so graciously supplied by the pollster. We further saw that many respondents chose options well beyond the reasonable agenda (e.g., a national parental training program). Several totalitarian-flavored panaceas also drew ample support. Especially disconcerting was a widespread inability to hypothesize potential problems policies might produce. In the case of hiring one hundred thousand new teachers, 47 percent could not imagine *any* possible disadvantage. Respondents performed only marginally better when asked to envision problems with federally assisted daycare. Clearly, debates among experts over potential liabilities do not resonate well among ordinary citizens. Deficiencies here suggest a public ready to accept magic beans in return for a cow. Are we to trust citizens oblivious to drawbacks and so easily seduced?

Finally, we found uncertain evidence in the public's willingness to pay, at least according to our special meaning of that notion. In the case of education, nearly a third of those endorsing the Clinton plan were personally willing to expend funds necessary to reduce class size to intended levels. Others desired this outcome, but only at bargain rates. To be sure, if told the true cost, many might change their minds, but the fact remains that nearly everyone is seeking a bargain. A comparable exercise with the daycare initiative again showed a similar disconnect between supporting a policy and willingness to pay for it. The huge range of responses also advises caution in assuming that policy consumers grasp what they are buying.

Admittedly, we explore only two items from a vast number of policies. Still, these findings fit exceptionally well with similar observations regarding public knowledge and sophistication. Experienced politicians do not give speeches filled with budgetary information that will confuse their audiences, no matter how great their respect for public wisdom. Only those who have labored to extract "competence," when none seems plausible, might disagree with our verdict. These less-than-flattering conclusions also have the advantage of being plain vanilla obvious without statistical manipulation or word play. Face validity is the technical term. Eventually, however, generality can only be established empirically, and on an item-by-item basis. Skeptics are invited to pursue similar inquires to expose contrary findings.

Supporters of direct democracy may conceivably interpret these findings as doubting public worthiness, even challenging their versions of "democracy." However, since when does democracy require a nation of Philosopher Kings, unexpectedly summoned by telephone, to direct public officials expertly? Policy aptitude, displayed via the surprise telephone poll, is *not* a democratic prerequisite. Indeed, this capacity to navigate multiple policy mysteries unlikely ranks high on any expansive "democratic citizen necessity" list. It is certainly trivial next to national loyalty, obedience to the law, and similar traditional civic virtues. Only among those academics infatuated with populism would our revelation of policymaking incapacity be judged troublesome.

Steadfast Fidelity

For public policy pronouncements to be granted legitimacy, they must be truthful. Respondents must mean what they say, and, since we cannot probe innermost thoughts, this earnestness is interpreted as steadfastness. Put differently, answers are not to be whimsical reactions to a mood swing. We are not demanding strict overtime continuity, for it is expected that views will shift as circumstances evolve. Fluidity may even reflect well on the public's acumen. Our test is the firmness of poll-expressed mandates at any one particular moment. If such constancy is lacking, then what the public "says" merely reflects haphazard questionnaire details. Uncovering such pliability does not violate some democratic ideal or challenge the pollster's scientific pretensions. Far more important is that it undemocratically awards political power to pollsters. This shift far transcends the more familiar technical debates over terminology or the ability of simple questions to capture multi-faceted opinions.

This problem of response elasticity is well known to industry experts though it is rarely confessed when heralding the democratic wisdom of the poll (see Schuman and Presser 1981; Tversky and Kahneman 1982, Tom Smith 1987; and others). It is well-documented that expressions can take on unique interpretations across varied contexts, seemingly clear words might hold ambiguous overtones, and so on. Kenneth Rasinski (1989) has shown, for example, that the phrase "improving the conditions of blacks" will draw more public support than merely saying "assistance to blacks," while "aid to big cities" is far less popular than "solving the problems of big cities" (393). Yet, some continuity across varied settings must exist if public messages are to be seriously regarded. The *vox populi* is not a postmodern "text" susceptible to endless interpretations.

Our own polls further confirm this fluidity. The introduction of cost/risks demonstrated that inserting realism undermines enthusiasm. To be sure, majorities seldom became minorities, but the overall direction is unambiguous, and litanies of liabilities may well execute that majority-to-minority trick. While warnings about unanticipated budgetary overruns shifted support only modestly, mentioning nonmonetary drawbacks often proved decisive. When confronted with the possibility that many newly hired teachers would be unqualified, a mere 15 percent of previous supporters continued their endorsement. While most drops were not this sharp, smaller falloffs were common elsewhere. These were most pronounced in the daycare issue when broaching less parental choice or abolishing religious instruction.

Our experiments that offered respondents choices beyond federally funded daycare or hiring new teachers are of special political relevance. Rivals routinely outshined the widely heralded Clinton initiatives, especially when relief via the tax code was mentioned. Indeed, nearly every alternative solution on childcare was more popular than Clinton's proposal. Evidently, what is most received in the stand-alone poll is not necessarily the most preferred. Determining the public will given the multiplicity of these "most preferred" picks could prove difficult. After all, there are dozens of realistic solutions in both education and daycare. This is not to argue that these rivals, versus Clinton's proposals, should be embraced. There is no guarantee that support for these choices is any more sensible than the two less-favored proposals.

Must desires conveyed through polls be consigned to the scrap heap? Matters are a bit more complicated, and the accustomed "imprecise question elicits varied responses" verdict ignores the larger political message. A more compelling (and politically germane) read is that public appetites are contingent on multiple circumstances, most of which go unexpressed in interviews. Remember that consumer behavior is typically directed by numerous factors, and dramatically shifting behavior hardly disconfirms consumer reasonableness. Imagine that a respondent is asked about his interest in acquiring a new Mercedes for $8,000. The potential beneficiary of this great deal would surely probe further. Almost any consumer would know that $8,000 was too good to be true, so there must be a catch. Perhaps the car has been wrecked, or stolen, or too temperamental to maintain. Depending on the information given, a decision would be reached, and would vary by the respondent's circumstances (e.g., did they really need a car, was the $8,000 obtainable, and so on).

Ideal surveys would permit similar dialogues. Respondents might request time to speak with those more knowledgeable. It is not everyday that one is suddenly asked to "to buy" multibillion dollar schemes. If someone could prove that hiring thirty thousand teachers would significantly boost academic achievement without harmful side effects or unexpected costs, citizens could genuinely endorse Clinton's plan. However, even a "great deal" like this may be rejected if funds were scarce. Similarly, cheaper daycare is no bargain if one's favorite babysitter cannot be hired or Bible readings are prohibited. At least in principle, selecting a policy is comparable to shopping, but—and this is a huge "but"—the usual poll question is a very poor substitute for what is often a time-consuming, laborious process. Presenting only the tiniest fraction of the relevant information does the respondent no good, though it is a boon to the questionnaire writer wishing to shape the results.

More telling, *why* should policy consumers navigate these obstacles, if presented or, for that matter, should pollsters attempt to impose near-impossible realism? This is wholly unnecessary, if not wasteful. Surely citizens themselves are not agitating to be polled (many even refuse to participate!), to help guide government. Meanwhile, those impatient to offer wise counsel enjoy more effective alternatives—they can always hector officials or join lobbying groups. More to the point, thousands are ever willing to shoulder these intimidating tasks with the guarantee that, if they should fail, removal is quick and painless. These compliant surrogates are called "office seekers" and, if elected, enjoy innumerable advantages over ordinary citizens in grappling with policy, for example, superior resources, more time and (usually) better training. Using polling to guide policymaking is nothing more than adding something unessential in a democracy.

Instrument Capacity

Deeply imbedded in the polling industry is the idea of inevitable progress. It is seemingly moving ever closer to recovering the real public voice. However, as demographers are cautious about extrapolating today's numbers into the future, we cannot assume the poll's steady progress to the desired end. The poll's limitation are especially evident when extracting exceedingly complex social welfare choices. Save an unexpected breakthrough, this aim may be unreachable. Gloom lies at the very center of the enterprise, namely a mismatch between the survey's modest extractive capacity and the exceedingly complicated material to be ascertained.

Recall those survey devices introduced in Chapter Three—the social judgmental approach, budget pies, Contingent Valuation Methods, among others. All suffered conspicuous flaws, and have vanished entirely or exist exclusively in highly specialized enclaves. Even among aficionados, however, problems remain to be solved. At best, instruments overburden respondents with formidable instructions or require immense policy knowledge among questionnaire designers. In today's world of telephone dominated "quickie" surveys, these alternatives are even more impractical. If anything, the rush to the cheap telephone poll has moved the enterprise away from the in-depth probing so necessary to recovering complex, nuanced preferences.

Admittedly, our own foray into new and improved techniques was an imperfect venture despite greater realism. The task's innate nature, not commitment, was the obstacle. It proved difficult to create instruments to accomplish all we had hoped to and, to be frank, we often settled for a few cents on the dollar. It is still hard to see how this can be improved. The problems afflicting this extraction, such as realistically assessing willingness to pay or enduring arcane statistical risk, constitute horrendous methodological challenges. That well-funded, technically skilled economists also have struggled with these measuring variables should be kept in mind. There may be a brick wall here.

More generally, there is not enough time available for respondents (especially during telephone polls) to acquire all the information vital to formulating hard choices (not wishes). The background behind policy debates on issues like class size reduction and daycare could *never* be presented in polls, even in elaborate face-to-face interviews. Nor could we expect respondents to spend weeks carrying out tiresome library and Internet research. Without exaggeration, a fully realistic poll might last for days, and whether most respondents could acquire such information or even grasp it fully if presented, is doubtful. Nevertheless, hard choice polls demand this expertise. Interviewer dexterity or other polling trade tricks are irrelevant when faced with this dilemma. The usual poll interview is incommensurate with the task.[7]

Extracting hard choices from pop-quizlike interviews would be most effective if the respondent said, "I'm totally baffled by your inquires, but just ask my elected representative what he or she would do. That's probably okay with me, too." The task would be sensibly outsourced to full-time specialists. If this division of labor proves unsatisfactory it is still possible to vote the rascal out when disasters ensue. If the next batch of leaders likewise fails, we can keep repeating the tactic until things improve. Intelligent people take a similar stand when cold-called by shady stockbrokers. The best answer is always, "I already have a trusted broker, so no thanks." If one's broker then fails, get another.

Augmenting Democracy

Of all the justifications advanced by supporters of public opinion polling, none is more forceful than its alleged democratic role. The accurate poll, made available to the powerful and expertly interpreted by the best and the brightest is promised to be the next installment in democracy's inevitable historical triumph. Given that heeding public sentiment is a key element of "democracy" in its many definitions, this argument easily attracts converts.

At a minimum, it seems as though polling does not hurt anything. And, if dangers were present, how is one to explain the survey's soaring popularity in democratic politics?

Of course we explained our unease regarding this in Chapter Six. Even if the polls faithfully reproduced public sentiment on an issue, creating a mandate across multiple issues is perhaps impossible with only these survey data (see Riker 1988 for this quandary). Our tradeoff exercise, it will be recalled, revealed that the simple "more/same/less" menu obscures a mystifying array of dollar figures. To state that, "democracy *requires* a close connection between poll outcomes and policy" is nothing more than duplicitous rhetoric. *This cannot be done when respondents can freely pick and choose across a vast expanse of choices.* Such democratic coloration by pollsters is either naive or self-serving. One might, for good measure, also add that multiple definitions of democracy exist, and faithfully heeding public sentiment is not the common thread. In fact, the public itself has not requested this "improvement," so if we were to heed public opinion we would have to reject government by *vox populi.* If these popular intrusions were so welcome, how is one to explain low turnouts in initiatives?

Pollster unaccountability is another democratic complication. Making survey advice authoritative takes power away from elected officials. With public debate framed by polls, murky choices regarding questionnaire design, sampling, terminology and all else regarding survey technique becomes a political act. Antipathy toward poll results show public support for endless entitlements might read as mean-spirited, even a tad "undemocratic." How is one to oppose beguiling nostrums "nearly everyone" wants? Rejoinders that poll questions are inattentive to risk or offer unrealistic seductions might be dismissed as mere caviling or an abandonment of "responsibility." Worse, as our own data hint, basing rejoinders to certified public poll pronouncements upon technical details plays poorly in Peoria.

This political power shift is not limited to usurping the duly elected. Reality itself may be subverted if the artful pollster can transform a policy disaster into victory. This is not as preposterous as it might seem. A blizzard of high-profile government education initiatives might all fail, but subsequent polls (all mysteriously interpreted behind closed doors) might nevertheless find that more people now believe that education has "improved." After all, are we not "moving forward" and "addressing the problem"? Success has become "beliefs about success" as expertly certified by the survey. The publicized poll and public relations become indistinguishable. Recollect how Clinton's supporters repeatedly pointed to high approval ratings (among other helpful survey tidbits) during the president's impeachment trial as "proof" of his worthiness. Tales of would-be candidates quickly dropping out of the race due to dismal poll showings are many. Who would fund office seekers with single digit poll ratings? In a phrase, polls create a powerful virtual reality.

Most evidently, those responsible for terrible poll counsel cannot be removed from their positions as one might evict blundering officials. The capacity to punish incompetence is no trifling matter; it is *absolutely* essential for democracy. Federal judges with lifetime tenure are more accountable than obscure technicians in the bowels of barely known organizations. Who ever heard of a pollster being punished for ambiguous questions leading elected leaders astray? Recall from chapter one how factually erroneous polls about the Panama Canal Treaty infiltrated legislative debate (Smith and Hogan 1987). This is more than just the blind leading the blind—if such "advice" is given credence, it may bring a reign of error. Interestingly, this accountability is standard in commercial relationships. Woe to the firm providing disastrous marketing advice. Misinforming one's client that Americans dislike four-door minivans is serious business for one's future livelihood;[8] notifying elected officials of strong public support to hire more grade school teachers is, by contrast, personally inconsequential.

Accountability is further undermined by the multiplicity of voices claiming genuine authority. Pinning blame (or credit) is already difficult in our system of dispersed authority, but imagine leaders heeding multiple and conflicting polls. Under such confused circumstances "authority" may well derive from the sheer power of publicity. The highly respected *New York Times* necessarily speaks louder than a group like the National Taxpayers Union releasing contrary poll results. Similarly, eye-catching, easy-to-grasp survey outcomes can easily eclipse more complicated findings, even among sophisticated leaders.

Who is sufficiently trustworthy for this momentous task? Every survey involves hundreds of technical considerations, and the most innocuous can be politically consequential. Blatant bias may be invisible to the uninitiated, particularly when it masquerades as a professional, technical consensus. It is likewise unsettled whether the *vox populi* can be monitored by private, for-profit companies eyeing expenses. In addition, awarding government funding to insure quality raises nightmarish conflicts of interest.

Our greatest fear, however, is the quiet subversion of constitutional safeguards. If a resurrected Madison heard all this poll-driven democratic marching orders prattle, he'd roll over in his grave. He'd assuredly describe this modern impulse as arousing dangerous passions, not requesting reasoned judgment. Recollect that the constitutional order imposes dispersed power;

agreements must be fashioned across multiple, often antagonistic, constituencies. It purposely encourages gridlock. Though often exceedingly frustrating to some, this venerable arrangement is less designed to protect the status quo (regardless of ideological content) than to safeguard liberty. It is a praiseworthy bargain between accomplishment and insulation against tyranny. To say that the public opinion expressed via polls is the long-awaited solution to overcome this lamentable gridlock reveals a profound political misunderstanding. Let us not conflate the hype from the poll industry with solid constitutional doctrine.

What Is To Be Done?

Today's infatuation with the *vox populi* is surely impervious to our arguments. Provided our office seekers are anxious to enchant citizens, polls will entice citizens to express their wishes, no matter how unrealistic. Perhaps only government regulation might reverse this unfortunate inclination, and these intrusions are deservedly unthinkable. For Washington bureaucrats to meddle, as they now license TV and radio, is a cure infinitely worse than the disorder. Even if the Federal Communication Commission did legally demand poll "honesty," regulations would almost certainly cover only superficial details—labeling rules regarding sample size, dates, poll sponsorship, and similar issues of disclosure. Imagine if an agency demanded that pollsters include costs and drawbacks in their descriptions of proposals? The protests would be loud and energetic, and rightly so. Nor, by the same token, might we expect pollsters impose self-restraint-much like the way Hollywood "voluntarily" rates its films to preempt more government interference. Polling is not under scrutiny like the tobacco or handgun industries. The issuing of polls depicting rapacious (and expensive) public desires will endure.

Pessimism equally applies to practitioners mending their ways and asking more hardheaded questions. Oscar Wilde once quipped that Socialism will never work—it takes too many evenings. It is the same for tediously extracting hard choices from an ill-equipped public. Practitioners are justifiably disinclined to expand terse interviews into information rich dialogues. Closely scanning the public mind (as we have done) requires resource commitments unnecessary in today's academic and mass media settings. Why add substantial costs if the product is already acceptable? Polling is unlike commodities trading where slight mathematical model imperfections invite bankruptcy. Those commissioning or buying public policy poll results lack a compelling motivation for guaranteeing political relevance. Conforming to modest industry-wide methodological standards is sufficient.

Present-day academic irresponsibility for passing off polls as worthy deserves a special mention. Here, at least in principle, a deeper duty to escape hazy flimsy information would be expected. Professors are hardly obligated to concoct news, when none is evident, or spin the data for appreciative benefactors. Surely analysts must realize that these foggy top-of-the-head sentiments gathered in polls can never constitute sound counsel. Does any sensible public opinion expert honestly believe that citizens typically know much of anything about issues that befuddle experienced lawmakers? One cannot extract blood from a turnip, even with powerful high-tech instruments. Unfortunately, such data continue to be taken at face value.

As chapter one confessed, we cannot peek into the hearts and minds of those embracing the *vox populi's* appetites. Only speculation is possible. If one hazarded a guess, however, it is that these practitioners and academics fashioning the poll created *Weltanschauung* welcome these expanding federal entitlements. It is not malicious bias; it is an easygoing acceptance of agreeable findings. That majorities crave government generosity for medical care, education, relieving poverty and all else is "natural" in settings where modern liberalism is *de rigueur.* Bigger government thus passes unnoticed, a fate distinctly different from when the public expresses ill-liberal views on, say, race relations or homosexuality.

Since today's pollsters will not mend their ways, the only sensible response is to generate a "counterliterature." Its purpose would *not* be to argue against today's standard wisdom, namely, that majorities favor growing entitlements. One should not fight bias with bias, no matter how artfully this one-sidedness is dressed up in technical verbiage. Instead, polls would simply confirm what we have demonstrated here, that the public is uncertain about such dilemmas as educational reform or federal daycare assistance. Poll responses are, predictably, shaped by information regarding costs, risks, tradeoffs, and all the other ingredients inherent in reasonable decisions.[9] And when these facts add up to a less-than-enticing proposition, the public clamor cools.

This proposal hardly attempts to push the polling industry—both commercial and academic divisions—into the dustbin of history. These social welfare enticements comprise only a tiny portion of the polling agenda, and if they vanished tomorrow, their disappearance would pass largely unnoticed. Other newsworthy probes would surely take their place and everyone, from mass media client to academic data cruncher, would be happy. If pollsters refused to repent, at least they could honestly label these data as public "hopes" or "wishes." In fact, if our admonitions about inserting realism into entitlement wants were heeded, this might be a godsend to all parties. For the for-hire practitioner, this expensive new polling process would justify higher client fees, while new technical rigorousness might well enhance the pollster's scientific prestige. In addition, those academics on the verge of exhausting available public data sets will enjoy fresh technical frontiers to conquer. Judged by the problems that await them in accurately extracting hard choices, this task may provide gainful employment until the next millennium.

The ultimate goal, however, is not reforming a polling industry still swayed by George Gallup's plebiscitory vision. We have no qualms with the thousands of garden-variety polls cataloguing the public's moral judgments, idealizations, beliefs, and all else that is strictly a matter of opinion. In short, public opinion should be about opinion, not advice giving. Democratic governance is our concern. Infusing our discourse has been a desire to see citizens *controlling* government, not dictating policy. The two are not interchangeable. Nor is direct citizen policy-making the proper historical evolution of elections. Achieving popular control is not rocket science: it already exists (though less than perfectly) thanks to our constitutional and two hundred years of practical innovation. Elections are the mighty vehicle of this control. Polls certainly have their estimable place in civic life, but to insist that they should guide government on extremely complex issues much more than it could ever help.

APPENDIX

The Daycare Questionnaire

Introduction

Hello, my name is (NAME), from The Angus Reid Group, a national market research company. We want to assure you we are not selling anything and are only interested in your opinions. For this short study we are speaking to Americans of voting age. Are you 18 years of age or older?

IF NO, ASK TO SPEAK WITH SOMEONE WHO IS, REPEAT INTRO/ WATCH QUOTAS/SKIP TO SCREENER B. IF NOT AVAILABLE, ARRANGE CALLBACK—RECORD DETAILS

IF YES, WATCH QUOTAS/SKIP TO SCREENER Q.B

WHEN TARGET RESPONDENT IS NOT AVAILABLE: RECORD TIME, DAY AND DATE OF CONVENIENT TIME TO CALLBACK AND FIRST NAME OF DESIGNATED RESPONDENT. (MAKE 2 ATTEMPTS TO INTERVIEW DESIGNATED RESPONDENT. IF NOT AVAILABLE AFTER 2 ATTEMPTS, DISCONTINUE AND TALLY. GO ON TO NEXT PHONE CALL.)

B. For classification purposes only, what is your age, are you .... READ LIST. RECORD ONE ANSWER ONLY.

[DO NOT READ] Under 18 [disqualify]

18–24
25–34
35–44
45–54
55–64
65 and over

[DO NOT READ] REFUSED [disqualify]
[IF REFUSED or UNDER 18, DISCONTINUE. ALL OTHERS CONTINUE.]
[NOTE TO FIELD: WATCH AGE QUOTAS]

C. AREA
New England [**NORTH EAST**]
Middle Atlantic [**NORTH EAST**]
East North Central [**NORTH CENTRAL**]
West North Central [**NORTH CENTRAL**]
South Atlantic [**SOUTH**]
East South Central [**SOUTH**]
West South Central [**SOUTH**]
Mountain [**WEST**]
Pacific [**WEST**]

[NOTE TO FIELD: WATCH REGION QUOTAS—QUOTAS APPLIED ON
FOUR MAJOR CENSUS REGIONS—BOTH TO BE RECORDED]

INTERVIEWER TO RECORD SEX
Male
Female
[NOTE TO FIELD: WATCH SEX QUOTAS.]

We would like to ask you about your opinions on politics and current events. In particular, we would like to hear your opinions on child care.

1. First, do you have any children under 12 years old in your household?

Yes
No
Refused

Baseline

[ASK ALL]

2. Do you think the federal government should spend more, less or the same amount of money on child care programs for low-income and working parents, or don't you think the federal government should play a role here at all?

More
Less
The Same
Government should not play a role
[DO NOT READ] No opinion/nothing/DK/Refused

Competence
"Easy question" and estimated costs

3. President Clinton has proposed having the federal government spend $22 billion over five years for a new federal daycare program. The program would benefit up to 8 million families. Do you strongly support, somewhat support, somewhat oppose or strongly oppose this proposal?

Strongly support
Somewhat support
Somewhat oppose
Strongly oppose
[DO NOT READ] Not sure/depends
[DO NOT READ] Refused

[ASK ALL]

4. The proposed daycare program will cost $22 billion over five years.

How much do you think this program would cost the average taxpayer each year?

[PROBE—"we are just looking for your best guess of the **national average**"]
[RECORD EXACT DOLLAR AMOUNT VERBATIM]

[ASK ALL]

5. As you know, there is only so much money to go around and choices have to be made on how best to spend taxpayer money. Suppose you were in Congress and your task was to decide how to divide **20 billion dollars** between several options: education, fighting crime, daycare, national defense and cutting taxes.

[READ LIST][ROTATE]
How much would spend on [ITEM]?
And how much would you spend on [ITEM]?

daycare
education
fighting crime
national defense
cutting taxes

[DO NOT READ] DK
[DO NOT READ] INCOMPLETE/CONFUSED/REFUSED
[ONLY IF RESPONDENTS INQUIRE: INDICATE TOTAL DOLLARS
  SPENT—DO NOT PROMPT]
[NOTE: THE TOTAL **NEED NOT** EQUAL 20 billion dollars—the purpose is not to force respondent choice into the total]
[NOTE: **ALLOW** DKs and INCOMPLETES BUT TALLY]

[ASK RESPONDENTS CODED 2 OR 9 IN Q.1]

6. How much tax money a year would you, personally, be willing to pay so that families with children under 12 could receive more federal subsidized childcare?

[PROBE—"we are just looking for an estimate"]
[RECORD EXACT DOLLAR AMOUNT VERBATIM; if 'nothing' enter 0]

[ASK RESPONDENTS CODED 1 IN Q.1]

7. Would you be willing to raise your own federal income taxes say $40 a year to fund government subsidized daycare for your children or would you just prefer to have the money to spend anyway you want? [RECORD ONE ANSWER ONLY]

Yes
No
DK/Refused

[ASK ALL]

8. President Clinton's daycare proposal has drawn some criticism. Can you think of any reason—**other than cost**—why a person might oppose this plan?

[DO NOT READ LIST]
There are other priorities for the government
Families should look after their own expenses
Daycare is not helpful for families
The government would have too much influence
Too much debt in government
Government too large/too many programs already
No reasons but cost
None/No reasons/nothing
9. OTHER [SPECIFY]

[ASK ALL]

9. Federal government subsidized daycare is one of many ways to help families with raising children. Here are some other possibilities for improving childcare. For each one of these options, please tell me which ones you think should be tried. **Choose as many as you like.**

Should we... [READ LIST] [ROTATE]:

Lower taxes so parents are responsible for their daycare expenses?
Establish national, government-run daycare centers, required for all children?
Expand public schools so that they can also offer free daycare?
Provide more money to government agencies to enforce laws regarding home childcare?
Give parents larger tax deductions for daycare expenses?
Create a national parents training program?
Make it easier to remove children from their home if parents are inadequate?
Create national standards for how parents raise their children?

Have the federal government pay all daycare providers directly as they now pay government employees?
Make quality daycare a constitutionally protected right for all citizens?

YES
NO
[DO NOT READ] DK/REFUSED

Costs and Preferences

[NOTE: RESPONDENTS ARE ASKED *ONE* OF 10, 11 OR 12; ONLY RESPONDENTS CODES 1,2 AT Q.3]

[ASK ONLY OF CODES 1,2 AT Q.3]

Net cost per taxpayer

10. You mentioned that you [ANSWER AT Q.3] the proposed daycare program. If enacted, this daycare program would add approximately 36 dollars per year to the average tax return.

Do you still support this program?

YES [SKIP TO Q.13]
NO [SKIP TO Q.13]
DK/REFUSED [SKIP TO Q.13]
[PROBE—IF RESPONDENT HESITATES, REPEAT FIRST TWO SENTENCES OF Q.3]

Marginal tax increase

[ASK ONLY OF CODES 1,2 AT Q.3]

11. You mentioned that you [ANSWER AT Q.3] the proposed daycare program. If enacted, this would increase the average tax bill from $6832 to $6868.

Do you still support this program?
YES [SKIP TO Q.13]
NO [SKIP TO Q.13]
DK/REFUSED [SKIP TO Q.13]

[PROBE—IF RESPONDENT HESITATES, REPEAT FIRST TWO SENTENCES OF Q.3]

One more program on top of all the others

[ASK ONLY OF CODES 1,2 AT Q.3]

12. You mentioned that you [ANSWER AT Q.3] the proposed daycare program. Both the national government and the states already have multi-billion dollars daycare assistance programs, especially for the poor and disadvantaged.

Do you still support the new program?
YES [CONTINUE]
NO [CONTINUE]
DK/REFUSED [CONTINUE]
[PROBE—IF RESPONDENT HESITATES, REPEAT FIRST TWO SENTENCES OF Q.3]

Support when considering possible downside

[ASK ALL CODES 1,2 AT Q.3]

13. President Clinton's daycare proposal has been criticized on non-cost grounds. Would you support this program if there were a *reasonable* chance that this federal assistance would:

[READ ITEM] [ROTATE]
Would you support if it might [READ ITEM]?
reduce the daycare options available to parents
put out of business small, independent neighborhood programs
reduce parental control over how daycare are run
encourage non-working parents to take jobs
make it difficult for daycare centers to offer religious activities
increase the authority of the federal government at the expense of
state officials

YES
NO
[DO NOT READ] DK/REFUSED

[IF RESPONDENT ASKS, A REASONABLE CHANCE IS 50%]

Non-governmental alternatives

14. President Clinton's federal assistance is one way that the government can assist parents needing additional child care help. I am now going to read you a list of other proposals to assist families with children. Please tell me whether you think they are **better** or **worse** than the proposal to spend 22 billion on a new childcare program.

[ROTATE]

[READ ITEM] Is this a better or worse idea than the childcare proposal?
reducing taxes so people have more discretionary income
increasing the tax deduction of parents for childcare expenses
eliminating government rules to facilitate more low-cost options for childcare
giving businesses incentives to provide workers with childcare
permit parents greater freedom to hire childcare help from overseas

Better
Worse
[DO NOT READ] The Same/DK
[DO NOT READ] Refused

NOTE: CODE REFUSALS SEPARATE FROM DKs

[ASK ALL]
Demographics
Now I have just a few more questions for classification purposes only.

Marital Status

15. What is your marital status? Are you...? [READ LIST. RECORD ONE ANSWER ONLY.]

Single
Married
Living common-law
Divorced or separated
Widowed
[DO NOT READ] Refused

Education

16. What is the highest level of education you have completed? [READ LIST. RECORD ONE ANSWER ONLY.]

Some High School or Less
High School Graduate
A Technical Diploma
Some College
College Graduate
Post Graduate Degree
[DO NOT READ] REFUSED

Occupation

17. Which of the following best describes your current employment situation? [READ LIST. RECORD ONE ANSWER ONLY.]

Work full-time (30 hours or more per week)
Work part-time (less than 30 hours per week)
Self-Employed
Full time homemaker
Student
Retired

Unemployed and not looking for work
Unemployed and looking for work
[DO NOT READ] REFUSED

Income

18. Which of the following categories best represents your total household income last year before taxes? Just stop me when I reach the proper category. [READ LIST]

Less than $20,000
$20,000 to under $30,000
$30,000 to under $40,000
$40,000 to under $50,000
$50,000 to under $60,000
$60,000 to under $70,000
$70,000 to under $80,000
$80,000 to under $90,000
$90,000 to under $100,000
$100,000 or more
[DO NOT READ] Refused
[DO NOT READ] DK

Race

19. In which of the following groups would you place yourself? [READ LIST. RECORD ONE ANSWER ONLY.]

White or Caucasian
Black or African American
Asian, Oriental or Pacific Islander
Native American or American Indian
Other (specify)
[DO NOT READ] Refused

20. And, are you of Hispanic or Latino origin? [DO NOT READ LIST]

Yes
No
Refused

THANK AND CONCLUDE INTERVIEW:

TIME STARTED:

TIME ENDED:

TOTAL TIME:

Notes

1 Public Opinion, Polling, and Politics

1. Richard Wirthlin who ran these polls also developed a "speech pulse" technique by which respondents could indicate exactly which words and phrases of the president's speech evoked positive or negative reactions. Speeches could thus be fine-tuned, with "bad" ideas eliminated and "good" phrases recycled.

2. Verba's speech is remarkable for its painless conflation of politics with empirical social science, a merging once virtually unthinkable in a discipline supposedly priding itself on dispassionate objective inquiry. Here, the adroit sampler differs not from the get-out-the-vote partisan activist. By pleading for more inclusiveness in the sample and raising the survey up as the supreme voice of popular sovereignty, Verba *de facto* advances aggrandizing the welfare state. It would be a miracle if these freshly recruited, once ignored respondents did not insist on more government programs to help the downtrodden. His views on the social scientist as the handmaiden of enlightened democracy ironically recall "old-fashioned" normative political science.

3. Those unfamiliar with political science as a discipline may not appreciate the significance of Brady's words. That this paean appeared in *PS* (the official journal of the American Political Science Association) suggests an almost official certification of this idea within the profession. Brady also acknowledges the help of several disciplinary notables in crafting this essay, further credence to the idea that this "polls-assist-democracy" relationship is now disciplinary dogma.

4. Organizations advocating reduced welfare spending are obscure players in poll-driven public discourse, but they do exist. Predictably given question drafting leeway, these results paint a picture quite different from the more familiar "we-want-it-all" outcomes offered by mainstream polling organizations. Over the years, for example, polls sponsored by the National Taxpayers Union find widespread public resistance to tax hikes to expand entitlement programs. Repeatedly, citizens here favor rolling back the Welfare State, for example, constitutionally imposed spending limits. In principle, this is the identical public who elsewhere clamors for big government.

5. Our argument is essentially indirect—the poll-fabricated consensus defines policy "reasonableness." A stronger argument would show that these polls *physically*

infiltrate decision making and are carefully heeded, if not decisive. A superb investigation of the survey's roll in foreign policy during the 1970s and 1980s strongly suggest this more direct impact. Robert Mattes (1992, especially Chapters Six and Seven) recounts that all presidents during this period spent lavishly on polling, and these results daily accompanied specific policy recommendations. Top officials also sought these data, sending aides daily to the White House to obtain this information. More telling, poll results were absolutely integral to executive branch and legislative debates, often being decisive in close, contentious situations. Here officials used polls to calculate damage control for taking controversial stands. Repeatedly, few public figures evidenced a "Profiles in Courage" willingness to buck poll delineated majority sentiment. Of course, whether this tendency strictly applies to social welfare is an empirical matter. Still, we suspect that hefty majorities on matters such as Social Security or childcare easily cower doubters.

6. A particularly important aspect of this agenda-building lies within the polls conducted by government agencies that rarely see the light of day. This can sometimes be viewed as "test marketing" public policies. Brehm's (1993, 8–12) overview of government run poll finds that in Fiscal Year 1991, the government itself conducted some 1.5 million interviews. Some were directed on behest of congressional committees looking into specific problems. How these polls shaped legislative initiatives is, unfortunately, unknown.

7. Creating this putative entitlement consensus often occurs via selectively publicizing polls that, predictably, reveal public desires for Washington supplied "good things." For example, a November 15, 1999 *New York Times* op-ed column by Princeton University professor Sean Wilentz asserts that the public appetite in the 1960s for expansive social welfare has returned (if it vanished at all) despite all the government cutbacks and downsizing talk. Data from two polls are tersely noted yet, says Wilentz, the evidence shows that politics "… is moving for universal health care and federal financing to hire 100,000 new teachers." These well-hidden data are evidently deemed authoritative. Liberalism is back, moreover, despite contrary signs—even welfare cutbacks demonstrate this resurgent liberalism for these prove that government can be effective. The Reagan-Bush era is over, concludes, Wilentz ("For Voters the 1960s Never Died," *New York Times*, November 16, 1999). By contrast, a National Taxpayer Union poll conducted almost simultaneously reports that a majority of voters want the federal budget slashed by at least 5 percent. (http:www.ntu.org/P9911newspendingpoll.htm). Both polls are suspect, no doubt, but what is notable is that the prowelfare poll-based story reached a huge audience via the prestigious *Times,* while the NTU was distributed largely to conservative cognoscenti.

2 From Wishes to Hard Choices

1. Our discussion obviously simplifies the immense obstacles that inhere in translating individual preferences into collective choices in institutional settings with

varied rules. Analysts with a mathematical bent have shown that the possible nonobvious outcomes abound, especially where actor preferences are not strictly orderly. Our point is the very modest one that institutional outcomes are not mere aggregations of individual first choices.

2. In 1995, the per capita state and local tax burden for education was $1006 (*U.S. Statistical Abstract 1998*, Table 500). What the precise percentage figure was in 1999, when the poll was conducted, is unknown at this moment, but 50 percent hike for education seems plausible. This poll was sponsored by National Public Radio, the Kennedy School of Government, Harvard University, and the Henry J. Kaiser Family Foundation, all organizations capable of doing the simple arithmetic. One might hypothesize that withholding the baseline figures had more to do with soliciting this generosity than technical insufficiency.

3. The strategy adopted by Wilson (1983) takes this approach. Citizens in two cities were quizzed regarding expanding services. Only after stating their position was the payment issue raised. Most citizens were consistent and thus received the label "sincere." Obviously, however, a gap still remains between verbal support and writing the check.

4. This connection between the proliferation of surveys and the legitimization of participatory democracy can be reversed: polling reduces citizens to passive spectators cheering on factions within government. Simple-minded answers to simple questions replace serious public discourse. The poll is thus an easy escape from more demanding citizenship responsibilities. This argument is developed in detail by Dryzek (1988), and we shall return to it in Chapter 5.

3 Civic Competence

1. Educators, predictably, have sought to associate virtually every type of instruction with "civic competence." One listing includes ecological attentiveness, awareness of global issues, familiarity with social problems, being a skilled consumer, knowing how to act morally, participating in social change, possessing critical skills, and being patriotic, among other virtues (Remy and Turner 1979). Morse (1989) would add a faculty for talking, judgmental capacity, the courage to act, and a knack for reflection, among others. Without doubt, a careful compilation of such admonishments might well exceed a hundred "worthy" traits essential for civic competence.

2. As this Converse-influenced literature developed, multiple terms were employed to capture cognitive dexterity: ideological thinking, rationality, political sophistication, and the like. Clearly, terminological distinctions here are important, but for the present, we can assume that all centrally touch on "civic capacity."

3. A notable example of this tenacious conflation of structure with dexterity can be found in Gastil and Dillard (1999). What makes this exemplar remarkable is that it commences with the question of whether bringing citizens together for an information-intensive series of assemblies (the so-called Deliberative Poll) will

yield "... better public decisions" (3). And how is this "better" assessed? The answer is by examining the interconnectedness and differentiation of resultant, post discussion preferences. In other words, the statistical form of one's views is, definitionally, equated with good judgment. Logically, this is a non sequitur. We offer this exemplar only to illustrate that thirty-five years of post-Converse scholarly rumination does not guarantee thoughtfulness.

4. Justifying this joining of Medicare, education, and highways into one question receives only a few Appendix lines plus a footnote sentence. It inescapably seems *ad hoc* (the chief rationale seems that all involve lots of money). Needless to say, each policy represents distinct constituencies, and positions on one need not predict stands elsewhere. Indeed, highways and education may itself be a tradeoff. Remarkably, thousands of words explore methodological nuances, while actual policy choices are nearly neglected entirely. Recall earlier comments regarding pollster familiarity with real world politics.

5. A further complication is that we do not know the amounts involved in these spend-cut exercises. What may appear entirely logical may, in fact, be nonsensical if the dollar amounts do not balance. For example, cutting defense by a dollar and rising social spending by ten dollars hardly demonstrates "competence" yet this would be construed as such in this research design.

6. We should likewise reiterate that in those few polls where shouldering a tax burden is seemingly assessed, the questionnaire masks what it truly being solicited. Recall Chapter Two's examples whereby majorities "agree" to pay $500 a year more in local taxes for improved education. This would be approximately a 50 percent increase per capita in education spending, a message hardly drawing even the most proeducation office seekers. Shades of the "pennies-per-day" tactic to fleece the gullible.

7. A remarkable feature of this analysis is its neglect of hard data on tax referenda. Here the public clearly has an opportunity to increase its tax burden and, as it is well known, the collective answer is often "no." Recent research relating voting to budgetary expansion also cautions us against a picture of public generosity. Peltzman (1998, ch. 5) in his analysis of both national and state data from 1950 to 1988 finds that incumbents at both levels are electorally punished for expanding government spending. This is particularly true for social welfare spending. Of course, there is no inherent contradiction here since the voting and the public opinion universe are not identical.

8. The effort here to let people escape the onus of ignorance is ingenious. In one chain of reasoning, cognitive skills are depicted as a function of education and this, in tern, is said to be determined by cultural and structural factors (271). This casual linkage is patently open to multiple, and far more plausible interpretations—for example, educational attainment flows from native ability and cannot be boosted by cultural manipulation (an interpretation on which substantial hard empirical evidence exists). The important point is that this rush to flattering judgment almost unthinkingly disregards credible rival hypotheses. This issue of conquering civic incompetence via remediation will be discussed at length in Chapter Six.

9. Delli Carpini and Keeter's odd reasoning is hardly unique. Verba, Scholozman and Brady (1995, ch. 11) take a similar approach to civic skill—individual capacity is merely a function of access to resources. Those at the bottom are there *only* because they have limited access to skills such as language proficiency, job-related expertise, or organizational membership. Being proficient thus resembles shopping—if you want a product you have to go where the product is available, and anybody can acquire the goods if they only know where to shop and have the money. Logically, then, inserting the untalented into an environment awash with enrichment would do the equalizing trick. Untold educational failures speak loudly to the foolishness of this reasoning.

10. Contrast this social policy resourcefulness to similarly ascertained race-related opinions. Here "bad opinions," that is, negative views of blacks, are reactively dismissed as defective, nonrational, and even a sign of mental illness. Imagine the outcry if researchers sought to redeem these disapproving views as investigators now rescue cravings for social welfare enhancement.

11. It is exceedingly difficult in today's contented environment to affirm the greatness of this loyalty and legal obedience accomplishment. To appreciate it fully, one is well advised to read early critics of Republicanism for they assumed, with ample reason that a Republic such as ours could not count on the affection of citizens. For them, only the glory of a monarchy or force could bind citizens to a government of humdrum men like themselves. It was asserted that such a Republic would inevitably degenerate into anarchy (see Wood 1969, 65–70, for this account).

4 Public Opinion I: Policies and Questions

1. While the Tennessee experiment (Student–Teacher Achievement Ratio, or "STAR" in acronym language) is always heralded as the Great Hope, skeptical studies have been relegated to academic obscurity. Among other STAR study deficiencies, each grade had a 20 to 30 percent drop out rate, often concentrated among lower performing students; no pretests were used to establish a legitimate benchmark to assess future test score gain; and neither the schools or classrooms were selected randomly. Teachers and administrators also were given incentives for increased performance. Mention should also be made of pundits who have conflated "statistical significance" with "educationally significant" (see Hanushek 1999 and Hoxby 1999 for an overview of these limitations).

2. Lurking below the surface in these discussions is the touchy issue of student discipline. It is difficult to teach effectively if students run wild. This fact may well explain why students in Japan or Korea excel in classes of forty-five plus students—they are better behaved. Unfortunately, disciplining miscreants is a "hot button" political issue given commonplace disparities across different groups.

3. The escalation of costs is seldom grasped by smaller class advocates. Harvard economics professor Caroline Hoxby (1999) finds that costs and class size tend to be proportional across the entire range. To reduce classes from twenty pupils

to eighteen, raises costs ten percent; going from ten to nine similarly adds a ten percent increase. In other words, the marginal cost of each reduction grows as class size diminishes.

4. The hidden heavy burdens on inner-city schools are easily swept aside in this rush for a miracle cure. Not only are construction costs exceedingly high here (and these include extra security measures), but teacher salaries must also be larger to reflect cost-of-living differences and physical riskiness. In one 1984 survey of Los Angeles teachers, some forty percent indicated that they would resign rather than accept an inner-city school assignment in a dangerous neighborhood (cited in Ross 1999). A detailed analysis of classroom size reduction in California reports that poorer school districts cannibalize other remedial programs to free up funds to reduce student–teacher ratios (Stecher and Bohrnstedt 1999). Simply allocating funds according to poverty levels does not capture this gap since many impoverished areas are lower-cost rural localities. Again, Clinton's assistance plan is little more than a gesture and may well nourish appetites for vastly greater outlays.

5. An especially troubling question concerns administrative flexibility. If the class ratio is legally mandated at, say, 18 : 1, and the class has eighteen students, and a single new student arrives, must an entire new class be created? This may entail additional construction and hiring a new teacher, all for a single student! Local administrators might also quietly manipulate district boundaries or how students are classified to secure federal funds.

6. Our analysis does not intend to equate "uncertified teacher" with "bad teacher." In fact, it is often argued that the certification process itself, with its emphasis on irrelevant pedagogical theory, often discourages good instructors from education careers. Still, it is doubtlessly risky to suddenly open the schoolhouse doors to those who would not otherwise prefer teaching jobs.

7. For example, classroom size can be artificially reduced by reclassifying administrators or paraprofessionals as teachers or mixing in highly specialized small-scale instruction with normal education. Some Massachusetts school districts solved the space limitation by dividing classes in half with coteachers. Minnesota has attempted to address the lure of chicanery with strict definitions of "teacher," but, interestingly, it still allows social workers to be counted in teacher/student ratios. A few legislators have even coined the term "class-size police" in this uproar over student–teacher ratios. The important point is that fakery is not unknown in educational data, and it would surely be encouraged if funds were narrowly tied to usage and performance.

8. In fact, a 1998 Phi Delta Kappa/Gallup poll asked respondents to choose *one* item from an array of twelve that would best improve schools in their community. "More teachers" received the endorsement of 10 percent of the respondents as the first choice. "Stricter discipline" was slightly more popular but no one idea received majority endorsement.

9. Official Census data collected in 1993 showed that monthly cost varied by income group, with those below the poverty line spending 17.7 of their monthly income on child care; only those with incomes below $1,200 spent a quarter of their

income on childcare, the highest percentage. The average was 7.5 percent but, and this is critical, 61 percent of those with incomes below $1,200 received childcare *without* any payment (figures are from "Greenbook" 1998, 671).

10. Research on daycare is predictably highly politicized and the same "facts" can be given entirely different meanings. Much depends on assumptions regarding "good" social policy, for example, whether it is indeed admirable to encourage more women to enter the workforce or to stay at home. Our analysis, admittedly, stresses government-funded daycare's possible drawbacks, given that such consideration is absent in polls. For an account that stresses the positive side of government intervention, especially assistance directed by professionals, see the articles in "The Silent Crisis in U.S. Child Care" 1999, *The Annals of the American Academy of Political and Social Science"* ed. Suzanne W. Helburn 563: 8–219. Note the term "silent" in the title, a descriptor suggesting public indifference to this "crisis."

11. The federal government's own Consumer Price Index data for urban areas showed that between 1982/84 and 1997, the price of daycare and nursery school rose some 34 percent compared to 60 percent for all items. In particular, daycare increases lagged far behind food, housing and medical care (*U.S. Statistical Abstract 1998,* Table 773).

12. Indeed, recall that in 1993 about 60 percent of the very poor paid *nothing* for their childcare, although we must be cautious that such reports may reflect a fear of the IRS or represents a bartered exchange of services (data are from "Greenbook" 1998, 671).

13. As in the classroom size issue, the underlying science here is uncertain. Day care professionals insist that their version of "quality" impacts positively on children. The evidence is, alas, not nearly as conclusive. Consider the by-now well-demonstrated fact that intensive early intervention programs like Head Start do not produce the hoped for long-term cognitive gains among the economically dis-advantaged. The issue is not one of daycare versus no daycare but what, exactly, should this intervention entail (some of these impact data are summarized in Olsen 1997).

14. This religious issue in government subsidized daycare is a legal nightmare waiting to happen. No doubt, untold popular daycare center activities might be viewed as "religious" by those insisting on strict church-state separation, for example, celebrating Christmas or before meal prayers. The comingling of funds—as when the minister also serves as a childcare administrator—might also prove troublesome in a court case. Under Public Law 104-103, this issue is partially sidestepped by permitting religious training if the funds come from parents, not the state directly. Uncertainty abounds here and at least some religion-based childcare centers have mixed emotions about greater federal aid (see Davis 1994).

15. The ripple effects of government required "quality" can be surprising. For example, "quality" almost always means larger enterprises, and these may collide with zoning restrictions against businesses in residential areas, hardly a trivial fact for

the poor needing close-at-hand assistance. Size also means required compliance with numerous employment rules that hinder scheduling flexibility, another relevant factor for single parents and the working poor. Again, the convenient, sympathetic relative may be the superior choice though this option is deplored by professionals.

16. The public, in fact, seems to be of a divided mind when this " biological family knows best" issue is interjected in the debate. On the one hand, government financial assistance for daycare is immensely popular. On the other hand, according to January 1, 1999 Lou Harris poll, only 15 percent favored giving government primary responsibility in ensuring family access to childcare. Sixty percent said "families themselves" while another 23 percent said employers. Even more troubling to advocates of government assisted daycare, an October 1999 Princeton Survey Research/Pew poll found an overwhelming majority endorsing the proposition that "too many children are being raised these days in daycare centers these days." Perhaps the term "ambivalent" is best applied to this situation (though some might also add "guilty" to this mood).

17. The family financial hardships of returning to a single breadwinner family are deceptively complicated. Over and above childcare expenses, working entails many other costs (e.g., clothing, transportation) and some of the income loss is made up by lowered taxes. For a parent to quit the workforce due to lack of available low-cost daycare may not therefore be as financially burdensome as imagined. The choice to work also can transcend monetary calculations and thus may be pursed regardless of daycare expenses.

18. Although the Angus Reid Group is relatively unknown to those working with off-the-shelf political data sets, it is a major worldwide survey firm doing in 1999 some $50 million in bookings. It also has conducted academic surveys and, as a matter of policy, does not perform "political polls."

5 Public Opinion II: Fervent Desires

1. The education questions concerned hiring thirty thousand teachers in grades 1–3 and drew a figure of 83 percent in favor. The childcare question was the traditional "more/same/less" type. Here, 53 percent favored more federal money, 4 percent less, 19 percent the same, and 20 percent stating that the federal government should not play a role. The data come from the national Angus Reid "Express" poll conducted March 3–5, 2000.

2. Analysis emphasizes competency among those supporting the Clinton initiative, but we certainly do not imply that opponents are thereby excused from these requirements. Rejecting entitlement lures is hardly a sign of greater wisdom. As we shall see, policy proficiency differences between supporters and opponents tend to be modest and nonsystematic.

3. This figure was arrived at by estimating the number of future individual income tax return at 120,000,000. The most recent exact figure was 116,060,000 from

1996, and this "120" figure seemed a reasonable extrapolation based on the previous pattern of slow, but steady growth in the number of taxpayers.

4. It is worth noting, however, that this "spend whatever necessary" is not unknown in the polling industry. Between 1981 and 1989, the CBS/New York Times Poll asked on six separate occasions whether protecting the environment is so important that improvement should be pursued "regardless of costs." On five instances, the "yes" response was the majority, often overwhelmingly. One can only wonder what the questionnaire drafter had in mind. Cited in "Willing to Pay," *Congressional Quarterly Special Report,* January 20, 1990, p. 142.

5. Recent presidential campaigns easily confirm that office seekers find the sorry state of public education a useful topic for duplicitous rhetoric. Every candidate vies for the title of "the education president" with such unproven schemes as putting computers in every classroom, national student achievement tests, or massive federal subsidies to boost reading scores. This effort resembles the hawking of "surefire" medical cures to the desperate and, as in medicine, the real public policy debate damage may be in obscuring real, though modest, improvement designs. After all, why strive to improve school discipline when wiring every classroom to the Internet will (supposedly) bring instant improvement.

6. In a situation that might be labeled "politics imitating research," observers of the 2000 presidential context noted that Democratic contender Al Gore displayed a clear penchant for calling George W. Bush's ideas "risky schemes." In one Florida speech, for example, Gore invoked "risky scheme" a dozen times to describe Bush's tax proposal. One of Gore's press releases used eight "risky scheme" mentions. *The Weekly Standard,* April 17, 2000, p. 2.

7. Not unexpectedly, both here and in the hiring more teachers exercise even numbers such as ten, fifty, one hundred, even a thousand were very popular.

6 Bestowing the Democratic Mantle

1. The huge expense of polling has important implications if it is to serve as a "popular" counterforce to elite domination. In this research's preliminary stages, a prominent survey organization was approached for a one-shot poll involving five hundred face-to-face in a single metropolitan area. The estimated cost was about $160,000, hardly a sum available to "ordinary" citizens. Regularly running polls on various topics would easily exceed a half million dollars a year.

2. The penetrability of surveys to political influence is impossible to gauge accurately, but the financial nexus between pollster and client surely encourages such attentiveness. Those drafting questionnaire items can also easily "sneak in" ideologically tainted items given the laxity of supervision in organizations conducting numerous polls. A particular striking example is given by Sommers (1994, 251–253) of a radical feminist using the well-respected Harris Poll to provide a scientifically inaccurate picture of depression among married women. Such manipulation seldom goes detected given the general assumption of research professionalism.

3. The willingness of survey analysts to simultaneously rely on polls to "guide" public decisions while elsewhere acknowledging gross inaccuracy is a fascinating subject. In fact, improving survey performance is a major preoccupation among practitioners. The poll's shortcomings are evidenced in the failure of preelection polls to forecast accurate vote outcomes despite enormous technological advances. One commentator (Barone 1996) even argues that the 1996 preelection polls fared *worse* than the notorious 1948 polls that declared Dewey the winner over Truman.

4. Historically, the polling industry has strenuously resisted regulation. Yet, paradoxically, if polls are to be granted immense new authority, this regulation is virtually inevitable. This new insistence on quality will probably sharply reduce industry numbers since smaller operators will be unable to pass along increased overhead costs to customers. The parallel is the auto industry, where tough safety and emission standards drove marginal competitors from the marketplace.

5. Analysis skips those arguments asserting that even under idea circumstances, the initiative hinders the popular will given its vulnerability to manipulation plus its incapacity to prioritize. In this context, what its defenders label "success" would truly be democratic failure (see Clark 1998 for this countervailing perspective).

6. This indeterminacy partly flows from the inherent contradictions of protecting minority rights versus heeding the majority will. The majority's victory is not always certified as "democratic" if it violates what is judged to be substantively democratic. For example, when a majority of voters reject policies helping certain favored minorities (e.g., gays, blacks), analysts may score this action as "undemocratic." Yet, if a majority thwarts a business lead effort to pass "progrowth" legislation, this triumph is scored as "democratic." With decision rules derived entirely from who wins and looses, confusion is inevitable.

7. In 1994, proponents of the five major California ballot propositions spent an average of $7 million per measure. And, most attempts fail despite ample campaigns (Gerber 1998).

8. Those unfamiliar with "new and improved democracy" cannot possibly imagine the proliferating schemes to augment elections. Carson and Martin (1999) detail a plethora of putative advisory bodies: citizen juries, planning cells, neighborhood policy juries, citizen survey panels, and similar contrivances.

9. The paucity of hard evidence regarding the collective outcome's wisdom is hardly surprising if one closely scrutinizes the device's theoretical foundations. The alleged connection between collective discourse and superior outcomes is seldom empirically well demonstrated. Clichés regarding truth emerging from the "marketplace of ideas" is *not* proof. Groups are just as capable of folly as are isolates, and the phenomena of mob hysteria is commonplace. Once again, hope triumphs over an awkward reality. The shaky value of the marketplace of ideas to extract truth is discussed further in Weissberg (1996).

10. Public officials can also be perplexed regarding this electronic citizen feedback. In the Cube experiment, for example, officials often disagreed over how to treat citizen guidance and, most critically, there were no legal strictures. Reactions

seemed to be *ad hoc* and situational, a far cry from rule by law. Hollander (1985, ch. 2) depicts this confusion in detail.

11. The cause of death was not always resource insufficiency. One particular example deserves special mention—"Anticipatory Democracy." This device engaged thousands of ordinary citizens, supplemented with polls and other feedback mechanisms, to (ostensibly) help governments overcome gridlock. Popular in the 1960s, it instigated over forty projects and took ample credit for various policy innovations. It has, apparently, vanished (Baker 1978).

12. A revealing feature of this system was the lack of participation by elected officials and its relative domination by combative computer enthusiasts. Moreover, interchanges often resembled normal conversation with people one might not normally encounter, not new information seeking. Anonymity also spawned extensive personal abuse, a notable reason why elected officials avoided participation.

13. Even if intervention programs were successful, this does not prove that inequalities can be overcome. Bestowing educational enrichment on the disadvantaged will close the gap *only* if "the have's" are denied similar measures. Moreover, even if intelligence was entirely environmentally determined, successfully manipulation not guaranteed. Jensen's (1998) overview suggests that environmental factors are exceedingly complex, difficult to specify, and may be beyond systematic control.

14. The classic examples are the European Socialist parties. Here, ordinary citizens, thanks to expert party leadership, are able to impose extensive social welfare systems that are the envy of American workers. These parties, unlike the Democrats with their infatuation with "openness" and diversity, judge their effectiveness on substantive outcomes, not process.

15. The disdain for hard evidence in this oft-made appeal is impossible to exaggerate. Only one notable example must suffice to demonstrate this irresponsibility. In Barber's plea from "strong democracy" he expressly addresses the possibility of mass foolishness. He offers several assurances, including quotes from Machiavelli and Roosevelt plus the pledge that new empowered citizens will undoubtedly exercise self-control if only awarded these fresh responsibilities (Barber 1984, ch. 7). Not a shred of hard, scientific evidence is offered.

16. Our fear is hardly unique. When Ross Perot unveiled his 1992 Electronic Town Meeting scheme, numerous political commentators vehemently criticized its totalitarian possibilities. This reproach frequently came from notable liberals. Anthony Lewis in the *New York Times* (1992) evoked images of Mussolini and Fidel Castro plus end-runs around the Constitution. Sidney Blumenthal, another well-known liberal, blasted the proposal as facilitating demagogic manipulation, calling it "the Geraldo system" (1992).

7 Conclusions

1. Perhaps this disproportionate attention is ideologically rooted. Specifically, campaign contributions come from wealthy business groups, while poll elucidation is

the domain of journalists and academics. Campaign gifts thus help "the rich," while polls help "ordinary citizens." One could only imagine what might transpire if the polling industry were suddenly dominated by conservative analysts.

2. Even that punishment is rare. Our excursion into the twisted quest for "citizen competence" in Chapter Three should be recalled. Professional etiquette suggests subdued disagreement, not sharp rebuke. Even gross misrepresentation of data is seldom punished, unless, perchance, the fraud involves federal money. Truly egregious misinterpretations are generally chastised with nonpublication though, to be frank, this gatekeeping activity is often intertwined with judgments having little to do with accuracy.

3. A more complex (and perhaps more important) argument here concerns the relationship between the polling industry as a rival of political parties. Information gathering was once central to the party's purpose, and this if often rendered obsolete by the for-hire pollster. Similarly, survey data analysts now perform functions once executed by party officials, for example, appealing to distinct demographic groups.

4. This image of being glued to the polls is, of course, empirically correct. Chapter One noted, for example, that the Reagan White House spent a million dollars yearly on polls and that these data were integral to the information given daily to the president. This vigilance has by now become routine, even institutionalized, thanks to modern technology.

5. This is not quite true. In the televised debate among Republican candidates prior to the February 2000 South Carolina primary, Bush, McCain, and Keyes were asked how they would treat polling, if they were president. Each strongly denounced poll pandering on matters of national importance. Yet, at least the first two candidates extensively used polls in their campaign and would surely consult them if elected.

6. Our analysis consciously avoids that one issue lurking in the background—what Kuran (1995) calls "preference falsification" or misrepresenting one's true opinion in more plain-Jane language. We strongly suspect that this is common in the public's social welfare pronouncements given the "respectability" of this form of public compassion. Since everybody already knows that this prowelfare position is the public norm, disagreement might reflect an odious deviancy. The poll's redefinition of "compassion" as endorsing state intervention (as opposed to private efforts) is a Pandora's Box subject and surely does an inquiry beyond what we here can offer.

7. Our assessment of the Deliberative Poll, an instrument allegedly overcoming these deficiencies, should be recalled. To repeat, this "upgrade civic competency" task is side stepped when the instrument is evaluated. At best, respondents might emerge "better" informed, but better does not mean competent. Perhaps this "bait and switch" tactic is understandable given the hazy nature of "civic competence" and, speculatively, the dreary outcomes. No wonder, then, that analysis typically centers on peripheral issues like attitude change or increased attitude coherence.

8. Our example is not hypothetical. Prior to Ford launching its Windstar van, its market research inquired into three-door versus four-door preferences. The poll verdict was "stay with three-door models." When initially marketed against the new Chrysler four-door models, however, the Windstar fell flat. It cost Ford nearly half a billion dollars to retool their assembly line to correct this marketing misjudgment. What happened to those offering bad advice is unknown, however.

9. Interestingly, bits and pieces of the existing public opinion literature offer ample confirmation of this point, though the implication for plebiscitory democracy is not made explicit. Here, analysis discovers that responses can vary immensely by question details or the nature of supporting/opposing arguments (see, for example Lau, Smith, and Fiske 1991; Zaller and Feldman 1992; and others). Left unsaid is that this variability bestows greater power to those controlling the questionnaire. Perhaps this implication embarrasses those claiming scientific disinterest.

Bibliography

Abramson, Jeffrey B., F. Christopher Arterton, and Garry R. Orren. *The Electronic Commonwealth: The Impact of New Media Technologies on Democratic Politics.* New York: Basic Books, 1988.

"Al Gore's Risky Theme." *The Weekly Standard* April 17, 2000, p. 2.

American Almanac, 1996–1997. Austin, TX: Hoover's Inc.

"An Initiative's Fading Fortunes." CIS Congressional Universe, April 11, 1998 (online version).
   http://lexis-exis.com/congcomp/docum … 09655844636e45d48ae412ac973dd& taggedDocs=

Argetsinger, Amy. "Teacher Shortage Stymies Efforts to Cut Class Sizes." *Washington Post*, sec. A1. February 7, 1999 (online version).
   http://infoweb4.newsbank.com/bin/gate.ex … Y0OtoxOjc6MTMwLjEyNg& state=pgarn6.11.

Arterton, F. Christopher. *Teledemocracy: Can Technology Save Democracy?* Newbury Park, CA: Sage Publications, 1987.

Baker, David E. "State, Regional, and Local Experiments in Anticipatory Democracy: An Overview." In *Anticipatory Democracy: People in the Politics of the Future.* Ed. Clement Bezold. New York: Vintage Books, 1978.

Barber, Benjamin. "The Second American Revolution." *Channels* (Feb/March 1982): 21–25.

Barber, Benjamin. *Strong Democracy: Participatory Politics for a New Age.* Berkeley: University of California Press, 1984.

Barone, Michael. "Why Opinion Polls are Worthless." *U.S. News and World Report* 121(Dec. 9, 1996): 52.

Bartels, Larry M. "Post-Cold War Defense Spending Preferences." *Public Opinion Quarterly* 58(1994): 479–508.

Beardsley, Philip L., David M. Kovenock, and William C. Reynolds. *Measuring Public Opinion on National Priorities: A Report on a Pilot Study.* Beverly Hills, CA: Sage, 1974.

Bennett, Linda L. M., and Stephen Earl Bennett. *Living with Leviathan: Americans Coming to Terms with Big Government.* Lawrence: University of Kansas Press, 1990.

Birch, Alfred L., and Alfred A. Schmid. "Public Opinion Surveys as Guides to Public Policy and Spending." *Social Indicators Research* 7(1980): 299–311.

Blumenthal, Sidney. "Perotnoria." *The New Republic* (June 23, 1992): 15.

Bohman, James. *Public Deliberation: Pluralism, Complexity and Democracy.* Cambridge, MA: The MIT Press, 1996.

Brace, Paul, and Barbara Hinckley. *Follow the Leader: Opinion Polls and the Modern Presidency.* New York: Basic Books, 1992.

Bradburn, Norman N., and Seymour Sudman. *Polls and Surveys: Understanding What They Tell Us.* San Francisco: Jossey-Bass, 1988.

Brady, Henry E. "Contributions of Survey Research to Political Science." *PS: Political Science and Politics* 33(2000): 47–57.

Brayfield, April A., Sharon Gennis Deich, and Sandra L. Hofferth. *Caring for Children in Low-income Families: A Substudy of the National Child Care Survey.* Washington, DC: The Urban Institute, 1993.

Brehm, John. *The Phantom Respondents: Opinion Surveys and Political Representation.* Ann Arbor: The University of Michigan Press, 1993.

Brewer, Dominic J., Cathy Krop, Brian P. Gill, and Robert Reichhardt. "Estimating the Cost of National Class Size Reductions Under Different Policy Alternatives." *Educational Evaluation and Policy Analysis* 21(1999): 179–192.

Browning, Graeme. *Electronic Democracy: Using the Internet to Influence American Politics.* Wilton, CT: Pemberton Press, 1996.

Bryan, Frank M. "Direct Democracy and Civic Competence: The Case of Town Meeting." In *Citizen Competence and Democratic Institutions.* Ed. Karol Edward Soltan and Stephen L. Elkin. University Park: Pennsylvania State University Press, 1999.

Budge, Ian. *The New Challenge of Direct Democracy.* Cambridge, MA: Blackwell, 1996.

Budziszewski, J. "Why Are We So Bad, And What Can We Do About It: On the State And Civic Virtue." *International Journal of Public Administration* 17(1994): 2285–2296.

Burtt, Shelly. "The Politics of Virtue Today: A Critique and a Proposal." *American Political Science Review* 87(1993): 360–368.

Cantril, Albert H., ed. *Polling on the Issues: Twenty-one Perspectives on the Role of Opinion Polls in the Making of Public Policy.* Cabin John, MD: Seven Locks Press, 1980.

Carson, Lyn, and Brian Martin. *Random Selection in Politics.* Westport, CT: Praeger, 1999.

Center on Policy Attitudes. "Allocating the Discretionary Budget." 2000. Available online at http://policyattitudes.org.

Citrin, Jack. "Do People Want Something for Nothing: Public Opinion on Taxes and Government Spending." *National Tax Journal* 32(1979): 113–129.

Clark, S. J. "A Populist Critique of Direct Democracy." *Harvard Law Review* 112(1998): 434–482.

Clark, Terry Nichols. "Can You Cut a Budget Pie?" *Policy and Politics* 3(1974): 3–31.

Converse, Philip E. "The Nature of Belief Systems in Mass Publics." In *Ideology and Discontent*. Ed. David E. Apter. New York: Free Press, 1964.

Cook, Fay Lomax, and Barrett, Edith J. *Support for the American Welfare State*. New York: Columbia University Press, 1992.

Coughlin, Richard M. *Ideology, Public Opinion and Welfare Policy: Attitudes Toward Taxes and Spending in Industrialized Societies*. Berkeley, CA: Institute of International Studies, 1980.

Cowling, Maurice. *Mill and Liberalism*. 2nd edn. Cambridge, UK: Cambridge University Press, 1990.

Crespi, Irving. *Public Opinion, Polls, and Democracy*. Boulder, CO: Westview Press, 1989.

Cronin, Thomas E. *Direct Democracy: The Politics of Initiative, Referendum and Recall*. Cambridge: Harvard University Press, 1989.

Cummings, R. G., D. S. Brookshire, and W. D. Schulze. *Valuing Environmental Goods: An Assessment of the Contingent Valuation Method*. Totowa, NJ: Roman & Allanheld, 1986.

Dahl, Robert A. "The Problem of Civic Competence." *Journal of Democracy* 4(1992): 45–59.

Davis, Anna Byrd. "Public dollars for child care aid many, yet raise questions." *The Commercial Appeal*, sec. A1. Memphis, TN, May 31, 1994 (online version). http://infoweb6.newsbank.com/bin/gate.ex ... zNTQ1MjoxOjc6MTMwLEyN& state=ilpdjd.6.

Delli Carpini, Michael X., and Scott Keeter 1996. *What Americans Know About Politics and Why It Matters*. New Haven: Yale University Press.

Denver, David, Gordon Hands, and Bill Jones. "Fishkin and the Deliberative Polls: Lessons from a Study of the *Granada 500* Television Program." *Political Communication* 12(1995): 147–156.

Director, Aaron. "The Parity of The Economic Marketplace." *The Journal of Law and Economics* 7(1964): 1–10.

Donovan, Todd, and Shaun Bowler (a). "An Overview of Direct Democracy in the American States." In *Citizens as Legislators: Direct Democracy in the United States*. Ed. Shaun Bowler, Todd Donovan, and Caroline J. Tolbert. Columbus: Ohio State University Press, 1998.

Donovan, Todd, and Shaun Bowler (b). "Responsive or Responsible Government?" in the American States." In *Citizens as Legislators: Direct Democracy in the United States*. Ed. Shaun Bowler, Todd Donovan, and Caroline J. Tolbert. Columbus: Ohio State University Press, 1998.

Dryzek, John S. "The Mismeasure of Political Man." *The Journal of Politics* 50(1988): 705–725.

Eismeier, Theodore. "Public Preferences About Government Spending: Partisan, Social and Attitudinal Sources of Policy Differences." *Political Behavior* 4(1982): 133–145.

Elgin, Duane. "Revitalizing Democracy Through Electronic Town Meetings." *Spectrum* 66(1993): 6–13.

Elkin, Stephen L. "Citizen Competence and the Design of Democratic Institutions." In *Citizen Competence and Democratic Institutions*. Ed. Karol Edward Soltan and Stephen L. Elkin. University Park: Pennsylvania State University Press, 1999.

Eysenck, Hans J. *Intelligence: A New Look*. New Brunswick, NJ: Transaction Books, 1998.

Fishkin, James S. *Democracy and Deliberation: New Directions for Democratic Reform*. New Haven, CT: Yale University Press, 1991.

———. *The Voice of the People: Public Opinion and Democracy*. New Haven, CT: Yale University Press, 1995.

Gallup, George. *A Guide to Public Opinion Polls*. Princeton, NJ: Princeton University Press, 1944.

Gallup, George H. "Preserving Majority Rule." In *Polling on the Issues*. Edited by Albert H. Cantril. Cabin John, MD: Seven Locks Press, 1980.

Gallup, George H., and Saul Rae. *The Pulse of Democracy*. New York: Simon and Schuster, 1940.

Gamble, Barbara S. "Putting Civil Rights to a Popular Vote." *American Journal of Political Science* 41(1997): 245–269.

Gastil, John, and James P. Dillard. "Increasing Political Sophistication Through Public Deliberation." *Political Communication* 16(1999): 3–23.

Gaventa, John. "Citizen Knowledge, Citizen Competence and Democracy Building." *The Good Society: A PEGS Journal* 5(1995): 28–35.

Gerber, Elizabeth R. "Pressuring Legislatures through the Use of Initiatives: Two Forms of Indirect Influence." In *Citizens as Legislators: Direct Democracy in the United States*. Ed. Shaun Bowler, Todd Donovan, and Caroline J. Tolbert. Columbus: Ohio State University Press, 1998.

——— and Arthur Lupia. "Voter Competence in Direct Legislation Elections." In *Citizen Competence and Democratic Institutions*. Ed. Karol Edward Soltan and Stephen L. Elkin. University Park: Pennsylvania State University Press, 1999.

Ginsberg, Benjamin. *The Consequences of Consent: Elections, Citizen Control and Popular Acquiescence*. Reading, MA: Addison-Wesley, 1982.

Ginsberg, Benjamin, and Robert Weissberg. "Elections and the Mobilization of Popular Support." *American Journal of Political Science* 22(1978): 31–55.

———. *The Captive Public: How Mass Opinion Promotes State Power*. New York: Basic Books, 1986.

Gittlesohn, John. "State class reductions face pitfalls in coming phase." *The Orange Country Register*, sec. A1. January 2, 1997 (online version). http://infoweb4.newsbank.com.bin/gate.ex ... jY0OToxOjcMTMwLjEyN& sate=pgarn6.11.

Gottfredson, Linda S. "Why g Matters: The Complexity of Everyday Life." *Intelligence* 24(1997): 79–132.

Gould, Stephen Jay. *The Mismeasure of Man*. 2nd edn. New York: Norton, 1996.

Green, Donald Philip, Daniel Kahneman, and Howard Kunreuther. "How the Scope and Method of Public Funding Affect Willingness to Pay for Public Goods." *Public Opinion Quarterly* 58(1994): 49–67.

Green, Donald Philip. "The Price Elasticity of Mass Preferences." *American Political Science Review* 86(1992): 128–148.

"Greenbook." "Background Material and Data on Programs Within the Jurisdiction of the Committee on Ways and Means." House Committee on Ways and Means. 105th Congress, 2nd Session, May 19, 1998.

Grissmer, David. "Class Size Effects: Assessing the Evidence, its Policy Implications, and Future Research Agenda." *Educational Evaluation and Policy Analysis* 21(1999): 231–248.

Hansen, John Mark. "Individuals, Institutions, and Public Preferences over Public Finance." *American Political Science Review* 92(1998): 513–532.

Hanushek, Eric A. "Some Findings from an Independent Investigation of the Tennessee STAR Experiment and from Other Experiments." *Educational Evaluation and Policy Analysis* 21(1999): 143–164.

Hanushek, Eric A. Testimony: "The Evidence on Class Size: Summary of Testimony" Subcommittee on Early Childhood, Youth and Families, Committee on Education and the Workforce, US House of Representatives, February 24, 1998.

———. "The Evidence on Class Size" nd. http://www.edexcellence.net/library/size.html.

Harris, John F. "Policy and Politics by the Numbers." *The Washington Post* (Dec. 31, 2000): sec. A1, A10.

Hausman, Jerry A., ed. *Contingent Valuation: A Critical Assessment.* Amsterdam: North-Holland, 1993.

Helburn, Suzanne, W., ed. "The Silent Crisis in U.S. Child Care" *The Annals of the American Academy of Political and Social Science* 563(1999): 8–219.

Herrnstein, Richard J., and Charles Murray. *The Bell Curve: Intelligence and Class Structure in American Life.* New York: Free Press, 1994.

Hill, Kevin A., and John E. Hughes. *Cyberpolitics: Citizen Activism in the Age of the Internet: Lanham, MD: Rowman & Littlefield.

Hochschild, Jennifer, and Bridget Scott. "Trends: Governance and Reform of Public Education in the United States." *Public Opinion Quarterly* 62(1998): 79–120.

Hoff, David J. "Clinton Seeks Teacher Hires, Small Classes." *Education Week on the Web.* February 4, 1998. Available online at http://www.edweek.org/ew/vol-17/21clint.h17.

Hofferth, Sandra L., April Brayfield, Sharon Deich, Pamela Holcomb, and Frederic Glantz *National Childcare Survey.* Washington, DC: The Urban Institute, 1990.

Hoffman, Tom. "Rationality Reconceived: The Mass Electorate and Democratic Theory." *Critical Review* 12(1998): 459–480.

Hollander, Richard S. *Video Democracy: The Vote-From-Home Revolution.* Mt. Airy, MD: Lomond Publications, 1985.

Hotakainen, Rob. "Student–teacher ratio alarms politicians." *Star Tribune: Newspaper of the Twin Cities,* sec. B1. August 5, 1996 (online version). http://infoweb4.newsbank.com.bin/gate.ex … jY0OToxOjcMTMwLjEyN& sate=pgarn6.11.

Houtz, Jolayne. "New teachers to have little impact." *Seattle Times*, sec. A1. Oct. 17, 1998 (online version). http://infoweb4.newsbank.com/bin/gate.ex ... Y0OtoxOjc6MTMwLjEyNg& state=pgarn6.11.

Hoxby, Caroline M. "Improving Student Achievement: Examining the Impact of Teacher Quality and Class Size." Testimony prepared for The Subcommittee on Postsecondary Education, Training and Life-Long Learning, April 29, 1999.

Hruz, Thomas. "Beyond Smoke and Mirrors: A Critical Look at Smaller Class Sizes." *Wisconsin Interest* (Fall/Winter 1998): 29–37.

Jacobs, Lawrence R., and Robert Y. Shapiro "The Rise of Presidential Polling." *Public Opinion Quarterly* 2(1995): 163–195.

Jacobs, Lawrence R., and Robert Y. Shapiro. *Politicians Don't Pander: Political Manipulation and the Loss of Democratic Responsiveness.* Chicago: University of Chicago Press, 2000.

Jacoby, William G. "Public Attitudes toward Government Spending." *American Journal of Political Science* 34(1994): 336–361.

Jensen, Arthur R. *Bias in Mental Testing.* New York: Free Press, 1980.

———. *The g Factor: The Science of Mental Ability.* Westport, CT: Praeger, 1998.

Johnson, Paul. *The Intellectuals.* New York: Harper and Row, 1988.

Kagay, Michael R. "Variability without Fault: Why Even Well-Design Polls Can Disagree." In *Media Polls in American Politics.* Ed. Thomas E. Mann and Garry R. Orren. Washington, DC: Brookings Institution, 1992.

Kagay, Michael R. "Presidential Address: Public Opinion Polling during Presidential Scandal and Impeachment." *Public Opinion Quarterly* 3(1999) 449–463.

Kahneman, Daniel, and Llana Ritov. "Determinants of Stated Willingness to Pay for Public Goods: A Study in the Headline Method." *Journal of Risk and Uncertainty* 9(1994): 5–38.

Kahneman, Daniel, Illana Ritov, Karen E. Jacowitz, and Paul Grant. "Stated Willingness to Pay for Public Goods: A Psychological Perspective." *Psychological Science* 4(1993): 310–315.

Kisker, Ellen Eliason, and Christine M. Ross. "Arranging Child Care." *The Future of Children* 7(1997): 99–109.

Kull, Steven. *Expecting More Say: The American Public On Its Role In Government Decisionmaking.* Washington, DC: Center on Policy Attitudes, 1999.

Kuran, Timur *Private Truth, Public Lies: The Social Consequences of Preference Falsification.* Cambridge, MA: Harvard University Press, 1995.

Ladd, Everett C. "What Do Americans Really Think About the Environment" *The Public Perspective* May–June 1990.

——— and John Benson. "The Growth of News Polls in American Politics." In *Media Polls in American Politics.* Ed. Thomas E. Mann and Garry R. Orren. Washington, DC: Brookings Institution, 1992.

Langer, Gary and Ben Fitzpatrick. "Tempered by Risk." ABC/NEWS Poll (April 9, 1999) online version.

http://www.acbnews.go.com/sections/politics/DailyNews/ kosovo_poll990409. html.

Lascher, Edward L. Jr., Michael G. Hagen, and Steven A. Rochlin. "Gun Behind the Door? Ballot Initiatives, State Policies and Public Opinion." *Journal of Politics* 58(1996): 760–775.

Lau, Richard R., Richard A. Smith, and Susan T. Fiske. "Political Belief, Policy Interpretation, and Political Persuasion." *Journal of Politics* 53(1991): 644–675.

Laudon, Kenneth C. *Communications Technology and Democratic Participation.* New York: Praeger Publishers, 1977.

Levine, Peter. *The New Progressive Era: Toward Fair and Deliberative Democracy.* Lanham, MD: Rowman & Littlefield, 2000.

Lewis, Anthony. "Governing by Television." *New York Times* (June 7, 1992): sec. C3.

Lewis, Justin. *Constructing Public Opinion: How Political Elites Do What They Like and Why We Seem to Go Along With It.* New York: Columbia University Press, 2001.

Lippmann, Walter. *The Pubic Philosophy.* New York: Mentor Books, 1956.

Los Angeles Times Poll, Study #406, January 1998. National Survey: State of the Union/Sex Scandal.

Lupia, Arthur. "Shortcuts Versus Encyclopedias: Information and Voting Behavior in California Insurance Reform Elections." *American Political Science Review* 88(1994): 63–76.

Martin, Claire. "The Cry for Child Care: Will Block Grants Force the Working Poor to Welfare." *The Denver Post* (March 21, 1995) sec. F-1 (online version). http://infoweb6.newsbank.com/bin/gate.ex ... zNTQ1MjoxOjc6MTMwLEyN& state=ilpdjd.3.

Mattes, Robert B. *The Politics of Public Opinion: Poll, Pollsters and Presidents.* Doctoral thesis, Department of Political Science, University of Illinois-Urbana, 1992.

May, Peter J. "A Technique for Measuring Preferences for Spending Reductions." *Social Indicators Research* 10(1981): 389–405.

Mayer, William G. *The Changing American Mind: How and Why American Public Opinion Changed between 1960 and 1988.* Ann Arbor: University of Michigan Press, 1992.

McIver, John P., and Elinor Ostrom. "Using Budget Pies to Reveal Preferences: Validation of a Survey Instrument." *Policy and Politics* 4(1976): 87–110.

Mead, Walter J. "Review and Analysis of State-of-the-Art Contingent Valuation Studies." In *Contingent Valuation: A Critical Assessment.* Ed. Jerry A. Hausman. Amsterdam: North-Holland, 1993.

Merkle, Daniel M. "The National Issue Convention Deliberative Poll." *Public Opinion Quarterly* 60(1996): 588–619.

Mitchell, Robert Cameron, and Richard T. Carson. *Using Surveys to Value Public Goods: The Contingent Valuation Method.* Washington, DC: Resources for the Future, 1989.

Morse, Suzanne W. *Renewing Civic Capacity: Preparing College Students for Service and Citizenship.* Washington, DC: The George Washington University, 1989.

Murray, Charles. "IQ and Economic Success." *The Public Interest* 128(1997): 21–35.

National Taxpayers Union, "As Washington Wails Over 1% Spending Cut, 8 out of 10 Voters think Budget Should Be Trimmed by at Least 5 Times as Much" http:www.ntu.org/P9911newspendingpoll.htm.

Nie, Norman H., Sidney Verba, and John R. Petrocik. *The Changing American Voter.* Cambridge, MA: Harvard University Press, 1977.

Nie, Norman, Jane Junn, and Kenneth Stehlik-Barry. *Education and Democratic Citizenship in America.* Chicago: University of Chicago Press, 1996.

Niemi, Richard G., and Jane Junn. *Civic Education: What Makes Students Learn.* New Haven, CT: Yale University Press, 1998.

O'Connor, Debra. "Sizing up the Research." *Saint Paul Pioneer Press* (Feb. 7, 1999) sec. A1 (online version). http://infoweb4.newsbank.com.bin/gate.ex ... jY0OToxOjcMTMwLjEyN& sate=pgarn6.11.

Olsen, Darcy. "The Advancing Nanny State: Why the Government Should Stay Out of Child Care." Washington, DC: Cato Policy Analysis No. 285, 1997.

Page, Benjamin I., and Robert Y. Shapiro. *The Rational Public: Fifty Years of Trends in Americans' Policy Preferences.* Chicago: University of Chicago Press, 1992.

Peltzman, Sam. *Political Participation and Government Regulation.* Chicago: University of Chicago Press, 1998.

"Poll: Parents Are Looking for Alternatives." *School Reform News,* 1, 8. Vol. 3, October 1999.

Price, Vincent, and Peter Neijens. "Deliberative Polls: Toward Improved Measures of 'Informed' Public Opinion?" *International Journal of Public Opinion Research* 10 (1998): 145–176.

"Public Agenda Online." Available online at http://www.publicagenda.org/issues/.

Rasinski, Kenneth A. "The Effect of Question Wording on Support for Government Spending" *Public Opinion Quarterly* 53(1989): 388–394.

Reed, Lawrence W. "Citizen Initiatives Fertile the Grass Roots" *Policy Review* 78(1996): 11–12.

Remy, Richard C., and Mary Jane Turner. "Basic Citizenship Competencies: Guidelines for Educators, Policymakers, and Citizens" *Mershon Center Quarterly Report* 5(1979): 1–8.

Riker, William H. *Liberalism Against Populism: A Confrontation Between the Theory of Democracy and the Theory of Social Choice.* Prospect Heights, IL: Waveland Press, 1988.

Riley, Richard W. "Remarks as Prepared for Delivery by U.S. Secretary of Education." November 8, 1999. Available online at http://www.ed.gov/PressReleases/11-199/class_size.html.

Robinson, John P., and Robert Meadow. *Polls Apart: A Call for Consistency in Surveys of Public Opinion on World Issues.* Cabin John, MD: Seven Locks Press, 1982.

Roman, Nancy E. "Democrats to Push for More Teachers: Goal is to Reduce Classroom Size at Grade-School Level." *Washington Times* (Feb. 26, 1999): sec. A4 (online version).

http://proquest.umi.com/pqdweb?TS=940442 ... &Fmt=3&Sid=1&Idx=
35&Deli=1&RQT=309&Dtp=

Rosenblum, Nancy L. "Navigating Pluralism: The Democracy of Everyday Life
(and Where It Is Learned)." In *Citizen Competence and Democratic Institutions.*
Ed. Karol Edward Soltan and Stephen L. Elkin. University Park: Pennsylvania
State University Press, 1999.

Ross, Randy. "How Class-size Reduction Harms Kids in Poor Neighborhoods."
Education Week on the Web (May 26, 1999). Available online at http:www.edweek.
org/ew/1999/37ross.h18.

Sandel, Michael. "After the Nation-State: Reinventing Democracy." *New Perspectives
Quarterly* (Fall 1992): 4–8.

Schevitz, Tanya. "Small Classes Produce Little Gains So Far." *San Francisco Chronicle,*
(June 23, 1999): sec. A1 (online version).
http://infoweb6.newsbanak.com/bin/gate.ex ... xNTkwMToxOjc6MTMwLjEyNg&
state=27p98j.9.1.

Schudson, Michael. "The Limits of Teledemocracy." *The American Prospect*
11(1992): 41–45.

Schuman, Howard, and Stanley Presser. *Questions and Answers in Attitude Surveys:
Experiments on Question Form, Wording, and Context.* New York: Academic Press,
1981.

Schwartz, Evan. "Are You Ready for the Democracy Channel?" *Wired* 2(1994): 4–5.

Sherif, Carolyn W., Muzafer Sherif, and Roger E. Nebergall. *Attitude and Attitude
Chance: The Social Judgment-Involvement Approach.* Philadelphia: W. B. Sanders,
1965.

Sinopoli, Richard C. "Liberalism, Republicanism & the Constitution." *Polity*
19(1987): 331–352.

Slaton, Christa Darly. *Televote: Expanding Citizen Participation in the Quantum Age.*
New York: Praeger, 1992.

Smith, Daniel A. *Tax Crusaders and the Politics of Direct Democracy.* New York:
Routlage, 1998.

Smith, Ted J. III, and J. Michael Hogan. "Public Opinion and the Panama Canal
Treaties of 1977." *Public Opinion Quarterly* 51(1987): 5–30.

Smith, Tom. "The Use of Public Opinion Data by the Attorney General's
Commission on Pornography." *Public Opinion Quarterly* 51(1987): 249–269.

Snyderman, M., and Stanley S. Rothman. *The IQ Controversy: The Media and Public
Policy.* New Brunswick, NJ: Transaction Books, 1988.

Soltan, Karol Edward. "Introduction: Imagination, Political Competence,
and Institutions." In *The Constitution of Good Societies.* Ed. Karol Edward Soltan
and Stephen L. Elkin. University Park: Pennsylvania State University Press,
1996.

Sommers, Christina Hoff. *Who Stole Feminism? How Women Have Betrayed Women.*
New York: Simon and Schuster, 1994.

Stecher, Brian M., and George W. Bohrnstedt 1999. "Executive Summary of the
technical report Class Size Reduction in California: Early Evaluation Findings,

1996–99." CSR Research Consortium. Available on-line at http://www.classize.
org/techreprot/execsum.html.

"Steps to Improve Federally Sponsored Childcare" *Weekly Compilation of Presidential Documents, March 16, 1998.*
http://frwebgate3.accessgpo.gov/c ... 13119713101010&WAISaction+retrieve.

Sudman, Seymour, and Norman M. Bradburn. "The Organizational Growth of Public Opinion Research in the United States." *Public Opinion Quarterly* 51(1987): S67–S78.

Taylor, Humphrey. "Polling. Good Government and Democracy." *Public Perspective* (July/August 2000): 33–36.

Thompson, Dennis F. *The Democratic Citizen: Social Science and Democratic Theory in the Twentieth Century.* Cambridge, UK: Cambridge University Press, 1970.

Tsagararousianou, Roza, Damian Tambini, and Cathy Bryan. *Cyberdemocracy: Technology, Cities and Civic Networks.* London: Routledge, 1998.

Tversky, Amos, and Daniel Kahneman. "The Framing of Decisions and the Psychology of Choice." In *New Directions in Methodology of Social and Behavioral Sciences: Question Framing and Response Consistency.* Ed. R. Hogarth. San Francisco: Jossey-Bass, 1982.

US Bureau of the Census, *Statistical Abstract of the United States: 1998.* (118th edition) Washington, DC, 1998.

Varley, Pamela. "Electronic Democracy." *Technology Review* 94(1991): 42–51.

Verba, Sidney, Kay Lehman Schlozman, and Henry E. Brady. *Voice and Equality: Civic Volunteerism in American Politics.* Cambridge, MA: Harvard University Press, 1995.

Verba, Sidney, 1996. "The Citizen Respondent: Sample Surveys and American Democracy" *American Political Science Review* 90: 1–7.

Verhovek, Sam Howe. "A Ballot Full of Voter Initiatives Becomes an Issue Itself in Oregon." *New York Times* (October 25, 2000).

Vetterli, Richard, and Gary Bryner. *In Search of the Republic: Public Virtue and Roots of American Government.* Rev. Ed. Lanham, MD: Rowman and Littlefield, 1996.

Wachtel, Ted. *The Electronic Congress: A Blueprint for Participatory Democracy.* Pipersville, PA: Piper's Press, 1992.

Walzer, Michael. "Civility and Civic Virtue in Contemporary America." *Social Research* 41(1974): 593–611.

Weissberg, Robert. *Public Opinion and Popular Government.* Englewood Cliffs, NJ: Prentice-Hall, 1976.

———. "The Politics of Political Competence Education." In *Political Education in Flux.* Ed. D. Heater and J. Gillespie. London: Sage, 1982.

———."The Real Marketplace of Ideas." *Critical Review* 10(1996): 107–122.

———. *Political Tolerance: Balancing Community and Diversity.* Thousand Oaks, CA: Sage, 1998.

Weissberg, Robert. *The Politics of Empowerment.* Westport, CT: Praeger, 1999.

Wheeler, Michael. *Lies, Damn Lies, and Statistics: The Manipulation of Public Opinion in America.* New York: Liverright, 1976.

Wilentz, Sean. "For Voters, the 60s Never Died." *New York Times,* November 16, 1999, Section A, p. 27.

"Willing to Pay" *Congressional Quarterly Special Report,* January 20, 1990, p. 142. (Original data were CBS News/New York Times poll, nd.)

Wilson, L.A. II. "Preference Revelation and Public Policy: Making Sense of Citizen Survey Data." *Public Administration Review* 43(1983): 335–342.

Wood, Gordon S. *The Creation of the American Republic 1776–1789.* Chapel Hill: University of North Carolina Press, 1969.

Yankelovich, Daniel. *Coming to Public Judgment: Making Democracy Work in a Complex World.* Syracuse, NY: Syracuse University Press, 1991.

Zaller, John, and Stanley Feldman. "A Simple Theory of the Survey Response: Answering Questions versus Revealing Preferences." *American Journal of Political Science* 36(1992): 579–616.

Zimmerman, Joseph F. *The New England Town Meeting: Democracy in Action.* Westport, CT: Praeger, 1999.

Index

ability differences, *see* intelligence
academy, disguised agenda, 10, 15–16,
    53, 147, 170–3, 180, 213–14 (1),
    215 (9)
    see also false consciousness; faux
        populism
American Association for Public
    Opinion Research (AAPOR)
    (1999), 176
Angus Reid Associates of Winnipeg,
    Manitoba, Canada, 84, 95,
    210 (18)
Animal Farm, 160
anticipatory democracy, 213 (11)
attitude, 26
    see also terminology
attitude assessment, *see* social judgment
    approach
authority, political, *see* academy,
    disguised agenda

Bellamy, Edward, 148
budget pie, 43–4
    see also policies, costs of

California's Propositions 187 and 209,
    146
Captive Public, The (1986), 4
Center on Policy Attitudes, 44
childcare assistance plan, 72, 78–80
    problems with, 80–3
    see also questionnaire (of *Polling,
        Policy, and Public Opinion*)
citizenship, good, 67–70, 207 (11)
    see also competence, civic
Class-size Reduction and Teacher
    Quality Act (1998)

politics of, 72–4
problems with, 75–8, 208 (5) (6)
    see also questionnaire (of *Polling,
        Policy, and Public Opinion*)
Clean water Act (1972), 37–8
Clinton, William Jefferson, 1–2, 72–3,
    77, 80–1, 95, 180
competence, civic, 14–15, 40, 44–6,
    49, 51, 67, 95–130, 134–7,
    150–1, 181–4, 192
    criteria of, 64–6
    definition of, 205 ch3 (1) (2),
        205–6 (3), 213 (15), 214 (7)
    discrimination and, 63–4
    patterns of answers, statistical, 55–8
    power and, 52
    sham, 53–62
    see also citizenship, good; false
        consciousness; intelligence;
        polls, deficiencies and
        distortions; polls, military
        spending; social reality,
        constructed
consensus, achieving of, 29–31, 41,
    204 (1)
    see also polls, legislation v.
Contingent Valuation Method (CVM),
    36–41
Contract with America, 12
cooptation, *see* academy, disguised
    agenda
cost-benefit analysis, *see* policies, costs of
cover story, *see* academy, disguised
    agenda
CVM, *see* Contingent Valuation
    Method
Cvrly, 21–2

Deliberative Democracy, 153–5
see also democracy, direct
Delli Carpini, Michael X, 60–1
democracy, direct
  Alaska Department of Transportation
    (1980) and, 155
  Alaskan Teleconferencing Network
    and, 152, 157–8
  Alternatives for Washington and,
    151–2, 156
  apathy and, 156–7
  communal projects and, 147–8
  cyberdemocracy and, 155
  deliberative poll and, 153–5
  Democracy channel and, 156
  *Electronic Congress, The: A Blueprint
    for Participatory Democracy*
    (1992), 155
  Electronic Democracy and, 158
  Electronic Town Meeting (ETM)
    and, 153
  Hawaii Televote and, 157
  initiatives and, 148–9
  Manchester England and, 154
  Minerva and, 152, 156
  New England Town Meeting and,
    150–1
  New Harmony and, 147
  NORC, 154
  Owen, Robert, 148
  problems with, 141–7, 156–9
    see also competence, civic;
      intelligence; polls, deficiencies
      and distortions
  quantitative conceptualization of,
    160–2
  Qube electronic town meeting and,
    152–3, 156, 158
  SES unrepresentative and, 157, 160
  Televote and, 153
  traditional, 148–51
DeWitt, Charles C(linton), xii
direct democracy, *see* democracy, direct

easy spontaneity, 50
education, *see* Class-size Reduction and
  Teacher Quality Act (1998)

educational problems, suggested
  solutions to, 106–8
Environmental Protection Agency
  (EPA), 35
equivalency test, 20, 23–4
Etzioni, Amitai, 152

false consciousness, 10–13
  see also academy, disguised agenda;
    social reality, constructed
faux populism, 149–51
  see also academy, disguised agenda
Fishkin, James F., 3, 153–5
free rider problem, 37

Ginsberg, Benjamin, 4, 11
gullibility test, 106–8

Hansen, John Mark, 56–7
hard choices, 19–21, 23–5
  see also terminology
height versus college success example,
  51–2
hidden agenda, *see* academy, disguised
  agenda
hierarchy, 168–70, 213 (14)
  see also intelligence

ideology by constraint, 54–5
inclusive democracy, *see* democracy,
  direct
inequality, economic, 160
  see also intelligence; political party;
    hierarchy
informed activism, 50–1
integration, racial, 27–8
intelligence (IQ), 161–8, 206 (8), 207
  (9), 213 (13)
  see also hierarchy

Jacoby, William G., 55–6

Keeter, Scott, 60–1

*Living with Leviathan: Americans
  Coming to Terms with Big
  Government,* 12

Madison, James, 4
moral competence, 50

National Education Association, 73–4
National Taxpayers Union (NTU), x,
    203 (4)
NORC, 92

Page, Benjamin I., 57–60
Panama Canal Treaty (1977), 10, 190
participatory democracy, *see* democracy,
    direct
plebiscitory democracy, *see* democracy,
    direct
political disengagement, 172–3
political party, 168–9
    see also intelligence
policies, costs of, 9, 12, 24–5, 31–2,
    34–6, 42–5, 86–92, 97–101,
    110–2, 114–25, 127–33, 211(4)
    actual experience and, 38
    free rider and, 37
    nonmonetary and, 33
    rare risks and, 38
    see also polls, deficiencies and
        distortions of
polls
    accuracy in answering of, 33–4, 37,
        39, 205 ch2 (3), 214 (6)
    biased, left wing, viii–xii, 6, 62
    car example, 21–2
    complexity problem with, 39, 44–5
    contingent valuation method
        (CVM), 36–41
        see also policies, costs of
    criteria, methodological of, 143–6
    deficiencies and distortions of, 5–9,
        12–15, 17, 25, 28–31, 36,
        46–8, 88, 96, 102, 105,
        117, 134, 187–8, 206 (6) (7),
        211 (2), 212 (3), 214 (2) (6),
        215 (8) (9)
        see also competence, civic; policies,
            costs of; social judgment
            approach
    democracy and, 2–4, 139–47,
        188–93, 203 (3)

legislation v., 7, 20, 29–31, 48,
    190–1
    see also consensus, achieving of
    legitimate use of, 16, 136–7,
        175–81, 193
    military spending and, 7–10
        see also competence, civic
    paradox and, 13
    Polling, Policy, and Public Opinion, see
        questionnaire (of *Polling, Policy,
        and Public Opinion*)
    response elasticity and, 185–6
    selective reporting and, 204 (7)
    social welfare policies and, viii–x, 6,
        11–12
    ubiquity of, 1–4, 10–11,
        203–4 (5) (6)
    use of, how to improve, 191–3
    which ones to listen to, 141–3, 190,
        204 (7)
power, civic, 52
preferences, 19
    see also terminology
progressives, 148
"Public Attitudes toward Government
    Spending," 55–6
public opinion, 6–7, 18

questionnaire (of *Polling, Policy, and
    Public Opinion*), 15, 83–93,
    195–202
    discussion and results, 97–138,
        183–6

*Rational Public, The (Fifty Years of
    Trends in Americans' Policy
    Preferences)* (1992), 57–60
Reagan, 1, 12–13, 59
revolutionary agenda, *see* academy,
    disguised agenda

science, normative versus positive, ix,
    203 (2)
Shapiro, Robert Y., 57–60
Sherif, Carolyn W., Muzafer Sherif, and
    Roger E. Nebegall (1965), 26–7
social judgment approach, 26–9

social reality, constructed, 10–14, 54,
176–8, 203–4 (5), 204 (6) (7)
see also false consciousness; polls,
deficiencies and distortions;
polls, ubiquity of
speech plus technique, 203 (1)
Strategic Arms Limitation Treaty
(SALT), 142
Student–Teacher Achievement Ratio
(STAR), 207 (1)
Survey Research Center, 92

terminology, 18–20, 26, 37
totalitarianism, *see* academy, disguised
agenda
tradeoffs, 42–5, 171–3
see also policies, costs of
truth in polling, 83

University of Michigan Center for
Political Studies, 55–6

University of Michigan Survey Research
Center, 31
University of Oklahoma, 27–8

Verba, Sidney, 3, 203 (2)
voting, 46–7

*What Americans Know about Politics and
Why it Matters* (1996), 60–1
willingness to accept (WTA), 37, 39, 40
willingness to pay (WTP), 37–9, 40,
65, 87, 111
wish, 18
see also terminology
words versus deeds, *see* polls, accuracy
in answering

Zimmerman, Joseph F., 150–1